Classroom Voices on Education and Race

Students Speak from Inside the Belly of the Beast

Daniel Frio

ROWMAN & LITTLEFIELD EDUCATION
A division of
ROWMAN & LITTLEFIELD PUBLISHERS, INC.
Lanham • New York • Toronto • Plymouth, UK

Published by Rowman & Littlefield Education
A division of Rowman & Littlefield Publishers, Inc.
A wholly owned subsidiary of The Rowman & Littlefield Publishing Group, Inc.
4501 Forbes Boulevard, Suite 200, Lanham, Maryland 20706
www.rowman.com

10 Thornbury Road, Plymouth PL6 7PP, United Kingdom

British Library Cataloguing in Publication Information Available

Library of Congress Cataloging-in-Publication Data

Frio, Daniel.
Classroom voices on education and race : students speak from inside the belly of the beast / Daniel Frio.
p. cm.
Includes bibliographical references and index.
ISBN 978-1-4758-0135-4 (pbk. : alk. paper) -- ISBN 978-1-4758-0136-1 (electronic)
1. Minorities--Education--United States. 2. Racism in education--United States. 3. Discrimination in education--United States. I. Title.
LC3731.F728 2012
371.829--dc23
2012025094

The paper used in this publication meets the minimum requirements of American National Standard for Information Sciences Permanence of Paper for Printed Library Materials, ANSI/NISO Z39.48-1992.

Printed in the United States of America

For all my students past, present, and future whose voices will never cease to inform, inspire, and amaze me.

For my loving and supportive wife Deena and daughter Lindsay, who believed I had a book that needed to be written,

And to our Maltese, Kelsey, our incredibly loyal and loving companion who will forever live in the hearts of our family.

Table of Contents

Preface

By the time I graduated high school I realized that my dream of playing major-league baseball would remain just that—a dream. Teaching had always been my "second dream," one nurtured by my love of the stories of history. However, I really knew little about the realities of classroom teaching. After obtaining a master's degree and teaching certificate I knew more history, but not much more about teaching.

When I first entered the classroom my teaching repertoire included mainly my own life experiences, including those as a student, and some media images. I soon found that listening to my students helped me both connect with them and, subsequently, become better able to teach them. Eventually, my students helped shape me into the teacher I wanted to be. Their stories, needs, and desires expanded my teaching skills, and also my awareness of and respect for the diversity of learners entering our public schools.

Like all teachers, I brought my own experiences to the classroom. Working-class Italian Catholics constituted nearly my total world as a child. My parents, Joseph and Clara, raised their five children in Knightsville, a neighborhood that can still claim 85 percent of its current residents as being of Italian ancestry, sitting in the center of Cranston, Rhode Island, the "most Italian of All American Cities" (Anne Romano, *Distant but Loyal*, Inkwater Press, 2007, ix), in the most Italian American state in the nation. Diversity clearly did not exist in my early years.

By junior high school I had developed a strong friendship with Dean Barrie (Jewish but part Italian). This was my first significant introduction to the diverse world outside my neighborhood. Without a doubt, I still had a lot of "life education" to learn, especially about the racial realities that confronted many kids, and the teachers who needed to reach such students in the classroom. Confronting racial issues within the classroom would ultimately produce the most profound lessons in my education as a teacher.

Given the overwhelming whiteness of my immediate world, my early racial education came mainly from books and the media's portrayal of the prolific racial battles of the sixties. Unfortunately, throughout my high school years (1966–1968), my teachers ignored the struggles of the civil rights movement. I was told that such topics were not "history" and they would "disrupt the classroom environment." Race issues, both in and out of the classroom, would persist throughout my lifetime, but unfortunately so would the reluctance of schools to address those issues.

Despite all the tumult of the sixties, public-school administrators continued to maintain a school environment that emphasized administrative and teacher power that demanded student compliance. In 1968, however, the times were indeed a-changin'. My early attempts to find my own student voice and challenge school authorities consisted of breaking dress-code rules. Initially, I would wear forbidden clothing such as shirts without collars (T-shirts!) and jeans.

Then, over winter break of senior year, I devised my most audacious assault on the rules by growing a mustache and wearing the forbidden facial hair to school. I was led into the principal's bathroom and handed a straightedge razor, and the cold water was turned on. A few excruciating minutes later I was clean shaven. He then handed me a bottle of rubbing alcohol and commanded me to finish the job. Apparently he had taken my "rash" explanation for the hair as an inspiration for his punishment. The good news was that he had at least heard my voice! I would leave high school with the desire to pursue teaching, along with a new image of what it could be like: Sidney Poitier's character Mark Thackeray in the movie *To Sir, With Love*. I admired how he managed to adapt to the needs of his unmotivated students by employing unorthodox teaching methods. He *listened to them*, jettisoned the required curriculum, and found common ground by connecting to the real world of his students. Coincidentally, that movie also contained a racial presence that would also follow throughout my career.

My college years at Northeastern University encompassed the most tumultuous student-rights activism of the sixties. College administrators reacted much like their public-school counterparts, looking primarily to maintain control. Their resistance to student feedback, especially with regard to curriculum, provided some significant lessons about the need for student voices to be empowered and respected.

After several postgraduate years of traveling the country, I entered the classroom and remained for thirty-five years. A minor event near the end of my career proved significant in the evolution of this book. Dewey, a senior, asked if I had heard my name mentioned on WEEI's morning sports show. He informed me that the co-hosts had read a quote of mine from the *Boston Herald* (October 30, 2002). They proceeded to mock my opinion, call me an idiot, and suggest I should lose my job. Dewey failed to gain access on the air due to an age requirement, and the matter was dropped.

However, that evening I discussed the story with Gay Vernon, a friend and newscaster on a Boston radio station. She asked me to calculate the number of students I had impacted over the years, and then proceeded to enlighten me about the "numbers book" for that morning show. Apparently tens of thousands more people now knew me as an idiot. Now that's having an audience!

About a year later those same morning co-hosts, John Dennis and Jerry Callahan, became embroiled in a major scandal over the following on-air exchange about a picture of a gorilla that had escaped from the Franklin Park Zoo:

Callahan: They caught him at a bus stop, right—he was like waiting to catch a bus out of town.

Dennis: Yeah, yeah—he's a METCO [Metropolitan Council for Educational Opportunity, i.e., the desegregation program] gorilla.

Callahan: Heading out to Lexington.

Dennis: Exactly.

This incident resulted in a two-week suspension for the co-hosts, but in no way was the callous and damaging emotional harm they had inflicted on society in general, but particularly on black students, addressed. Those "gorillas" in the METCO program will also now have their voices heard. I submit that their voices will prove to be far more worthy of being heard than the radio celebrities who demeaned their humanity. And perhaps these student voices will reach an even larger audience.

As I entered my final years in the classroom, my career came full circle when a former student, then a mother of four children, paid one of her several visits over the years. Rachel Cibley and I sat in the commons when she surprised me with the ultimate tribute, one that spoke to a fantasy that had faded across three decades. Rachel looked into my eyes and told me that I had been the *To Sir, With Love* influence in her life. I knew then that I could retire with a sense of fulfillment.

A year into retirement, Nicole B. a former student, expressed the following sentiment: "I hope you feel as liberated walking away from Wayland High School as I did!" Indeed, I felt liberated from the constraints of life within the belly of the beast. But, more importantly, a much larger audience than a single classroom teacher could now hear the raw and powerful voices of students in search of impacting their lives and education.

Acknowledgments

First and foremost, this book owes its existence to the students I worked with during thirty-five years in the classroom. They sustained me then, and their words have continued to engage me well after the end of my teaching career. Without them the book simply does not exist.

To my wife Deena, special-needs teacher and guidance counselor over the course of a thirty-six year career, I am in debt for both her inspiration and her enthusiasm regarding the writing of this book. Her feedback proved invaluable at every step of the process. More importantly, her collaboration and wisdom on all things education over the decades always kept me focused on listening to student voices. For this I owe an immense debt of gratitude. I also thank our daughter Lindsay, who provided needed motivation and encouragement, especially when finding a publisher seemed like an improbable task. I would also be remiss to not mention that Kelsey, our family dog, cuddled at my side during the entire writing process.

My good friend Mark Olken provided well-considered feedback from the perspective of an outsider to the education profession. Mark's insights consistently brought a necessary viewpoint to the text. His comments and observations as a reader astutely addressed everything from minute errors to major themes. Our regular breakfasts also served as an excellent sounding board throughout the process.

Mark Liddell's observations as a reader and as a strong advocate for all children provided exceptional insights into the racial themes prevalent throughout the book. As an African American coordinator of a METCO program, his feedback proved vital in confirming that the presentation of racial themes resonated with his work in the schools and in life.

Of course, I owe much of my work in teaching to the values and encouragement of my mom and dad. Neither of them had the opportunity to attend college, but they worked hard to raise five children who achieved a variety of degrees. Whenever I faced promotion setbacks by advocating for students, they stood by my decisions.

Thanks to assistant editor Mary McMenamin and production editor Carly Peterson.

I thank Tom Koerner, Rowan & Littlefield vice president and editorial director, for providing the encouragement and editorial feedback that finally enabled me to focus the book through the voices of the children. Each of his recommendations brought the kind of reflection and reframing necessary for bringing their voices into sharper focus. In the end, he made this book happen.

Along the way, various friends contributed words of support and encouragement, including Pat Olken, Dean Barrie, Bob Buchbinder, Lynn Pearson, and Bob West. A special thanks to Jack Levin, who lent his advice as a prolific author in helping me negotiate the publishing process.

Many former colleagues contributed to my professional development and gave personal support, particularly around issues of race. The material in this book might never have developed without the friendship and expertise of Manuel Fernandez. I also found consistent support from John Brande, Gini Buckley, Brian Newmark, Anne Gray, Christine Truffant, Nicole Stewart, Mary Holland, Marion Howe, Mark Thema, Chris Siggers, Deborrah Dorman, Linda Thompson, Jim Miller, Heather Pineault, Tom Hermanowski, and Steve Feinberg.

I'd like to thank the many Wayland parents who supported me throughout the years with invitations to graduation parties and family dinners. Also, I wish to extend a special mention to Mary Ann Borkowski, Ann Landry, Sue Mack Brigham, and Janet Gundel. The race and racism course would not have happened without their advocacy.

A shout-out to some administrators who stayed true to maintaining their focus on the kids: Bill "Smitty" Smith, Larry Hines, Joanne Hadalski, Peter Sanchioni, Judy Caporiccio, Sandra Raymond, and Vic Palladino. Thanks to history-department head, the late Tom Brennan, who hired me at Wayland, gave me tenure, and believed in me.

Several teachers inspired me as a student and served as role models for my career. Ralph Napolitano encouraged my intellectual growth and nurtured the idea of college back in middle school. Joan Lonergan encouraged my love of history and took the risk of letting her ninth-grade student teach a class lesson on the Civil War. John Post supported my early writing as a mentor to my honors thesis at Northeastern University. His critical feedback always arrived with the understanding that the writer's voice was more important than the mentor's—a perspective that informed my career in the classroom.

Most significantly, I owe a tremendous debt of gratitude to Raymond Robinson, chairman of the history department at NU and my most inspirational teacher and mentor throughout my undergraduate years and beyond. He fostered my love of history and modeled so much of what I valued in teaching.

In my last few years I had the opportunity to supervise and work with a couple of fine young student teachers, Emily Gordon and Lindsay Torres, who allowed for invigorating professional dialogue and helped keep me encouraged about the future of the profession. Having young teachers to mentor also provided a spark in those last years. For that I'd like to thank Elizabeth (McNamee) Lantz, Dan Gavin, David Schmirer, and Kirstin (Walker) Lahey.

Finally, there are students, mostly not mentioned in the book, who stayed in contact as they grew into adults, inspired me to maintain my desire to enter the classroom each and every day, and, as adults, helped me feel good about my working years. Many thanks to students from my early years: Karina Roessel, Rachel (Cibley) Murokowski, Joe Ricciardi, Kristin (Hammerton) Murphy, Rachelle Engler, and Gloria Harrison.

From the "middle years" I had the pleasure of maintaining contact with Dan Turnbull, Shannon Marshall, Erica Licht, Ping-Hong Lu, Kirk Carapezza, Alyssa Parker Geisman, Giselle Tejada, Chris Cohen, and Atoya Josephs.

Most recently, Sasha Pansovoy, Priscilla Wright, Derrick Brisson, and Kate Purrington helped me keep my focus on the book and its major themes. Also, thanks to James Ivker, who inspired me to promote the book on Twitter. And to Bassma Sayeh, who tried to pitch the book to Oprah on Facebook. That didn't happen, but it did enable me to reconnect with and receive support from many former students. Finally, thanks to the audience for my first reading from the book, my former students at the E. W. Thurston Middle School in Westwood, Massachusetts.

Introduction

New visions of American education must start with the voices of children rather than the voices of politicians, private and public think tanks, philanthropists, and some education leaders who have dominated the debate over what's best for the nation's children. In order to reach the children in the classroom, the adults must first listen to those children. To ignore their voices effectively disenfranchises the very people whom the schools profess to empower as citizens in an increasingly diverse and complex world.

Education-reform efforts over the last half century have riveted the nation, yet no data suggest that educators have managed to overcome the socioeconomic and racial achievement gaps that challenge our nation's public schools. Indeed, as noted routinely by students and teachers, the emphasis on quantifiable data driven by standardized testing has shortchanged creativity and the critical social-emotional goals in all the public schools. Student voices won't supply all the answers, but their words should be the starting point of education discussions.

This book focuses on the issues raised by children in their attempt to satisfy their educational needs and desires, while also endeavoring to navigate the complex developmental issues in their lives, particularly those associated with race. Looking to make sense of their world both in and out of the classroom, students found ways to communicate their concerns in an effort to bring meaning to their education.

It became evident in early classroom experiences with nonmainstream children that teaching could not rely solely on forms of pedagogy such as a predetermined curriculum or textbook. Meeting the learning needs of these students necessitated constant attention to the unique needs of individual children. Subsequent experiences would gradually incorporate the need to gain access to student voices in the search for a connection between the world of school and the realities of students' lives. This emerging model proved to be the antithesis of the public-school experience in the sixties.

The first chapter presents the building blocks that established the prominence of flexibility in meeting the needs of children with significantly impaired cognitive functioning, along with emotionally and behaviorally challenged teenagers. The unique individual needs of these children at the margins of public education necessitated a flexible classroom such that, on a daily basis, *their* curriculum often took precedence over *the teacher's* curriculum.

The second chapter illustrates the challenges presented in developing a new program at Chinle High School, situated in the middle of Navajo Nation. The gifted-student program, the first such high-school program on an Indian reservation in the United States, offered a blank slate for educating students in a unique classroom setting. Accessing student voices across a large cultural divide proved difficult, but eventually student feedback provided the means to better meet their unique and complex needs. Once again, teaching proved to be a continually evolving process.

The following two chapters highlight voices from Wayland High School (WHS), situated in the western suburbs of Boston. WHS maintained an excellent academic reputation, yet it faced the challenges of increased student testing and ranking of schools, which brought added stress into the pressured lives of suburban students. Confronted with more work, less sleep, and intensifying competition for access to the most selective colleges, students often found themselves further immersed in what they referred to as the "suburban bubble" that isolated them from the "real world." They found themselves increasingly caught up in the drive for success . . . at any cost.

The middle chapters emerged primarily out of the presence of the Metropolitan Council for Educational Opportunity, Inc., the voluntary desegregation program begun in 1966. The separation of chapters by racial identity reflects the realities of how students generally identified in their lives. The exceptionally raw voices of students surfaced from the constraints conditioned by an education system that routinely denied the significance of race in their world. Their words increasingly revealed the hidden curriculum that comprised some of the most potent lessons learned at school.

These chapters culminate with some updates on the lives of students whose stories and voices speak from their days in high school, along with some commentary on people or events featured in the chapter. Also, a summary of the *lessons learned* about teaching, derived from student feedback, functions as the *takeaways* for the reader. Since good teaching involves change and growth over time, these lessons evolved as well.

The final chapters summarize the lessons, reflections, and recommendations with which to approach a truly child-centered education in the twenty-first century.

The voices presented throughout the book owe their existence to a mutual trust built on relationships established in and out of the classroom. By high school, the vast majority of students had learned silence. To question the orthodoxy of educators often brought disdain upon low achievers or the fear of losing one's privileged position in the educational hierarchy that rewarded the highest achievers. Once students felt empowered to speak, however, they revealed not only their uncensored words on life and their formal education, but also the hidden curriculum at school.

Access to student voices evolved over time, through a variety of methods. Asking students to critique their education through course evaluations provided some important feedback. However, that feedback paled in comparison to the incredibly raw material that would flow from the introduction of student journals into the curriculum.

This major shift occurred when a colleague, Marcia Wilk, shared this alternative to traditional homework assignments in the senior psychology course. A consultation with a former colleague, John Brande, demonstrated how journal assignments could work in U.S.-history classes or, quite simply, *any* class. Allowing students to express what *they* were learning, rather than what the teacher expected them to learn, opened up important channels of feedback from students. Most importantly, students felt increasingly empowered to speak their truth.

Eventually, as part of a course called "Race and Racism in the United States," the most successful tool for accessing the greatest variety of student voices surfaced. An interview project empowered students to open up exceptionally rich and uncensored conversations with each other about their world, specifically with regard to race issues. In 1999, Sue Mack Brigham (Souter) and Mary Anne (Porecca) Borkowski made these voices available to the school and the greater community through the publication of *Race across the Generations: Many Voices, One America.* That volume, ignored by administrators, provided an early impetus to expand the reach of their voices to a greater audience.

This book is not intended as an academic tome, one filled with statistics and citations. Instead, the student voices should serve as case studies that provide insights into the world of education directly experienced by children. Background information on students, teacher commentary, and institutional issues serve as vehicles to provide a context and complement to the student voices, along with some commentary so often missing in school-reform debates. Scholarly works are occasionally mentioned, but the text resides mainly in the real-world perspective so passionately expressed in students' voices.

The student excerpts in this book were selected because they represent common themes that emerged from thousands of journals and interviews, reflect the variety and complexity of the many issues confronting teens, or present some unique perspectives. In no way do they speak for all students, a conceit that denies the inherent individuality and humanity of any class of students.

Their words have been excerpted from journals with little editing, except to maintain the anonymity of specific people or families. Students generally chose to retain their real names, though others asked for pseudonyms. Adult names have mostly been omitted in order to maintain a focus on the themes and the students rather than the individual adults involved.

Uplifting and positive journal entries occasionally surfaced, but just like most of the media and society, teens proved to be more drawn to the dark side of their lives. And since students recognized the complexities of their world and often were seeking some advice or resolution for problematic situations, there was often no inclination to write about a stress-free academic life or a *Leave It to Beaver*–type family.

Students certainly do not provide all the answers to the myriad of education problems, but they do offer keen insights into the direction that education reform should be taking, one that winds its way back to the core of education, the students. Democracies can only thrive when citizens believe there is power in their voices. Students who feel unheard learn powerlessness with regard to their world. Unfortunately, powerlessness may be the most salient attribute that students are currently learning in our schools.

In the fifties, TV personality Art Linkletter coaxed a lot of truth, funny as it was, out of young children. Yes, kids did say the "darndest" things. Contemporary teens may need some coaxing, but they will say the "damnedest" things, if they trust they will be heard. These journals inspired students to freely express their uncensored voices, particularly their keen awareness of how race had impacted their education and personal growth.

The honesty, poignancy, strength, insight, and power of all these student voices deserve to be heard. They had a way of "keepin' it real." Their feedback proved more rewarding and provided more professional development than any feedback ever generated from professional evaluators. Their trust in putting their words to paper and tape cannot be underestimated. Hopefully, the reader will extend that same trust to the selection and presentation of student voices in this book.

Chapter 1

The Education of a Teacher

A junior girl standing down at the end of the hallway appears very distraught. A male teacher, using the power of his body and authority, has cut off her space and is forcefully reprimanding her. Should another teacher intervene? He departs, and it's obvious that the approach of another teacher only serves to heighten her anxiety and fear. A look of concern and soft words of empathy help to diminish her apprehension. Cautiously, the girl begins to explain the drama that has just unfolded. After receiving support for her feelings, a perplexed look overtakes her face as she stammers, "But I thought all teachers stuck together!"

Dealing with a situation where a teacher is bullying a student had never been addressed in any teacher-preparation program or professional-development workshop. As with the challenges of handling most of the really tough issues faced by teachers, no formal training had transpired. As exemplified in the case of this girl, certainly there existed a tacit understanding that teachers would unequivocally support the discipline procedures of other teachers. And both students and teachers would accept the authority of administrators. There should be no surprise that students would learn to be silent.

Armed mainly with their own educational experiences as children and classes mostly focused on theoretical approaches to education, teachers are pretty much thrown into the belly of the beast.

If they are ill equipped to handle some routine problems in the classroom and the school building, it's not hard to imagine how difficult it must be for most teachers to deal with the tougher issues such as bullying, racism, and sexual harassment. Students, however, in their innocence, expect otherwise. They expect the adults to possess the wisdom and skills to address the most vexing issues in their world.

When tough issues are left unaddressed by the adults, the students' education on these issues, by default, enters into a school's hidden curriculum, which produces significant learning outcomes.

Unfortunately, these outcomes generally contradict the formal curriculum. The lesson that this junior girl had learned, along with so many of her peers, was that school adults protected bullies within their ranks. In order to understand the hidden curriculum, the adults have to first engage and listen to the students. Once revealed, those hidden lessons can be mitigated within the formal curriculum. This process can only occur in school buildings where student voices are respected.

Since teacher-training programs mostly avoid any "real-world" issue, most teachers are ill prepared to cope with most aspects of teaching. Ultimately they learn their trade within the isolation of the classroom, informed mainly through their own student experiences, a little professional development, and a lot of trial and error. However, lucky teachers encounter some wise mentoring and some challenges that enable a sharp learning curve.

Taking an aide's position at the East Somerville Community School in Massachusetts would offer just such an opportunity with students, presenting issues well outside the parameters of a typical classroom. Being armed with a master's in U.S. history and certification as a secondary teacher offered virtually no help in educating a class that consisted of "trainable retarded" students (children with significantly impaired cognitive functioning), with the primary responsibility being that of working with a twelve-year-old autistic boy.

The class certainly posed significant problems, but also some out of the ordinary learning experiences. That year would indeed produce some lessons beyond any initial comprehension. Working under the guidance of Barbara Meagher, an equally young professional who possessed expertise and consistent devotion to her students, afforded an excellent role model for any teacher at any level of education.

Accessing strong educational models and mentors would provide the best professional development, especially because they respected the needs of the students.

The primary goal for this boy involved learning to communicate with the outside world, specifically his mother. His disabilities kept him fundamentally locked inside his own private world, which specifically troubled his mother, who wished that he could at least tell her when he was hungry. Over the course of the first few months a portion of each day was spent working directly with him, using Sugar Pops as a reward for learning the sign for "I'm hungry." Barbara provided the necessary procedural guidance, though patience turned out to be the most important piece of the process.

Although the class was self-contained, there were many opportunities for the students to participate in the larger school community. One particularly memorable day, the autistic boy accompanied the class to a play in the auditorium, where he sat in a row among the whole student body. His loud, shrill noises and physical outbursts ultimately necessitated that he be escorted back to the classroom. He immediately snatched a deck of cards off the desk and tossed them on the floor. He then proceeded to lean his back against the wall and throw his legs up.

Such aberrant classroom behaviors always warranted consequences intended to produce proper behaviors. In this case, his feet were placed back on the floor and his attention directed to the cards in a manner that clearly communicated his responsibility to pick them up. After what seemed like an eternity, all the cards ended up in their proper place. A hug let him know that his behavior was commendable.

At that moment of resolution, the sound of hands clapping resounded throughout the room. In a far corner sat a man who had silently witnessed the whole process. He introduced himself as the assistant superintendent for special needs and dispensed his own verbal reward with a reference to "exceptional professionalism." That moment of direct administrative approval would not be replicated much over the course of the next thirty-five years, but it certainly proved to be very powerful and memorable.

Working with other students in the class presented a variety of tough challenges, all requiring patience and flexibility in order to meet their individual needs. Each child possessed clearly defined goals, but achieving those goals necessitated alterations to the curriculum on a daily basis.

This process was exemplified in the case of a girl identified as having "happy puppet syndrome," renamed Angelman syndrome in 1982. This neurogenetic condition consisted of mental and motor retardation characterized by hand flapping, jerky gait, absent speech, and excessive laughter. The main "trainable" goal involved helping her to become independent in feeding herself. Each morning would begin with a breakfast routine that necessitated helping her open her cereal and milk and pour them into her bowl. A mess would generally ensue because of her immediate desire to eat.

However, at any time, toileting issues could take precedence over the independent-eating lesson. At such times the child's needs clearly dictated that the teacher's predetermined schedule had to be instantly modified. A child's feedback about the need to use the bathroom would immediately become the lesson. Sometimes that feedback came too late or went unread, which would then present another disruption to class routines.

This situation occurred routinely with another member of that class, who had suffered brain damage at birth due to seizure activity. Her primary education goal concerned independent toileting, a process that involved many accidents in the classroom. One day the whole class was visiting the "educable retarded" class next door, when it became apparent that she was missing. A quick look into her regular classroom revealed her standing, grinning, in the opening to the bathroom with her face, hair, arms, and hands covered in her feces.

The clean-up required a lot of wet and dry paper towels before her appearance promised a much more pleasant ride home. Of course, dealing with random toileting accidents also required patience, and they always disrupted whatever lessons were occurring throughout the classroom.

The daily routines with these children placed an emphasis on patience, flexibility, and listening to their "voices" in order to advance their education.

Throughout that year in East Somerville, there were considerable frustrations and very few significant educational advances . . . for the students. For a novice in the classroom, however, the learning experiences were considerable. The staff who worked closely with the two programs acted with unmitigated professionalism throughout the year. Their constant focus on the needs of the children enabled them to utilize the skills of an aide, an approach that set high expectation for future classroom experiences.

The school year that started the following fall brought some entirely new experiences, beginning with a stint on the substitute list for the City of Boston. The phone rang on the first day of school with a request for a sub at South Boston High School. On the trip out, the car radio reported the lead story, with police chief Robert DiGrazia expressing his concern over the expected violence at South Boston High School that morning. A significant piece of history would be experienced that day.

The early seventies had catapulted Boston into the national limelight as arguably the most racist city in America, primarily due to opposition to busing for desegregation purposes. The Boston Public Schools had remained virtually segregated despite the *Brown v. Board of Education* decision in 1954 and passage of the Racial Imbalance Act (1965) in Massachusetts. South Boston HS had become a focal point of the crisis due to the ongoing rowdy protests at the school and the highly publicized stabbing of a white student by a black student, which had further enflamed the anger of white residents.

On that September morning, South Boston High School would not disappoint for historical drama. Being situated at the top of the stairs leading to the main entrance provided a close view of that morning's events. Soon, at the base of the steps, there congregated mainly white women and children whose demeanor and placards spoke to Chief DiGrazia's comments on the morning news. Trouble was clearly brewing. The initial approach of the non-white students gave visual confirmation to the imminent tempest as motorcycle-mounted police in riot gear topped the hill ahead of yellow buses surrounded in blue.

The pent-up venom of enraged whites, in the form of words and spit, began to swallow up the single file of students who disembarked between a gauntlet of police, who seemed inextricably caught between their racial identity (some of the protesters cited their lack of racial solidarity) and their duty to uphold the law. Fortunately, no violence occurred in the classrooms, due to the presence of police officers throughout the halls and a near-total boycott by white students.

That day certainly brought to life memories of the Little Rock Nine, especially the denigration that these kids had to endure in pursuit of their education. Clearly, race issues associated with desegregation had continued to plague the public schools. Those issues would become a consistent focus in the classroom, beginning with the next step in an educational career that would eventually give expression to the racial voices of the students living in the midst of desegregated classrooms.

Eventually a steady job opened up at a Boston middle school, after an aide had been stuffed in a locker as a final act of intimidation. Fortunately, the position meant working again under the direction of a confident young professional. Deena possessed an amazing intuitiveness about her curriculum and her students. She realized that all her special-needs training needed to be adapted flexibly in order to successfully run this classroom. She also possessed the confidence to share her doubts and concerns about the many difficulties of educating these students.

This learning and adaptive behavior (LAB) class operated within the special-needs department as a substantially separate program for emotionally and behaviorally challenged teenagers. Typically, these students were black and Latino boys who lagged well behind their peers academically, but were ahead of them in criminal-court involvement. The goals of the program were to keep the students in school, gradually integrate them into mainstream classes, and eventually close the achievement gap between them and students without emotional or learning disabilities.

This assignment proved unusual right from the start. After I found the front door of the school locked, a young man assisting the door monitor provided an escort to this new classroom. On the walk to the second floor he counseled caution in accepting the position, citing the outrageous behaviors of these "crazy" kids. Upon entering the classroom, Deena, with reproach in her voice, turned to the boy and asked, "Stephen, where have you been?" Such was the introduction to a young man who played an important role in this very exacting and exciting classroom.

Right from the start, Deena bestowed the utmost respect, predicated clearly on an educational philosophy that prioritized the need for teamwork in helping these students try to meet their academic and behavioral potential. Whatever ego she possessed, it would never be allowed to hinder the educational job that needed to be done. That year would be spent with a number of highly dedicated teachers, all engaged in the immense challenge of educating middle-school children, most of them bused in during a time of intense racial turmoil.

That year would provide excellent modeling for a most fundamental lesson of teaching: no matter the circumstances, working toward the best interest of students should always be a non-negotiable.

The numerous issues presented by very badly behaved boys with very strong libidos convinced Deena of the need to share much of the classroom discipline, since the students seemed more willing to listen to a male. She also acknowledged a weakness in math, so this position also included new experiences with curriculum creation. However, given the students' mercurial moods, both the math lessons and behavioral expectations demanded constant flexibility.

The constant daily adjustments in class, along with regular consults with other school personnel, also provided substantial opportunities for growth. Listening to the insights provided by special-needs teachers provided significant insights into individual student needs. Follow-up conversations with Deena about these consults and daily classroom practices also added significantly to a very sharp learning curve.

The principal also proved to be a consummate professional and a strong role model. Dr. William Smith, a young and barely experienced principal, possessed an amazing strength of self, even if it meant deferring to a newly hired aide. This remarkable attribute surfaced early in the year, when Stephen instigated a raucous scene in the middle of the school lobby. The noise level prompted Dr. Smith to exit his office and approach an increasingly out-of-control Stephen. Dr. Smith's first attempt to gain control of the situation only prompted a more venomous outpouring from Stephen.

Upon arriving in the foyer, the scene presented a lithe, soft-featured white boy disrespectfully confronting an imposing black man with Wake Forest College football credentials, who looked ready to employ a few football moves to subdue that unruly student.

Quickly catching Dr. Smith's attention, he took the cues to back away from Stephen. Recognizing his own inability to effect any change in Stephen's actions, while also observing confidence in his recently hired aide, Dr. Smith retreated to his office.

Almost immediately the situation became defused, at which point Stephen expressed the desire to apologize to Dr. Smith. After the apology, which Stephen made sure to declare a scam, Dr. Smith disclosed that he had been close to putting his hands on Stephen and expressed how much he appreciated help in handling the situation.

Dr. Smith's ability to recognize the limits of his power, put aside his ego, and then turn over this disturbing situation to an aide demonstrated arguably the most impressive single administrative action to be encountered over a long career in education. Far too many administrators would fail to recognize the limitations of their skills and the strengths of those in their building.

Unfortunately, Dr. Smith's career in the Boston Public Schools proved to be very brief. In 1978, Smith authored a piece in the *Boston Globe* in which he spoke to his understanding of high-risk students and their unusual needs:

> The consequences are to be expected: in the absence of respect for the student on the part of teachers and school the student feels some official suppression of spirit. He seeks support elsewhere ("underground"), which leads him to antisocial, "illegal" behavior. The string runs out as expected: recognition and respect by (illegal) peers replaces positive responses from teachers and school. (*Boston Sunday Globe*, September 17, 1978)

Dr. Smith wrote intuitively and passionately about the challenges faced by students often rejected as "losers," but, more importantly, he acted on those beliefs as a principal.

Explosive situations at the school proved to be far too common. These students earned most of the attention because of their propensity for causing trouble in and outside of the classroom. Rosario, one of the Puerto Rican kids in the class, presented a crude, defiant, loud and obnoxious demeanor throughout the school building. Quite frankly, he seemed to possess no discernable socially redeeming value.

When questioned about his goals in life he immediately responded with his intent to become a pimp. With reference to his real world, Rosario expressed a desire for money, power, and women—and in the projects where he lived, these people were not corporate executives. In addition, he also expressed the goal of "graduating" from the Junior Homicide to become a member of the Latin Homicide gang. Any urge to point out the merits of an education needed some time and patience.

Listening to Rosario and learning more about his life brought a much better understanding of and respect for the obstacles he had to overcome before educational demands could possibly gain traction. His life outside of school encompassed urban life on the streets in ways that most people encounter only in books and movies. He came from a very unforgiving neighborhood . . . and home. His education had to be a more forgiving place.

This classroom consisted of likely "throwaway kids," and they deserved the opportunity to be educated despite all their behaviors to the contrary. Listening to them opened new doors to educating them.

Since these students couldn't function well in the passive environment of a traditional classroom, the curriculum placed a heavy emphasis on a very comprehensive program by which students could earn rewards upon achieving clearly delineated academic and behavioral goals. A token board hung upon the wall displayed their achievements as they worked toward a couple of hours at the West End pool hall, a meal at a local restaurant, or popular items such as record albums (all subsidized by Deena). Sometimes the whole group was rewarded with field trips to places such as Faneuil Hall Marketplace or other downtown locations.

One such trip proved to be quite memorable and produced another profound lesson. The Bunker Hill Monument presented an exceptionally tricky proposition. Driving into the heart of Charlestown with black and Latino students during the busing crisis warranted some strategic planning. So the students were prepped well in advance on a plan that included a *quiet* walk from the car to the entrance of the monument and then a trip to the top, to be followed by a hasty return to the car. Basically, the main goal placed a premium on drawing no unnecessary attention during this field trip.

Upon exiting the school that day, the students' immediate actions indicated that this field trip probably wasn't going to proceed exactly as planned. As the kids ran across the street to the car, they were loudly informed that the vehicle was locked. They laughed and proceeded to pop the lock with some sticks they picked up off the ground. Not quite the skills rewarded on the achievement board, but nonetheless very impressive.

No one ever made it to the monument. No sooner did the students step onto the sidewalk than a loud torrent of Spanish emerged powerfully from Rosario's mouth. Immediately they were piled back into the car, and the monument became a blip in the rearview mirror. When asked what he had said, Rosario's reply confirmed the prudence of such a hasty departure: "If you white people want a piece of this Puerto Rican ass, then come and get it!" Despite the poor timing, Rosario's voice reflected a sense of pride and some inner strength.

Having entered education with the intent of empowering student voices, that day with Rosario provided me with an early indication that those voices might come from very unexpected, and quite challenging, places.

At the end of the year Rosario's family granted permission to have Rosario spend a Saturday with his teachers, which resulted in a trip up to the quaint coastal town of Marblehead, so that he could have some fun running around the rocky coastline. The outing culminated with a pizza lunch, at which point he declared, "I wish you could be my parents." No one quite like Rosario ever surfaced in any future classes, but meeting any students seemingly universally disliked by adults would bring Rosario to mind.

The students who present the most difficult challenges, those who seem to be rejected by both their peers and the adults at school, deserve an education as much as any other student. Quite simply, "Somebody has to advocate for them."

Stephen presented as the antithesis of Rosario. Stephen possessed a charm that worked as effectively on most peers as it did on the adults in the building. As a skinny white boy living on the streets of a predominantly black neighborhood, Stephen had managed to survive through his ability to talk his way out of trouble. Charming Dr. Smith after his outburst in the foyer had been early proof of the skills that enabled Stephen to successfully navigate the streets as well as school.

Monitoring these students in the lunchroom, since that less-structured environment offered the greatest potential for trouble, offered insights into the ways that these students operated on the streets. Every day meant constant attention to the game of cat and mouse, since escape for them meant trouble for the school. However, being closely monitored at lunch did not eliminate the potential for a variety of deviant behaviors.

It eventually surfaced that their primary scam at lunch involved Stephen and Rosario cooperating to steal food. Stephen would sweet-talk the lunchroom staff with compliments about their hair or other pleasant adult talk that kept them engaged, while Rosario filled his pockets with snacks. It certainly did not reflect poorly on these women, because Stephen's prime skill was smooth-talking.

Devon proved to be the enigma of the class, given that he pretty much kept to himself, did his work, and stayed out of the messes created by Stephen and Rosario. That all ended on the one day that it seemed safe for me to leave the building for a sub sandwich. Upon my returning to school with sandwich and soda in hand, an active ambulance outside the front door indicated something was seriously amiss. Within seconds, Deena was being carried out on a stretcher!

The story began in the second-floor hallway, where Deena attempted to direct Devon into the classroom, only to be ignored. Totally at wit's end, she grabbed the "skully" that he had pulled down over his face from his head as a lure to bring him into the room. Instead, Devon started hitting her in a fit of rage. Later that evening, Deena explained the lesson she had learned from that day. She understood the very personal and private qualities Devon attributed to his cap: the very understanding that led her, in her anger, to seize it from him. She blamed herself for having escalated a confrontation that she, as an adult professional, should have de-escalated.

In educating hundreds of diverse students, a lot of mistakes can be expected along the way, but the focus must be kept on trying to learn from those mistakes—and moving students forward in the process.

Later in the year Devon turned up on a windowsill overlooking the street below, engaged in some very inappropriate behaviors with the bus drivers. The adults who gave him audience were more problematic, but Devon's refusal to return to class necessitated immediate attention. Eventually, a consequence more respected on the streets, one that instilled some fear, brought him back to the classroom—but also brought a terse request to report to Dr. Smith's office for a meeting with Devon's parents.

Up until this point I'd had no troublesome interactions with Dr. Smith, but walking down to the office generated a whole lot of trepidation. At the conference table sat a grave principal and two very irate parents. Politely asking Devon's parents if they truly wanted to hear the uncensored story of what had precipitated the confrontation brought an emphatic response from his dad.

So they heard the unvarnished, detailed truth. Immediately, the father turned to his son and said something to the effect of, "You should thank this man for having far more patience with you than I would have. I will take care of you at home." He then offered thanks for making an effort to discipline his son.

That year in the LAB class contributed immensely to the education of this teacher. Dr. Smith's strong leadership established a model by which to judge all other administrators. The students presented the most outrageous classroom-management problems, which would lay the groundwork for any classroom issues in the future. Also, experiencing the amazing perceptiveness and sensitivity to student needs exhibited by Deena provided a model for all future teaching positions. Fortunately, a July wedding would ensure a lifetime of consultations on all matters educational with Deena.

The lessons from that year were profound—especially the realities of the huge gap that separated school from home in the lives of so many students. For many, their lives away from school easily overpowered the limited time at school. Basically, all the school's efforts in support of Rosario would never be acknowledged or understood in the public domain. Instead, the schools would likely be judged as having failed this student. A lot of people at the middle school tried their best to provide a sound education, but sometimes the streets won out.

Unfortunately, there are far too many students like Rosario—kids stuck at the wrong end of the socioeconomic hierarchy. As most teachers learn, you can try your very best, but there are students that you may still fail to reach. Sometimes the streets or unsupportive homes win out. Yet respecting the voices of children and providing a classroom experience that connected the real-world experiences of students to the curriculum could reach many more students. Those lessons, however, would take years of classroom experience to be fully learned.

POSTSCRIPT

Over the summer, a lunch date with Stephen proved to be one of the last contacts with the class, as gradually these students faded into the past. Several years later, we encountered a former administrator who informed us that Stephen had graduated high school and looked to pursue a career in law enforcement.

Thirty-two years after leaving that school, on March 18, 2008, I received a random e-mail that asked, "Are you the same Danny Frio that taught at the Taft Middle School in the late seventies?" It was signed "Devon." My initial reaction went something like, "This can't be . . . but then it must be." He cited two profound moments in his educational life. On the verge of dropping out of high school, he recalled a day at the Taft when I recommended that he move to a higher level because he was really smart at math. Devon took that confidence and proceeded to focus on math.

At another critical juncture, during a rough time at college, he contemplated giving up, before recalling another lesson he had learned from that LAB class at the Taft. He recounted how he and his classmates had deliberately acted out to see if they could drive us to either take days off or just plain quit. He had come to realize that many of their most outrageous behaviors were intended to test our belief in them. To their surprise, we never missed a day. So when he stood on the verge of dropping out of college he remembered how we never gave up on them, and now he would not give up on himself.

Today, Devon, a certified public accountant with a graduate degree from Northeastern University, runs a company he founded called Allgood Products in Watertown, Massachusetts. He also has been married for twenty-one years and is the proud father of four children.

Devon's story only served to reinforce what energizes so many teachers to struggle with difficult students—you just never know when you're making a difference.

In 2000 Dr. Smith organized the historic Joint Congressional Resolution establishing a National Day of Honor to recognize the service of African American and other minority soldiers in World War II. In conjunction with that event, he gave voices to heroes lost in history through his award-winning documentary film *The Invisible Soldiers: Unheard Voices.* Currently, Dr. Smith serves as the executive director of the National Center for Race Amity based at Wheelock College in Boston. If his next dream comes true, the nation will annually celebrate racial friendship on the second Sunday in June as part of National Race Amity Day.

LESSONS LEARNED

Within school buildings, students learn a hidden curriculum that often contradicts the formal curriculum.

Professional development increased dramatically by working with and consulting with an excellent mentor.

There is an absolute need for patience and flexibility in meeting the needs of students who can't learn at the "teacher's pace" and on the "teacher's schedule."

The needs of students should always be non-negotiable.

Strong administrators possess a self-awareness and self-confidence that places student needs above personal ego.

Even the toughest kids want and deserve an education; there should be no "throwaway" kids.

Empowering student voices will likely produce many unexpected words; that should not diminish their importance, but rather stimulate more empowerment.

All students deserve teacher advocacy, but those most rejected by peers and adults need it the most.

Teaching involves a lot of trial and error, and mistakes should serve as prime lessons.

Race plays a very significant role in the lives of some students.

Chapter 2

The Rez

Chinle High School

It is hard for an Indian like myself to make a decision. I mean when I finish high school, I don't want to leave the reservation. I want to be close here with my family and my very close friends.

—Navajo senior

After a couple of thousand miles, the car faced west in a high-altitude forest on the shores of Tsaile Lake in eastern Arizona. In the distance, at the mouth of Canyon de Chelly, sat Chinle, a dusty town at the center of Navajo Nation. Skirting the canyon for the last thirty miles of the journey, the long drive ended with a descent into the "Beautiful Valley." Over the course of the last half hour's drive, however, the trees gradually shrank and then disappeared, giving way to long stretches of sand, clay, tumbleweed, and sagebrush. But initial moments of doubt would eventually fade, as the most fulfilling journey in the field of education was about to commence.

In the spring of 1868 Theodore H. Dodd, Indian agent to the Navajo, reported to General William T. Sherman on the situation of the Navajo at the Bosque Redondo, where they had been forcibly transplanted via the Long Walk from Arizona. After several devastating years in New Mexico, Sherman determined that the Navajos would be better off and the federal government would save money if the Navajo were to be sent to a reservation west of the Rio Grande, where they could be "civilized" and self-sustaining.

Dodd's report eventually resulted in the longest-lasting treaty between the United States and its conquered Indian people: a treaty that would return the Navajo to their sacred lands, primarily located in northeastern Arizona. Under the terms of the Navajo Treaty of 1868, education was to be provided in order to "insure the civilization of the Indians." Along with a schoolhouse for every child between the ages of six and sixteen, the Navajos were to be provided "a teacher competent to teach the elementary branches of an English education . . . who will reside among said Indians, and faithfully discharge his or her duties as a teacher" ("United States–Navajo Treaty of 1868," art. VI).

Just over a hundred years later, Ross Caputo and the Chinle school district looked to take that education to a new level in creating the first high-school gifted-student program on a reservation in the United States. Hiring someone with two years' experience as an aide who had just secured secondary social-studies certification illustrated the desperate nationwide search to fill the position, which had ended in Massachusetts.

Though the term racial achievement gap did not have much recognition at that time, Caputo must have been prescient. First, the students were expected to graduate high school with academic performances that would qualify them for college. Second, they were to be academically prepared to achieve four-year college degrees. Third, they would return to the reservation to assume professional positions that were routinely held by Anglos (non-Indians). In 1977, these goals had no statistical support, but this administrator expected nothing less.

The enormity of this challenge was initially dwarfed by all of the start-up concerns of a new program. The power of near-total control, from scheduling to curriculum and instruction, presented opportunities that would obviously never occur again. Having a blank slate to create an academic program produced some anxiety, of course, but mostly it stimulated a lot of brainstorming about every facet of the curriculum.

Initially, the desolate terrain and extremely rural nature of Chinle tempered some of the professional excitement. A relatively large reservation town of 25,775, Chinle attracted significant attention from tourists, especially Europeans, due to the presence of the Navajo people in the nation's only continually inhabited national park. Canyon de Chelly, a stunningly beautiful and historically significant canyon, provided incredible vistas on each rim, its walls rising a thousand feet high from the valley that was Chinle.

The recent growth of Chinle symbolized the continual transformation of reservation life from an almost completely rural lifestyle into something closer to the way of life of off-reservation citizens in the United States. In 1978, The "School and Community" section of the high school's accreditation report cited this change:

> Within the past ten years tribal utilities have come to the Reservation making it possible to open private enterprises . . . Essentially all of the few businesses Chinle now has have been opened within the past ten years. Pickups have replaced wagons and house trailers are rapidly replacing hogans as the Navahos move closer to available utilities and jobs.

The economic boost provided by the installation of utilities did not dramatically change the exceptionally poor nature of the town. Unemployment stood at a staggering 69 percent, and, of the 31 percent who did have jobs, 45 percent earned less than $5,000 a year. The education level of adults in Chinle was not statistically reported, but expressed as "reflected in the data listed" and "far below national norms."

The Chinle public schools actually serviced children from as far as forty miles away. At the time, a child who lived more than a mile and a half from a road (dirt or paved) qualified for Bureau of Indian Affairs (BIA, now the BIE, Bureau of Indian Education) boarding schools, while the rest attended public schools such as Chinle High School. Overall, the school contained 887 students, of whom all but 36 were American Indian, overwhelmingly Navajo with a small minority of Hopi. The Anglos were all children of school personnel, public-health professionals, or trading-post operators.

Quite starkly, every relevant socioeconomic statistic, especially income and parental education, underscored the factors tied to educational failure in the United States. Both the socioeconomic and racial achievement gaps confronted teachers at Chinle .

The Gifted Student Program represented the vision of a school district that wished to make a very bold step toward mitigating these vast achievement gaps so evident in the local schools. Success at this task also included overcoming a vast cultural gap that separated teacher from students.

Living in trailer 20, a singlewide surrounded by Chinle clay with no discernible amenities, proved challenging, though far less than the cultural and academic issues present in a classroom housed in one side of a doublewide trailer behind the main high school. The extraordinary language barrier initially presented the most obvious problem. Research indicated that this language barrier was pretty much insurmountable, given that after the age of around thirteen it would be virtually impossible for an Anglo to learn the Navajo language.

The physical ability needed to speak this tonal language, with its vowels that changed with pitch, was nearly impossible to replicate, except for some basics such as *yatahey* (hello) and *aoo'* (yes). Whole blocks of time were spent listening to student conversations, with absolutely no understanding of a word being said. Clearly, listening to and accessing feedback from student voices would prove to be a daunting challenge. In fact, a good deal of early communications would involve a form of improvised sign language on both sides of the language barrier.

Essentially, it became evident that gaining access to student voices would have to proceed much more slowly and carefully than in any situation previously encountered. This difficulty was mitigated by the fact that any student who could be considered for the gifted program had to have some reasonable bilingual skills. Even so, most of those students were reluctant to speak with an unknown Anglo man.

This cultural barrier had to be transcended—a process that would require patience, given the necessity for first developing trust, a trust that had to overcome present cultural gaps and a long history between Anglos and Navajos. This gap was especially spacious with the female students, who were culturally prohibited from looking straight into the eyes of Anglo men.

Also, the cultural norm of pondering one's responses rather than risking a poor but rapid answer to questions proved costly on tests geared to the *Jeopardy!* style of response. This reluctance to offer a response without long and serious contemplation, which would be viewed negatively in traditional Anglo schools, would ultimately provide some early and constant exposure to what would much later appear in educational research as "wait time." The efficacy of waiting for responses would be a valuable lesson for the years ahead.

The state required IQ tests for funding purposes—the very style of test that proved unsuited to the culture of the Navajo students. Thus, it made more sense to emphasize qualities that identified potential and achievement. For example, given the goals of college graduation and a return to the reservation, the inclusion of social assertiveness and independent study habits weighed heavily in the selection process. Without some semblance of these essential qualities of the Anglo educational system it seemed highly unlikely that Navajo students would be able to compete in a college world of mainly Anglo students.

At that time, a very small percentage of American Indian students were surviving their first year of college, and the main factor appeared to be lack of confidence in competing with Anglos at school. The intimidation involved cultural norms as much as a learned sense of intellectual inferiority later termed a *stereotype threat*, a phenomenon substantiated by Claude Steele and Joshua Aronson in *Stereotype Vulnerability and African-American Intellectual Performance*.

Navajo cultural pride existed alongside a pervasive sense of intellectual inferiority to Anglo peers. Aside from Shirley, who already possessed the confidence of a successful student, the Navajo students entering the program generally needed enhanced confidence and competence in order to compete in a predominantly Anglo school setting. The obvious dilemma involved building more assertiveness and competitiveness without promoting assimilation. All of this had to be considered before a student set foot in the classroom.

Navajo attributes of cooperation, humility, and public timidity had to be maintained so that the students could successfully walk in two worlds. In effect, two "real worlds" had to be constantly taken into account, a daunting task for sure.

Initially, the classload was set at twenty, with students to be pulled out of their regular classes for a more advanced curriculum. The students would take courses including Algebra I and II, American History, Free Enterprise (an Arizona required course), and Research and Writing. In order to maximize the impact of the program, students were enrolled into as many as three periods a day. Needless to say, some teachers resented having their "best" students removed and their professional competence called into question by a young newcomer.

This response was certainly understandable since the transfer of students to another teacher suggested different levels of competence. However, there could be no wavering on what seemed to be in the students' best interests. Basically, the success or failure of the program could best be determined if students participated as often as possible.

Some staff members also expressed some disdain for the notion that a "gifted teacher" had been hired, as opposed to the program's own official designation of a "teacher of the gifted." One day in the teacher's room, while I was working on some lessons, the hostility toward this new program boiled over. One teacher in particular expressed his hostility very bluntly.

He began with statements such as "I bet you think these Indians are smart," followed by something about how anyone who did must think that blacks were "our" equals; this set the tone for the confrontation. It became more personal when he stated, "You must think you're so much smarter than us 'cause we're from Oklahoma and Texas while you're from Massachusetts." Avoiding the teachers' room would prove to be a worthy strategy. However, for the students in any classrooms where these sentiments also existed, there could be no avoidance.

Eventually it became apparent that Chinle High contained mostly dedicated and honorable teachers, including some who lent much support to the program. Unfortunately, it doesn't take more than few poor teachers to negatively impact the achievement of individual students and potentially alter the environment of a school. Reservation schools often have a difficult time attracting *any* teachers. Therefore, as would soon become apparent, teachers could expect less risk of losing their jobs. The poorest districts around the country understand this dilemma quite well.

A much broader issue confronting the program surfaced during a full-school assembly in the fall of 1977, when tribal chairman Peter MacDonald spoke to the students on the issue of education. The most controversial portion of his speech occurred when he encouraged the students to pursue a college degree so that they could better serve their people by replacing the Anglo professionals on the Rez. This declaration clearly affirmed the goals of the gifted program, but any sense of a shared academic mission quickly dissipated when some fellow faculty members began to voice anger about how the "chief" had threatened their jobs.

Despite many hurdles, the program progressed very smoothly. Within a month potential participants had been identified, tested, and placed in a variety of courses. In a school where whites represented around one percent of the student population, they ended up with nearly 25 percent of the slots in the program. Although this unforeseen development initially proved disconcerting, the inclusion of whites actually provided a positive element to the class, since competition with whites had to be experienced in order for the Navajo students to succeed at college.

Approaching the cultural gap with no past training created the need for a lot of assistance. The most honest and often trenchant insights into the struggles faced by Navajo students came through a close friendship with Leroy and Sally Mitchell of Many Farms. Sally taught social studies at Many Farms BIA School, which provided a natural connection, while Leroy, native to the reservation, provided frank cultural insights. Having lived off-Rez for a number of years, Leroy was particularly adept in both worlds, though totally committed to his Navajo culture.

A very early "cultural adventure," one that set the tone for a budding friendship, involved exploration of Canyon de Chelley. On an excursion into the park, Leroy fell victim to the canyon's dangers, when his *chitty* (a vehicle, in this case his pickup) became mired in quicksand. A favorite picture from that day shows Deena reaching toward the sky exhorting for help, while Leroy attempts to get some traction under a front wheel. Our inability to dislodge his pickup meant a long, hot walk through the sand with the intense midday sun beating down on the inner canyon floor.

About a half hour into the walk, with Leroy in the lead, Deena's misery from burning feet led to an amusing cultural episode that would set the stage for a lifelong friendship. At one point, Leroy turned to behold what appeared to be a truly ridiculous sight, an Anglo man carrying his wife so that she could have relief from the hot sand. Leroy's burst of laughter was followed by his uncertainty as to who deserved the greater pity, the woman who asked to be picked up or the man who consented. The ability to laugh about such cultural differences would prove very helpful in trying to navigate the predominantly Navajo world.

For Navajo students, however, living in two worlds was not a part-time exercise. Throughout history, American Indians had been forced to deal with the Anglo world, mostly from a position of less power. An Anglo teacher could choose to step across cultural lines, but they faced the constant tension of clashing cultural values.

The initial method for opening up the pathways to communication with the students involved working with them individually. Small class sizes provided the ideal circumstances for such close personal attention. These conversations helped to establish the trust necessary for opening the door to future class discussions. Of course, much research has continually reaffirmed the benefits of small class sizes, especially for those students most disaffected or disadvantaged.

A second means to accessing their voices arose at the end of the first semester, when the students provided feedback on a course-evaluation sheet. The sheet probed with a number of questions, including what they liked about class, what teaching styles interested them most, and how the classes could be improved.

Their responses used phrases in support of discussions/debates as the most interesting and informative classes: "we have open discussions with the whole class"; "making comparisons helped me to pinpoint the differences"; "interesting when both student and teacher get involved"; "with the participation of ourselves we are able to learn more"; "broadens our horizons"; "the discussions are usually lively and quite extensive about the subject"; "I love to get different people's points of view on a subject"; and "in this class we are able to discuss what we do and don't understand."

The students also cited, multiple times, the merits of small classes, with wording such as the following: "the individual attention; get more time with the teacher"; "the personal help we receive, because it helps us to more readily see and correct our mistakes"; "I feel that the teacher . . . determines what would be the best way to approach a situation for a certain student"; and "I like how the teacher can get around to everyone, since this is such a small class." The last significant response cited the way the class dealt with the "real world."

The several references that students made to the "real world" aspects of class discussions inspired the creation of a social-history course that emphasized contemporary, mainstream American culture. This course became especially important in trying to prepare the students for the off-reservation college experience that would place them in a predominantly Anglo environment. It also served to partially replace a principal component of the original program goals that included experiential education.

Clearly, the students felt most engaged with pedagogy that emphasized active learning over passive, and connections to their world. Without a doubt, the students expressed their desire to speak and be heard. The next thirty years of teaching would unquestionably corroborate the cross-cultural nature of this aspiration.

The initial plan to connect student learning to the "real world" by pairing up students with local professionals who could serve as role models and mentors failed to take root. Basically, the town of Chinle simply lacked sufficient commercial and professional opportunities for students. Instead, the social-history course would be complemented by some additional exposure to the commercial, postsecondary world that they would experience more regularly in off-reservation college towns.

The difficulty in achieving this goal, however, was epitomized in the case of Patty, a model student in the classroom, despite the large cultural gap she faced on a daily basis. She possessed a bright-eyed interest and intellectual curiosity that surfaced in every topic she studied. Though Patty struggled with writing in English, she managed to convey some interesting insights into her world, for instance when she described family life: "For example, in my family we all have to share the daily tasks, our belongings . . . and lectures."

Patty was the youngest daughter in a very large family, who had regular chores that were quite simply awe inspiring. On one memorable day, Patty's story emerged as a result of her lateness to class. She felt that she had let the teacher, and herself, down by not having accomplished her morning tasks as efficiently as necessary to get to school on time. This apology opened the door to a fascinating story about Patty's life.

Each morning Patty rose before dawn to take the sheep out to first pasture. Upon her return, Patty cooked breakfast and cared for her seriously ill father, who had taken up residence in his own hogan in the compound. After her chores were done that day, Patty rode her horse to school, got bogged down in the mud, and arrived late to class. And *she* felt badly!

Patty seemed to be an ideal candidate for a position in Chinle's commercial district, comprised of about ten small businesses. Full of spunk and energy, Patty possessed all the necessary qualities to successfully meet the goals of the gifted program. And when the owner of the hardware store in town agreed to hire her for the summer, the stage was set for this new aspect of the curriculum. The next day, Patty received this news with a most memorable look that so vividly expressed without any words, "How shall I let this man down?" Ever polite and respectful, Patty conveyed her appreciation for all the effort expanded on her behalf, but she declined the offer.

What transpired next opened the door to another fascinating cultural exchange. Patty explained that she simply preferred to herd her sheep during the summer. This prompted a response that came from a very honest place, and that always seemed the best way to approach these conversations. "I would think it's so boring being out on the range all day with nothing but sagebrush and tumbleweed. How do you do it every day?" Patty's incredibly bright smile spread across her face, exuding a look that combined understanding, appreciation, and innocent amusement at the ignorance of her Anglo teacher. Patty explained how her eyes saw something new and different every day, from plants to rocks to animals. Her sheep, all of which had individual personalities, brought her a sense of fulfillment that she eagerly anticipated each summer. Patty told some enthralling stories that day, as she turned her teacher into an apt student.

That summer, Patty would ride her horse, armed with a rifle in case coyotes threatened her sheep, but she would never return to the gifted program. In the fall, she visited to convey her decision to spend senior year at another school. She courteously accepted the offer of help with regard to any future guidance she might need in the college-application process.

Patty visited again late in the spring, with the news that she would not be attending college. Instead, she intended to follow her dream to be a heavy-equipment operator. Her decision could only be met with understanding and encouragement. Those bright eyes and that broad smile spoke to a passion that could not, and should not, be denied. Patty may have "failed" the program, but she didn't fail to leave an indelible mark on her teacher.

Sometimes a teacher's dream may not match an individual child's dream, which should not be considered a defeat, since children should always be free to pursue their own dreams.

Eventually, instead of job shadowing and placement, a new component to the curriculum was instituted to meet the goal of furnishing the students with some understanding of the social and educational road that lay ahead. The first of two major field trips required little in the way of logistics, given that Navajo Community College was only thirty miles from Chinle. This trip was intended to familiarize them with a college campus and provide the first step toward building some comfort being around a college campus.

The second field trip encompassed a great deal more planning since it involved a weekend trip to Phoenix. Since the intent of the program involved placement of students in off-reservation schools, a visit to Arizona State University seemed like a necessary step forward. This trip necessitated raising money, which inspired the showing of a movie to the whole school. Since the nearest movie theatre was about ninety miles away, this unusual event generated quite a crowd. That money helped fund a plan that included a tour of Arizona State University and a nighttime trip to an amusement park.

While processing the trip with the students, it became clear how it felt for them to be surrounded by Anglos "out in the world." This apprehension became quite apparent while walking around the ASU campus. One couldn't escape the preponderance of blond people and the dearth of Navajos on campus. Adding that blunt cultural presence to the competitive college classroom amplified the challenge faced by these students. Such experiences gave real life to the challenge of navigating the social and academic worlds dominated by Anglos, yet the goals of the program had to confront that challenge.

The college-admission piece necessitated an immediate and ongoing connection to the school's guidance staff, especially for their expertise on which institutions might be most suitable for Navajo students. In the spring, the junior guidance counselor, a relative newcomer to the department, invited all juniors to an important meeting, one intended to address the significance of the senior year. This figured to be an ideal time for them to begin thinking about how they would approach the college-application process.

The counselor's opening remarks proved to be quite stunning. She built the drama to a crescendo about an imminent and most significant life decision, one that would define their future. The words that followed closely approximated, "You will soon be selecting a mate for life." A subsequent story about how she had met her husband and how her careful search had been rewarded with a happy, lengthy marriage was followed by the lessons to be learned from her experience.

This meeting totally epitomized how the gifted program operated far out of the mainstream of the school. Absolutely no words were spoken about college or even the process of contemplating post–high school employment. Yet evidently reality had won out. Indeed, the majority of students would probably not attend college or find gainful employment—at least not in the commercial sense. This meeting starkly illustrated the task faced by students in the program. Once again, flexibility and adjustments in the curriculum were necessitated in order to equip students to achieve their goals.

Adjustments to life in Chinle tended to follow a similar learning curve. In the late fall when the monsoon rains arrived, pretty much the whole town turned to mud. Leroy, however, laughed at any complaints about the mud. He promised that the dry spring weather would prove far worse for Anglos. His dire warnings about blowing dust that would cover the floor of the trailer and wreak all kinds of havoc sounded like the usual Navajo humor at the expense of naïve Anglos. Come spring, however, sighting a cloud and the potential for rain seemed like a godsend.

When the first dust storm hit town it could be seen approaching Chinle as a wall of brown blowing from the west. You could see it coming from fifty miles away. And when it arrived, the dust blew right through the doors and windows! And it got worse. When you stepped outside, the dust choked up your breathing and tore into your face. At school, the halls and classrooms filled with dust, yet students and teachers continued their work. Leroy declared that the mud and the dust had been sent by the Creator to keep Anglos away from the Navajos' sacred lands. Indeed, the Creator had been wise. It was miserable.

That spring, as the school year came to an end, a strong foundation had been established for the gifted program. The process for identifying and placing students had been streamlined, new courses had been added, and trusting relationships with students helped provide important feedback. Students were progressing at their studies, which, with one more year, would hopefully prepare them for postsecondary success. The following year would also bring me new responsibilities, as I had received a promotion to head of the special-needs department. This leadership position certainly indicated a year of new challenges, along with potential for more growth.

However, the return to Chinle brought monumental challenges that were entirely unpredictable. At the teacher orientation, I found that the most incredible and immediate problem involved heading a department without any other teachers. School would start, and there would be no teachers in the rest of the special-needs classrooms. There are many inequities between a reservation school and a typical suburban school, but classrooms without teachers speak to the immense education gap in America, especially before the computer age.

Eventually, the assistant superintendent brought in a minister to cover some classes, shuffled around some other people to fill in, and then hired Greg, a retiree who looked to utilize a special-needs degree he had earned over twenty years before. Some students now had adults in the classroom, but the problems in providing them an adequate education would persist.

I helped fill in with classes with students who spoke little to no English. Communication was very difficult, and the situation necessitated the creation of new ways for generating feedback from students. Reading body language proved very valuable, along with building trusting relationships with students in the classroom and on an individual basis. Essentially, those two methods would remain fundamental tools that would later lead to vital ways to gain access to the hidden curriculum that was otherwise perpetuated through student silence.

Another lesson, one often forgotten in the aging process, was that beyond all the possible cultural differences that exist, kids are still basically kids. That lesson would always be quite valuable in building bridges across racial barriers.

Meanwhile, every position in the department had been filled, though the situation with Greg proved more detrimental than having the position vacant. In fact, he presented the most prolific and frustrating supervisory issue that year, and one that magnified the constant difficulty in finding teachers for reservation schools. Since his classes met in the same trailer as the gifted program, it was impossible to avoid his unprofessional behaviors.

Flags went up within the first couple of days when he asked to speak to me in private, evidencing a strong sense of concern and urgency. He opened an initial conversation with exasperation and disdain, saying, "These people are so primitive. They're so dumb. I can't believe that we let them live in our country." The school was certainly desperate for teachers; but though dismissal was not an allowed option, at that exact moment it became clear that very close attention would have to be paid to his classes. The students obviously didn't deserve to be subjected to those attitudes.

Subsequent problems seemed to surface on a daily basis. Sometimes his classroom would be filled with students . . . and no teacher. On numerous occasions he could be found asleep on a stuffed lounge chair in the trailer's book room. After a reprimand, Greg did spend more time in the classroom, though no discernible curriculum ever seemed to be taught.

With the hope of impressing administration with the urgency of the problem, many of his in-class comments were documented, including "I don't want any more Indian talk in here," and "That's why you're in special education, because you fool around and don't know how to act around people. You got some schoolteacher mad." In reference to the gifted students, he commented, "IQs don't mean anything. I don't want you in that room. It's for the smart kids. Did you know that they have more problems than you guys? When they leave here they can't talk to normal people because they are so smart."

Before Greg's arrival, these students had been attending class on a regular basis, during which times they were supplied with worksheets whenever no teacher was available. Not a great education, but still superior to the situation with Greg.

Now, the students were showing up and waiting for their education, and there was none to be had.

Within days, Greg's story reached a new nadir when an urgent message came from the principal to report to his office. The principal explained that Greg had accused two students of assault, a charge that the students had not argued. Without any refutation on the part of the students they faced expulsion, despite the belief that Greg's story lacked credibility. The principal wanted the truth from both sides, but up to that point the boys had refused to talk with him.

A visit with Greg started out with this initial response: "Have you ever been in a room surrounded by threatening Indians, and they have both exit doors blocked? I was so scared that I pulled out my can of mace, sprayed some, and ran for safety." Of course the story bore no resemblance to any behaviors remotely likely on the part of these two boys, or any students in the high school for that matter. However, cultural values strongly indicated that these boys would have a hard time disputing the word of a teacher, despite the ridiculousness of the story. Fortunately, the students' side of the story was deemed important, so the principal engaged someone he figured they would trust.

They spoke little English, but gradually they described the event in a way that resonated squarely with the many scenes observed in Greg's classes. Typically he just "hung out" in the class and, if no work had been provided, the students simply milled about. This typical day had turned into chaos when Greg's disdain for and fear of his students had spiraled out of control. "Surrounded by Indians," he indeed used his can of mace, but only out of an irrational fear that the students *might* assault him. The students were dismissed back to class without fear of expulsion.

Justice had been served, but only after listening to student voices and granting them the credibility they deserved in this case.

Despite these diversions, the gifted program continued to evolve, mainly adjusting to student needs, particularly those potentially related to their ability to access and succeed at the next level. A physics course was added to the curriculum, with the intent of building a stronger transcript for the students. However, the high school's ten-year accreditation evaluation took the school to task for having an uncertified teacher of physics and for the obvious lack of lab facilities. Fortunately, any teacher deficiencies in the non-humanities managed to be overcome by the students' innate intelligence.

A fairly typical class in math and science would involve circulating among the students or teaching to small groups throughout the period. This allowed for close personal attention and a general de-emphasis on teacher-directed instruction. Oftentimes, students had their learning problems resolved by other students or managed to resolve them on their own. Jameson exemplified how this process worked. He came to class and opened his algebra book, going chapter to chapter. Rarely would he ask for any help. Routine checks most often resulted in the response, "I'm OK."

Late in the year, his grade was administered the California Achievement Test in math. During the test Jameson worked quietly and methodically until placing his pencil down with about a half hour of time remaining. It seemed quite early for Jameson to be finished, and not like him to give up. An inquiry about any potential problems was met with Jameson's typical succinctness: "All done." Indeed, Jameson had responded to all of the questions, even those that went beyond what he had seemed to cover in the book. When the results came back to the school, Jameson had stunningly achieved a perfect score.

Perhaps Jameson's most lasting lesson, one that would be important for all future classes, called attention to the reality that teaching can often be accomplished by providing opportunities for letting students learn for themselves and through their peers.

Though Jameson possessed obvious cognitive skills and seeming confidence, a constant vigilance had to be paid to establishing a strong foundation for leaving the Rez and gaining a college degree. For some of the students, that step still proved to be very difficult. At that point the idea for this book had not yet surfaced, so only a small fraction of student writing remains.

The quotations that follow display the fundamental struggle of maintaining the family support system on the reservation while also feeling the allure of off-reservation opportunities. This student's words speak well to this dilemma: "It is hard for an Indian like myself to make a decision. I mean, when I finish high school, I don't want to leave the reservation. I want to be close here with my family and my very close friends." Of course, staying on the Rez posed significant issues, as he stated, "If I decide to stay I'll probably have a hard time in getting a job and . . . I won't have enough money to run a family."

Beyond the social issues, students generally lacked academic confidence and often competence, a dynamic that can be very difficult to overcome when students possess strong feelings of intellectual inferiority. What's internalized over sixteen years cannot be easily reversed. Karina exemplified this debilitating self-assessment that can prevent students from coming close to their academic potential.

Karina entered the program in a unique fashion. A teacher referred her with the hope that an exception might be made for a junior girl whom she perceived to be heading down a potentially self-destructive personal and academic path. Karina was arguably the most accomplished female athlete at the high school, but had not distinguished herself academically in any way that would have warranted inclusion in the program. However, this teacher believed in Karina's intellectual potential, and she felt that the gifted program might boost her self-esteem, which then might motivate greater achievement.

Karina could have easily rested on her athletic laurels, but this colleague felt she deserved so much more. Without question, Karina deserved a chance, and she ended up enrolled for three periods of the day and very quickly began to achieve the academic success that spurred further motivation. Karina maintained a constant focus on her studies, never wavering from the day she set foot in the program. In fact, her boyfriend Monty sat next to her in a couple of classes, and neither of them ever let that relationship interfere with their schoolwork.

Karina cited individual attention and class discussions in her first written evaluations of the program as prime reasons for her success. She also stated that her acceptance into the program indicated a show of confidence in her that she intended to validate. Karina's journey in education had just begun, as she would increasingly set her expectations to a higher level and proceed to achieve those goals.

Karina provided my most poignant moment at Chinle High, lingering after class with a very troubled look on her face before she asked, "Why do white people hate us?" Karina's compelling question had been prompted by an incident from a recent basketball road game. Upon emerging from the gym after a tough loss, the Chinle team faced a gauntlet of Anglo "fans" who spit and cursed at the girls. Many of the words focused on the whites' hatred for Indians. Chinle had lost the game, but apparently they needed to understand just how much they were hated.

The thought of anyone hating and taunting Karina was exceptionally sad and ludicrous. But this, she understood, was larger than her. Unfortunately, the blatant racism that Boston had unearthed with busing confronted Indian people on a regular basis. No easy answer existed to Karina's question, but it prompted a discussion on racism that really would continue to resonate for a lifetime.

Standing in that room with Karina on that day, after working so closely with this remarkable student, helped to personalize the race issue, as well as the self-doubt that permeates so many aspects of a child's life. Whereas disdain and disregard for Rosario could be rationalized due to his very aggressive and rude behaviors, no such logic existed for Karina. She deserved nothing short of total respect for her exceptional personal and intellectual qualities. However, when issues of racism surfaced in my future, it would sometimes be the faces of both Rosario and Karina that stimulated action over silence.

Listening to non-white students talk about their racial experiences in the white world certainly provided incentives to continue finding ways to hear their voices. They deserved no less.

At the end of the year, after much debate, personal issues brought the realization that I would no longer call Chinle home. The desire to start a family presented the most compelling reason. Despite some assurances from Anglo couples, the lack of local medical care, given that the public health services on the reservation did not service Anglos except in emergencies, seemed too risky. The dirt airstrip in town, the small plane owned by a staff member, and the short flight to a hospital about ninety miles away all seemed less than ideal, especially when compared to facilities in Boston and New York.

So in May I submitted a letter to the principal, declaring my intention to leave the gifted-program position and terminate all department-head responsibilities as of that notification. A follow-up meeting with the principal led to the longest and most surprising conversations of the year. The first surprise came in the form of the year's written evaluation. This document really affirmed the goals of the gifted program in ways that displayed real appreciation for the cumulative efforts, over two years in the making. The principal wrote:

Teacher and students have an excellent rapport with each other and have a constant listen/talk type of classroom so that the teacher learns as much as the students. Everyone is a teacher and feels a sense of self-worth. A variety of classroom activities leaves to the students the ability to work at their own pace which is determined by the students themselves since they themselves set the tone for the class with them being the catalyst. Mr. Frio works closely with students, counselors, parents and members of his department in order to make sure advanced students get the work they need. Mr. Frio works under adverse conditions with little relief during the day. What he does accomplish with these students is outstanding since he must fight against all odds to offer a program which is enriching the knowledge of superior students in a poor setting.

The ensuing discussion proved to be the most casual and honest one with an administrator over the course of thirty-five years in the classroom. And it ended with a couple of major shocks. The first involved his resignation due to insurmountable differences with the superintendent. His next statement, however, could never have been imagined. He wrote on my termination letter, "I agree with the above request. Other department heads have already withdrawn their duties. As of May 10, 1979, [Greg] will be responsible for the Special Education Department for the remainder of the year since he is the only certified teacher in the department and will be returning next year."

Of course, the consequences meant that administrative politics would take precedence over the needs of students. Unfortunately, this would occur very often with administrative decisions in the decades ahead.

Saying goodbye to Chinle and the Rez in general, along with the students and the Mitchells especially, came with lots of regrets, but also much hope for the future. As I left the Rez, heading south to old Route 66, a group of students followed the car, beeping and waving a last goodbye. They left an indelible image that will forever bring a smile.

The intelligence and motivation displayed by the Navajo students reinforced the belief that many schools underserved much of their underachieving poor and non-white populations. Perceived cultural "deficiencies" and racial stereotypes of intelligence often allow schools to assuage their guilt and shirk their responsibilities for meeting the needs of their most at-risk population of students.

At Chinle, socioeconomic factors certainly contributed to the lack of educational performance by many students, but they did not guarantee it. Each day there awaited a group of students dependent on their teacher's confidence, training, knowledge, and expertise. Meeting the needs of those students proved to be both very inspiring and humbling. Most importantly, their voices and the lessons they taught would never be forgotten.

POSTSCRIPT

We left the Rez in 1979, but the Rez would never leave us. Over the next decade we returned on several trips, catching up particularly with former students and the Mitchells. Karina and her high-school boyfriend Monty both graduated from the University of Northern Colorado in four years and subsequently returned to Navajo Nation. Monty worked as a reporter and editor at the *Navajo Times* before moving on to freelance photography and writing. In 1993, Monty provided both the text and photography in his first publication, *Kinaalda*. Eventually he moved into the education field, where he served as the executive director of the Rough Rock Community School. In 2011, Monty accepted a position as deputy director of Navajo education. However, he never achieved the other goal we had often discussed—to replace Carlton Fisk on the Red Sox.

On a very special late-summer visit in 1986, we had the extreme pleasure of greeting Karina as she emerged from an orientation meeting for her first teaching position at Ganado Public School. During a brief hiatus from teaching, Karina took her advanced computer skills degree and worked developing online American Indian curriculum for the National Indian Telecommunications Institute. Karina's skills and career would soon outpace those of her "gifted teacher." She returned to the classroom, became a science-curriculum leader, and then served as principal at Round Rock Elementary. In 2011, she reinforced her commitment to education on the reservation when she received a doctoral degree from Arizona State University; the title of her dissertation was "The Implications of the Navajo Nation Sovereignty in Education Act of 2005 on Arizona Reservation Public Schools." Karina currently serves as principal at Lukachukai Community School. Along the way she married Monty, raised four children, and became a lifelong Red Sox and Celtics fan . . . and proudly wears a Jacoby Ellsbury T-shirt.

Shirley entered the program with much confidence, leaving little doubt that she would succeed. Indeed, she received a BA in political science/business and public administration, along with a master's certificate in management information systems from Arizona University. Her minor in Indian law and Indian studies of the Southwest led her to continue her educational endeavors at the University of Washington in Seattle, where she currently serves as senior executive manager of bioengineering in the College of Engineering and School of Medicine.

Before leaving the reservation, I asked Leroy to recommend a book that he thought Anglos should read in order to understand his world. He recommended Rodney Barker's *Broken Circle*, which certainly pulled together many of the complexities confronting Indian people as they sought to maintain their cultural identities and dignity in an Anglo world that had so often attempted, at best, to marginalize them and, at worst, to eradicate them. As Leroy stated, Anglos had tried very hard to destroy his people, but they had persevered and would continue to do so.

The book became a well-read selection in the race and racism course. After forty-four years, Sally Mitchell continues to devote her heart and expertise to the history students and faculty at Many Farms High School.

One of the most heartening events with regard to the students' ability to assert their voices took place near the end of the school year, when Staci arrived as an emissary, visibly panting, to announce that all of the class had joined in a massive school walkout! Apparently, the principal had banned the student privilege of walking over to Kentucky Fried Chicken during lunchtime, and now hundreds of students had joined together in protest. Staci, one of the white students in the program, continues to find her voice as a reporter for the *Santa Fe New Mexican*.

Greg never made it through the first year as department head; the students reported that they drove him away. Evidently the students found their voices and advocated for their own best interests.

LESSONS LEARNED

The racial and socioeconomic gaps present daunting challenges, yet they demand constant attention.

Students who live in two worlds, particularly non-whites, need their primary identity affirmed as a foundation for academic confidence and success.

Teachers need to respect cultural differences with their students and make an effort to bridge the cultural gap.

One should constantly find ways to connect the curriculum to the real world of the students.

Students desire an active classroom instead of passive learning, and that means their voices must be encouraged and heard by the teacher and other students, too.

A teacher should be humbled by his or her own learning struggles and the patience of those trying to teach the teacher. Students deserve the same patience from teachers.

Student dreams, though they may not meet those of the schools, still deserve respect.

Teen bridges can be built across racial lines by bringing teens together as young people who share so many common interests and anxieties.

Socioeconomic issues matter immensely, from student readiness to school staffing—and they defy simple solutions.

Racial identity and racial pride denied can debilitate self-esteem and impede academic achievement.

The story of American Indians in U.S. history classes must extend beyond the nineteenth century.

Chapter 3

Wayland

Realities of Life in a Model American Suburb

Growing up in a white suburb means that there is a preconceived path to success in life. From an early age we are taught to follow our dreams and we are told that if we try hard enough we are guaranteed what we want. . . . I feel that because of this notion that any goal can be accomplished with hard work, white people have a bias towards poor people living on welfare because we expect them to do the same as we do, graduate and be successful.

—Jeremiah

Because the people [in the suburbs] had similar lifestyles, the system of conformity was not just encouraged in the school systems, but also at home. They reduced individuality to a point where it is not even much of an option.

—Alexandra

In 1979, for the most part, Wayland, Massachusetts, epitomized the American Dream. Large homes, spacious yards, varied recreational facilities, and a strong school system made the town very attractive to professionals wishing to live within easy access of both Boston and the burgeoning technology corridor west of the city. Yet there still remained some rural enclaves on the north side of town, along with dwindling remnants of its working-class past in the village of Cochituate.

The "dream" became more apparent as the working-class population disappeared along with the factories that had been a major source of employment in the industrial past. Rural areas also disappeared as the construction of new homes moved Wayland into the pantheon of elite Boston suburbs. Wayland's appeal would become inextricably tied to the reputation of its schools. That reputation received a boost when the schools transformed from providing a comprehensive education to one that reflected the higher "intellectual" demands of a professional, affluent community.

The demographic changes in town were reflected in student voices, as working-class kids were replaced by students who entered kindergarten with college in mind. Talk about shop and cooking classes was replaced by angst over advanced-placement classes and getting into a "good" college. Increasingly, the world of school came to dominate adolescent lives outside of school, as the competitive world of professional adulthood seemed to be further encroaching on the fragile lives of adolescents.

Student journals revealed how the high-stakes academic competition that had come to define their world produced debilitating stress and intensified the unethical behaviors that enabled them to manage more homework, more projects, more books, more tests, and more activities, with no more time. They also revealed the tremendous stresses of family life, the increased drinking and drugging as coping mechanisms, and the disconnect they felt from an education and town culture that had constructed a "bubble" to protect them from experiencing and knowing the "real world."

Before the construction of this protective "bubble," the town had to deal with the dramatic economic changes epitomized by Wayland's declining working-class section, located around Dudley Pond and Lake Cochituate. The once-vibrant industrial base, along with its working class, had begun to slide toward extinction, gripped in the manufacturing collapse that permeated the entire New England region. But that economic rupture would not occur in silence. The working-class tensions so evident in 1979 were not to go silently into oblivion.

The shifting of class plates just beneath the surface erupted in 1985 with a public splash when *Boston* magazine ran a story titled "The Bogeyman Comes Home" (John Strahinich, December 1985). The article focused on the class tensions evidenced in the controversy surrounding a "townie" with a criminal past who had been appointed as executive director of the Wayland Housing Authority. The more affluent newcomers who opposed the appointment, the so-called Waylandites, were accused by the townies of trying to usurp power in town government.

The townies went public, speaking bitterly about the whole affair. One townie exclaimed, "Wayland's a heartless town" (290), while another declared, "It's a bedroom town now. They don't want no [*sic*] industry. And they don't want any part of us. The blue-collar guys, they're just putting up with them" (293). Clearly, the townies understood that their power was waning and the world they once knew was quickly slipping away.

By the dawn of the twenty-first century, Wayland reflected a near-complete transformation into one of the "model" suburbs that filled a semicircular belt around the city of Boston. The town's website would cite its "semi-rural setting" and access to the "marshes and fields that surround the Sudbury River," which served to provide opportunities for "passive recreation." Along with the easy access to shopping, sightseeing, and dining, most emphasis was placed on "one of the finest school systems in the state." Wayland High School (WHS) stood as the capstone to one of the idyllic suburban experiences in the American Dream.

By 2009 the strong working-class identity maintained its existence mostly in the nostalgic memories of an older generation, with a few holdouts reminiscing about a sense of loss. A final spasm of the class struggle saw the creation of a "gang" called "Coch" in the first decade of the new century. Replete with colors and attitude, its immediate flourish petered out after a couple of years, perhaps the last tremor of seismic forces that had gripped the town for decades.

It was this new generation of adolescents growing up in a predominantly affluent town who would consistently term their suburban community the "Wayland Bubble." Typically, the term referred to the homogeneity of life in an affluent, predominantly white suburb. On the one hand, students acknowledged gratitude for the mostly safe and comfortable lives they lived, yet the term always seemed to be expressed with an overriding tone of derision.

Magda, a young woman with some strong first-generation-immigrant values, revealed the disconnect from the "real world" and the contempt for pressures within the bubble:

> The more I live in Wayland, the more it bothers me how the houses are so far apart from each other, how people don't know their neighbors, how parents freak out about college, how the focus is on homework, classes, and grades, how everyone has the newest popular gadget and still

manages to complain about something. People in high school aren't really focused on the outside world. Wayland is this little bubble where people can live in their houses, go about their business, and come home in the evening not ever having thought about the people who aren't living in Wayland. I do believe that in some ways Wayland is an awesome town. It has its advantages, but I think a lot of people don't UNDERSTAND what is going on in the rest of the world. I don't understand what is happening in the rest of the world. . . . Junior year was extremely stressful. All I remember is doing SAT prep, SAT II prep, college essays and applications, homework, etc. It was so depressing, looking back on it now. But what else was I going to do? I feel like I have been living in the little world of Wayland, focusing on MY academics, on MY extra-curriculars, and getting MYSELF into college. . . . It just seems so ridiculous, you know? Why do the people of Wayland get to grow up like this?

Lowell summarized his perception of Wayland relative to the real world outside of suburban American towns such as Wayland:

Wayland, the epitome of suburban life. We are middle class citizens not living in poverty. We do not have random acts of violence at our doorsteps. No gang warfare. We do not have kids selling drugs on the street corners. We are not being oppressed by our government. We are not denied the basic rights of man; in fact, we are afforded rights beyond the rights that people fight and die for every day.

A mix of suburban isolation, angst, and idealism surfaced routinely in their voices. Yet students also voiced strong gratitude for the safety and comfort of their lives, along with the benefits one acquired as a graduate of Wayland High School. This disparity between the privileges they enjoyed and the problems they grappled with fueled much of the frustration, fear, sadness, and guilt that surfaced in their journals. One student summed up the feelings of many students when he said, "I mean, we live in a rich white suburb. It's boring and bland but I like it."

As evidenced in the journals, students recognized that the town's growing affluence did not come without costs. The increased pressures at school and at home were often cited as causes of increasing problems with alcohol and drugs. This dynamic of alcohol and drug abuse in the midst of the American Dream evidenced the clear disconnect between the realities and image of their "perfect" suburban world.

Wayland became the face of the problem when it experienced public exposure on November 28, 1989, when the *Boston Globe* published an article titled "A Town with Money—and Drugs," coupled with the statement, "Despite the wealth, Wayland's teenagers have a problem."

Lt. Gerald J. Galvin of the Wayland Police Department addressed the myth of the ideal suburbs: "It used to be believed that only the indigent or ghetto dwellers had a drug problem. But the suburban community has found that they have it also. And they have been forced to come to grips with it." Further bursting the bubble, author Pamela Reynolds stated, "These days, though, even money can't insulate this tranquil community from some hard realities."

Students spoke to the intense pressure to "do better than their parents" in looking to explain the "hard realities" of suburban life. One student articulated a refrain expressed consistently by students throughout thirty years in Wayland: "The [school] pressure definitely ties into the drinking . . . Kids obviously want to forget about their school work. If you're drinking or you're buzzed, you're obviously going to forget about that."

The stresses and pressures of school, however, did not diminish over time. A decade later, one senior wrote about an increasingly typical life for the stressed-out suburban student: "I've been getting that feeling lately, the one that lets me know that soon I'm going to crack and just go nuts for a while . . . I have that feeling of . . . insanity, wanting to just sleep forever, being so tired and so pushed and so unhappy. This sucks."

The following quotes exemplify the many comments expressing how stress had intruded upon and adversely affected their lives away from school:

"This is not to say that I don't, along with many others, enjoy a dinner with my family sometimes during the week, but to be honest, I'm usually bogged down by homework."

"We quantify our work by the amount of sleep we got the night before the project is [sic] due."

"I just feel like I work myself so hard, like a dead, heavy and burdened mule, and I end up in the same place."

"My grades started slipping in junior high. I was too busy at home to keep up with schoolwork. I had to break up fights, pick up broken glass and stay up way too late to think clearly the next day."

"I have actually felt forced upon [sic] by my teachers to do things I absolutely detest."

"Students at Wayland High School live under the constant pressure to succeed. As students, we are pushed to excel and sacrifice a lot of our lives trying to obtain that goal."

"Sometimes, it just feels like I spend so much of my life studying and the only thing that happens is that the walls push in a couple of more inches each day. Why do I do this to myself?"

"More than ten minutes of relaxation in a day would be cataclysmic!"

Sadly, years later these students will probably reflect back on such a journal with a nostalgic attitude that will quite likely disregard the pain and emphasize the gain. It would not be surprising to find these same students regarding the stresses as necessary for success, an attitude that might enable them to ignore the voices of their own children.

Unfortunately, school-reform efforts in the twenty-first century continued to place more emphasis on ratcheting up the education process with more time on task, more homework, and more testing. Alfie Kohn covered this issue extensively in *The Homework Myth*. Suburban students would find themselves lumped together with all schools in a political process obsessed with standardization, which focused on the quantitative side of more work rather than substantive qualitative changes. Many journals dealt with the cognitive dissonance of the school's acknowledgment of the debilitating workload and its disregard for any serious consideration for the students' plight . . . and certainly for their voices.

In fact, the principal would find some humor in his attempt to reduce student stress when interviewed by the *Globe*. He told an anecdote about a failed attempt to hold yoga sessions after school, with this explanation: "The kids told us they didn't have enough time to take yoga because they were too stressed."

This response may have amused some adults, but it did nothing to address the problems that students, like Avery, faced upon entering the high school:

I'm crouched on the floor next to my bed, my knees pulled tightly to my chest in hopes of assuaging the involuntary shaking. Tears are racing down my cheeks in a merciless flow; my face and neck feel swollen and itchy. The room is suddenly swelteringly hot and the floor is spinning. There's an SUV driving back and forth over my chest. I can only choke short, shallow breaths. I can feel that familiar stab of searing pain in the pit of my stomach, like a hot knife has just been plunged into my abdomen. The pain just continues and I feel completely helpless, knowing there is nothing I can do to get rid of it. . . . This was a typical night for me during my freshman year at Wayland High School. I went from the occasional project and fifteen minutes of nightly homework in middle school to lab reports, pop quizzes, and all-nighters to finish six-page papers at the dreaded high school. It definitely wasn't smooth sailing during my freshman year—instead I was thrown in with the sharks, and expected to swim all on my own.

The grade and college competition, in conjunction with the social pressures to live a trendy lifestyle, tend to mimic the stresses of the adult world, a world that has increasingly encroached on kids before they are emotionally equipped to cope.

This persistent interrelationship between academic and social pressures in the area of student substance use often intertwined with various problems at home. Clearly, one of the most glaring differences between the adolescent world of the Baby Boom and twenty-first-century students can be found in the breakdown of the family. The consequences of divorce, along with the earlier onset of issues such as alcohol and substance abuse, popped up quite often in journals.

Of course, some of these family journals resulted in upbeat and encouraging descriptions of close, supportive families that fit the suburban ideal; but many provided emotionally provocative stories of pain. At school, many of these students managed to hide their private lives quite well. Nicole worked hard at school and persevered in honors courses despite all the difficulties she endured outside of school. As a junior, she managed to maintain a constant smile and upbeat demeanor that endured despite a very difficult home life, one she shared with more of her classmates than she realized:

> Honestly, all I remember about my Dad was that he worked until six thirty every night. He came home hungry, tired, and irritated that we were so noisy. I never realized it was strange that we used to say "Yes, Dad" or "Yes, Sir" to almost every command he issued. Man, could he yell, and when he yelled, he took his sweet old time. That's all there was to him. . . . Then he moved out. That was it, no more dad, one night when I wasn't home. I lived with my step-mom. I hated her guts. I don't think I've ever felt hate or rage or disgust so violently as I did then. I blamed her for my mother ditching me, my father leaving me, the sky's blueness, my sadness, and my life. I feel like I've been raising myself for almost eighteen years. And applying to college, grades, sports, plays, the three jobs I have . . . it's all part of the game. I can't wait until college. I want to get lost, in a huge school somewhere where it doesn't snow and the sun makes you happy. I want three thousand miles between home and me. I want to not think about the parents who bore me and don't exist anymore. Part of me thinks parents and parenting are shit. Sorry. But it's true. This self-parenting is tough. P.S. Sorry, I'm not sure why this all came up. It's been a long tiring week. I'm sorry.

Casey managed excellent academic success while maintaining the exterior mask of the "ideal suburban image" to cover the emotional turmoil of her home life. This student's personal strength, and the growth she evidenced over the years, elucidated the incredible perseverance of so many students who faced very challenging obstacles in attempting to reach the high expectations of the ideal suburban world. This short excerpt captures the essence of a very long and anguished journal:

> My dad is an alcoholic, yet I never realized that was why he acted the way he did. . . . When I lived with him I was too young to connect his violence with his drinking. . . . I have five or six vivid memories of family fights, screaming matches. . . . I have NO memory of living in [town] unless my dad was drunk, or I was at school or sports. My life before thirteen is like a big black hole with a couple islands (family fights, soccer, birthday parties).

The most disturbing cases of dysfunction evidenced in these journals certainly knew no cultural or economic bounds, though they sometimes contained elements that derived from circumstances more prevalent in an affluent culture. A student expressed exasperation with the drone of school, placing an emphasis on how "success and appearance is all that matters, emotional happiness is never stressed." She concluded with, "I can't remember the last time I heard a kid say their aspiration was to be happy."

This senior girl wrote about the adult demands she faced at home from parents who had a hard time coping with life and her inability to truly help. She ended a journal with the resignation to her situation as follows: "So tomorrow at school people will expect me to be happy and lively." Her ability to achieve strong academic success under these circumstances proved to be more common than unique.

Other students wrote about the mask they wore to school, with comments such as Theresa's: "I'm pretty outgoing, so tomorrow at school people will expect me to be happy and lively. . . . Anyway, tomorrow I'll have to put on a smile, so no one asks if I'm OK." One boy wrote, "The masks that we use to protect ourselves rarely come off . . . often we seem out of touch with our emotions, even robotic." Or, as Lowell put it, "We struggle with our internal crisis with a smile on our faces and go on our way."

A very kind and sensitive young man wrote a very long, gut-wrenching journal that involved a great deal of physical violence at home. Obviously he carried this pain with him every day, yet he came to class and did his best to achieve success at the honors level. Occasionally, his work would be a little late, but, like most of his peers, he never asked for any special consideration. He would take any applicable penalty and move on. At the end of a very lengthy journal he wrote about how good it felt to write down his story, ending with, "Thanks for taking the time to read all of this . . . I truly appreciate it."

Problems at home certainly had to impact a student's performance at school, yet so many students managed to maintain a strong academic profile despite struggling with a very unsettled home life. Overwhelmingly, students refused to use personal problems as a means of excusing any academic missteps, but rather they studiously insisted on taking full responsibility for their school performance.

Other students put their stories to paper, but that catharsis had little impact on their performance at school. These students simply succumbed to stress at home and their school performance suffered. These statements came from students who dealt less successfully with issues of abuse and alcoholism at home:

"I judge myself with little mercy—as hard as I try, I am super irresponsible, and what I think is most important, I am distrusting of men in general."

"My school work has never been consistent or up to its potential. When I concentrate I do good, but it seems like I never have time to do that. I'm always thinking about something else."

"The idea of productivity and self support has eluded me over the years. . . . My grades plummeted . . . I could be failing out of school."

The connection between the academic stresses and demands of both home and school were sometimes implicated in a student's feelings of low self-esteem and poor performance at school. One boy attributed his inability to feel competent and smart to the following: "In school I would be assigned projects, and my mom would do them for me so that when I came to class I would look good because I had such a creative and well-built project."

This student's situation was far from unique. With so much pressure for students to achieve and for parents to feed off of their children's success, the line between helping a child and doing the work had become blurred in many homes.

After mentioning a lot of complaints about parents that a typical teen would probably understand, one young man stated that "I know that this all seems wonderfully clichéd to you, but to me it is real, hurtful and very hard to deal with." Reading so many of these stories made it clear that those students living in a dysfunctional family can never be truly understood by outsiders. The stories may begin to sound like a cliché, but the reality is still elusive.

Without question, students throughout the public schools can find their academic achievement debilitated due to varied dysfunctional issues at home. For many in Wayland both the schools and community provided substantial support systems, though such efforts always seemed to be overwhelmed by student needs. However, in poor districts, both urban and rural, those services don't begin to provide support for the overwhelming issues facing so many children.

A disturbing number of children expressed anxiety and pain about living in homes where parents were either physically or emotionally absent, perhaps overwhelmed by job expectations of their own. Most of those children spoke about suppressing their feelings in order to maintain the ideal veneer of the suburbs, as well documented by Madeline Levine in *The Price of Privilege*. It appeared that they had learned how to keep their distress under wraps and present a controlled and happy exterior in public.

Students continually referenced academic expectations that they had internalized at a very young age. Emphasis placed on success or "failure" as early as elementary school made for some very trying years ahead. By their junior and senior years, all the stark realizations of all that earlier talk had peaked in ways that could hardly be imagined. From David Elkind's *The Hurried Child* to Roberta Golinkloff's *Einstein Didn't Use Flashcards*, many books have covered this subject matter, but experiencing these very emotional journals and discussions provided a different level of learning.

The inner pain revealed in these journals evidenced a world rarely exposed at school, where children had learned to perform as "good students" rather than complex human beings. Although family dysfunction knows no class or racial boundaries, the suburban "bubble" can convincingly lend itself to denial, especially since so many students wore the "happy mask" to school. The American Dream just didn't seem much like a dream; rather, it seemed a whole lot like reality.

Listening to their voices there emerged an understanding of a different form of pain, one that came not from want or discrimination, but from privilege. Their pain didn't necessarily equal or surpass that of people born into poverty or those forced to deal with racial discrimination, but it was real, and it was the pain they knew.

Another boy's struggles resulted very directly from the culture of status. Unable or unwilling to complete regular assignments and virtually always failing or struggling to keep his head above water in class, he did find time to write a five-page, typed journal in which he wrote in depth about a life of material wealth without emotional fulfillment. He stated, "I got everything a kid my age could want." However, he also noted that all that material wealth could not compensate for the lack of love that he evidenced in his parents' "anger and aggressions" toward him.

Abbey stated her situation quite succinctly in the midst of a long journal: "I understand that he grew up with nothing and worked hard to give us everything. I can say this only probably because I have everything I need, but I would trade everything to have my dad around more."

Another student took this last sentiment and broadened its application: "I see why so many of my friends who have the most expensive clothing . . . suffer. I see why so many mothers and fathers don't know how to reach out to their children, and why so many parents are never home and how they try to make up for their absence [with money]."

Another consequence of a high-stakes education with high stress involved the escalation of unethical means of meeting academic demands. Infusing various articles and excerpts from David Callahan's *The Cheating Culture* into the curriculum stimulated the students to routinely reveal evidence to substantiate recent research. Most students overwhelmingly owned up to their cheating with reference to the pressures to succeed, the weight of their homework burden, and the limited time to complete their assignments.

The following quotes represent many comments on how students rationalized their thoughts and feelings about the integrity of their academic lives:

"I think that the idea of getting a bad grade outweighs my feeling of guilt."

"Colleges don't accept the kid that tries the hardest, but they take the kids with the best grades."

"There is so much pressure from teachers, adults, and friends that sometimes we feel trapped. Also, everyone lets us get away with our wrongdoings."

"We are just mimicking our society."

"If people are looking only at results, why should we care how we get the results?"

"Kids are lying and cheating more to maintain the [image of the] 'perfect kid' according to adults."

"People obviously cheat when high expectations are made for them and they feel they mustn't let anyone down, especially themselves."

"This generation sees so much crime, drugs, and cheating that it seems natural, not wrong."

"Cheating is a risk people take to get what they want."

"The pressures of this society often spawn a competitive spirit so strong that morality is no longer at the forefront in the common student's mind."

Lowell acutely tied the pressures of school and how kids coped when he put this spin on the debilitating nature of his world: "I find myself writing these final words close to tears. . . . from exhaustion. These stresses push us to extreme actions that often betray our moralities."

These increasingly normalized behaviors of silenced voices and academic dishonesty in pursuit of prestigious college acceptance letters obviously troubled many adolescents. They understood all too well that their inner goals as both learners and humans had been commandeered by adults, who seemed to be motivated by their own goals—bragging rights for teachers, administrators, and parents when newspapers and magazines ranked the "best schools" and reported the list of college acceptances.

Students generally understood that a diploma from WHS, no matter how obtained, offered a ticket to college and eventual entrance back into the world of affluent suburbia. Yet many students expressed a lack of emotional fulfillment in the midst of this highly cognitive and rigorous academic regimen. On the one hand, they possessed the admirable goal of becoming educated, professional adults, yet they also questioned both the path to that goal and the ultimate nature of the American Dream as they lived it.

Both in class discussions and journal entries, students addressed the cycle of working hard in order to get into a great college, get a good corporate job, make a lot of money, and raise one's own family in the suburbs. One student questioned one of the earliest steps in that cycle: "Each step is followed by another harder task, but we are always told, 'Work hard now so that you can be happy later.' That happiness never seems to come."

Meg wrote a very lengthy poem after having read Tom Wolfe's *The Electric Kool-Aid Acid Test*. In this poem, she expressed a frustration with the escalating demands for conformity with the line "We all march around to desks in orderly lines"; and she touched on the loss of idealism when she wrote, "Our youthful idealistic tendencies were lost so long ago." In a four-page poem Meg saw an inexorable march toward solitary silence, unless "better ways" were explored:

> Rationed food, rationed lives
> We live and work in cubicles
> Where new ideas hardly ever seep through
> These walls that box us in
> were fragile when we were younger
> completely non-existent when we were children
> and will become stronger
> as we grow older.
> Until finally, we live in isolation
> Alone in our own ideas.

The silencing of children, which appeared to be directly correlated with the drive toward professional wealth and all the trappings of the American Dream, certainly brought many harmful consequences, including the dilemma best articulated by Matthew. In his own powerful way, he explained the situation as follows:

> The students in my class, myself included, are quiet, but they are not quiet due to a lack of thought (for the majority). Rather, there is a fear that forces them into silence, a fear that attacks the foundations of the type of race class that you have built. The origin of this fear brings us, inevitably, back to the suburban mindset. To be a suburbanite, it is *essential* that you be as non-confrontational as possible. You must avoid explicitly offending people like the black plague, and instead offend through implicit meanings hidden behind otherwise benign comments. Your race class feeds on uncensored thought, which is a concept that most students at [WHS] don't even know exists.

Matthew's analysis explains why most students, on the surface, presented the mask of content and control—a veneer that suggested a willing compliance with the educational system presented to them. This generation of students would find remarkable kinship with the voices that emerged from the free-speech movement of the sixties. Only their voices had found no outlet. By the twenty-first century, students seemed to have lost any hope of finding their voices. And to the outside world, silent students implied content students.

Wayland High School's mission statement, however, promised something very different, with phrases such as "personal responsibility" and "empathy for others" in the first sentence. And it ended as follows: "Our goal is to advance our students' growth into principled, informed, and capable citizens who help guide a democracy that follows humanitarian principles in the global forum, and shape a just society where individuals may reach their full potential." Such statements tended to represent what schools *should* be doing, but generally tend to ignore.

Unfortunately, the school's hidden curriculum taught some alternative lessons. The following voices address part of the hidden curriculum that might possibly occur in most schools. As one student noted, the lessons at school had little to do with student voices: "In my school today it is rare to find people who use school and their classes as a place to express themselves. Students these days just learn to obey. . . . We're like robots and we will continue to be robots as we get older."

Nina, whose journals always conveyed exceptional depth, put most of these issues into a perspective that her peers might find particularly perceptive and forthright:

My whole life I have been conditioned to believe a good grade affirmed that I was smart, and so my report card began to be part of my perception of self worth. I knew I shouldn't gloat when I received a better grade than my peers, but I could never suppress a small twinge of superiority. We're taught competition is good—for grades, colleges and even community service. No one studious and ambitious deeply questions this in Wayland because to do so would make one a loser or burnout. I agree that most exams are just measures of how well you can retain facts, and not truly indicative of your intelligence. I've learned that the dull, but methodical can get amazing scores on the SAT, while brilliant, but scatterbrained kids do abysmally. This all goes so against everything we believe in Wayland that it makes me squirm just writing about it. If the way we measure intelligence is flawed in our school, what else is wrong with our style of education? This is such a radical idea to me because it challenges my belief that I am a "smart kid" and that getting into the right school will affect who I am as a person. . . . There is still some yearning in my peers to rebel, but most are too afraid of the consequences of rebellion.

On rare occasions these sentiments would leap from the page and fill the emotional void that lurked in every classroom. One day in honors U.S. history Chelsea, a prototype for the best that Wayland had to offer—hardworking, friendly, happy, bright, and academically success-ful—found her voice in class. The words emerged with a force and passion that belied her well-crafted exterior veneer. Without faltering, she delivered a powerful monologue that pillo-ried her educational experience with remarkable precision.

After "breaking the code of silence" for about ten minutes, Chelsea released the last gasp of breath in her lungs with the resounding sigh of catharsis. Without hesitation her peers affirmed her words with their own emotional outburst. She was far from alone. For that moment in time, the students' curriculum had totally enveloped their rented space in a class-room.

This heartfelt disappointment and anger about school certainly belied Chelsea's cheerful exterior, but it still fell short of the bitter lesson learned by Jane, an excellent academic performer with a seemingly well-adjusted and well-measured personality. This journal entry came as a surprise, yet it shouldn't have—Jane certainly had a lot of company:

In a lot of ways, I resent Wayland for turning me into such a bitter person. . . . This school makes you hate people. We've been told since we were like five to do well in school, and as it's coming down to the wire now with colleges, every little thing makes a difference. Or it seems to. Maybe Wayland taught me to hate the grade-grubbers, cheaters, resume-boosters, and arrogant people. I know I dislike them, I just hope that I won't dislike everyone who shows a competitive side. This school turns people into all of the things that I hate. . . . I think that I have done everything I can for my education in this school, but I've gotten to the point where I think that being a happy, good person is more important than everything else, and that's all I want to do. . . . Whatever happened to learning for the sake of learning? I know it will never change and "that's just the way it is," but from an academic standpoint where every grade is public knowledge and if you get a C you may as well kiss your life goodbye, I just think that there has to be a better way.

A better way? The "better way" was already present in the school's mission statement, yet encouraging students to speak out and overcome a lot of "learned silence" had generally not found a place in the formal curriculum. Among a variety of issues, students learned to be silent about bullying, dating violence, racism, sexism, and homophobia, so it was not difficult to recognize that they kept silent about their educational needs.

Unfortunately, the lessons in the hidden curriculum will probably last a lifetime rather than fade quickly like all that content in their ever-expanding glut of tests.

Ultimately, the reality of Wayland presented a complex portrait of a modern suburban American Dream. It rightfully prides itself on being a community relatively safe from violent crime, with spacious open lands and a school system that consistently ranks with the top public schools in academic achievement. Indeed, thirty years in Wayland revealed a community populated with many remarkably friendly, well-intentioned, and supportive adults.

In many ways adults understood the increasing pressures to prepare their children for the competitive environment of college admissions and the upper-middle-class life that had become more expensive and difficult to access. For the most part, students generally recognized the privileges of living in such a community. However, in their private lives, they understood that their reality also contained the scourges of substance abuse, broken families, child abuse, and the stresses that come with high academic expectations and parents caught up in the escalating demands of the professional world.

It would be no surprise to find that the high school served, in many ways, as a microcosm of the greater community. The biggest difference, however, resided in a small room that housed the non-white students who were bused in from Boston to desegregate the high school. Their presence, in close quarters with the majority of white students, created a racial dynamic nearly nonexistent in the greater community, and provided an excellent opportunity to explore the secret world of race in a predominantly white suburb.

POSTSCRIPT

I was walking from the commons to the history building with Raesia, an exceptionally bright and assertive Boston student, when she stopped, looked at me, and declared, "You know these kids have just as many problems in their community as we do, but they just put a fresh coat of paint over them." Raesia often caught my attention with her insights, but this one struck me as exceptionally heartfelt, yet also tinged with some suppressed anger. Her eyes told me a story of personal issues in her life that transcended race, while also revealing the added angst of growing up as a black female in America. I had been at Wayland for over two decades before that day, and I realized that this young woman had poignantly, insightfully, and succinctly summed up a major piece of what I had learned over the course of those years. Kids really do say the damnedest things.

LESSONS LEARNED

The culture of status comes with a high price, and schools exacerbate this, especially when they focus too heavily on cognition and minimize emotional development.

Expectations can be excessive and/or rigid and ultimately debilitating—leading to emotional meltdowns, excessive drinking, and drugging.

Academic and social/emotional support services, at both the school and community levels, are critical for the achievement of many students.

Troubled lives among the privileged can be masked, but the pain is still real.

The ramping up of schoolwork and ever-increasing expectations fueled a culture of cheating.

Love of learning and idealism had been lost to the bragging rights achieved through college acceptances and school-ranking surveys.

Kids have a strong desire to explore the boundaries outside their immediate world.

Some suburban parents crossed the line from providing help to actually doing some of their children's assignments.

The hidden curriculum teaches some very powerful and long-lasting lessons.

Chapter 4

A Distinguished High School
Deals with Class and Race

If schools want to teach they need to create an environment where racist thoughts can be said without fear for [sic] getting sent to the principal's office or harassment from other students, otherwise schools aren't combating racism, they are sweeping it under the rug

—White male student

This way of learning is supposed to make us feel good about our achievements. However, most of the time school just stresses me out. I study way too hard and learn about a lot of pointless stuff.

—Lynn

Wayland High School (WHS) made a dramatic splash on the national scene in 1960, appearing on the cover of *Life* magazine, along with coverage from *Time* magazine, the *New York Times*, and the *Boston Globe*. The facilities at Wayland High School epitomized the cutting edge of progressive public education. Anchored by a domed field house at one end and a three-story administrative/media-center building at the other, the high-school campus boasted several additional buildings devoted to specific academic disciplines. The outer edges of the grounds offered sweeping vistas of sports fields and conservation land along the Sudbury River.

In a rare match of form and substance, the interior design facilitated an innovative delivery of instruction, including large classrooms with stadium seating for special presentations; middle-size classrooms to accommodate a typical class of students; and small, seminar-style rooms where teachers could interact with smaller groups of students for discussions and hands-on activities. Wayland High stood on one side of the great socioeconomic divide that separated public schools in America, worlds apart from Chinle.

By 1979, the physical plant had begun to wear down, but the facility still maintained the progressive architectural and educational design that had found its way from blueprint to reality. Over the course of the next thirty years, Wayland High School received much recognition for its academic prowess, beginning with recognition from *Red Book* magazine in 1987. The following year, WHS was designated a national Blue Ribbon school, which also brought a visit by Secretary of Education William Bennett. In December 2009, the high school was awarded a silver medal from *U.S. News and World Report*. Routinely, *Boston* magazine would cite WHS in its "Ten Best Schools in Massachusetts" issue.

Despite all the accolades, there existed some troubling realities that transcended the stress-es and coping mechanisms revealed by students who chafed at the concept of their idyllic American Dream "bubble." Certainly they spoke with passion about homework, drinking, increasing academic expectations, and their isolation from the "real world." These subjects even surfaced occasionally in class discussions and in the local press.

Yet deeply problematic issues, specifically those of class and race, remained primarily relegated to the domain of unspeakable discourse. Students clearly understood how both issues figured prominently in their everyday lives, but they found that most staff and the school's formal curriculum either avoided these topics or inadequately addressed them. For the most part, the working-class kids occupied a distant corner of the campus, and the main-stream of the school found students effectively segregated by race.

When students were provided opportunities to explore those issues, they would reveal a hidden curriculum replete with ignorance, isolation, misunderstandings, and stereotypes. Cou-rageously, some students publicly pushed to have these issues integrated into the formal curriculum, but their efforts were met with steadfast resistance from most administrators. However, perseverance, passionate parents, and a superintendent willing to take a risk would ultimately prevail.

The most salient issue in 1979 appeared to be the struggles associated with the town's transformation from a working-class and rural community into an affluent suburb. The com-prehensive nature of the original structure and curriculum had provided space for a decent variety of vocational programs, generally associated mainly with the Cochituate community. Yet the decline of the blue-collar community and the influx of well-educated professionals had decidedly shifted the focus of high school toward servicing primarily the needs of college-bound students.

In 1979, those blue-collar kids, along with the Boston students bused in to desegregate the Wayland schools, represented the largest group of marginalized students at the high school. Together, they were disproportionately represented within the "non-college" classes. The low self-esteem associated with these classes, along with a greater proclivity on the part of these students to vent frustrations, made for an explosive potential. Any racial tensions between students were sure to find an outlet in those classes. That volatility received a potent trigger when incendiary town events predictably entered the school building.

In July of 1981, two students and a local adult provided the fuse when they burned a cross on the front lawn of a Wayland home. The five-foot-high wooden cross burned an area of fifty square feet on the lawn of a black editorial writer for the *Boston Globe*. Later, the stoning of a black man in a canoe on Dudley Pond further heightened racial tensions.

The brewing storm reached the middle of the U.S.-history classroom at the beginning of school in September, when a Boston girl realized that a participant in the cross burning was actually sitting about ten feet away from her. This young woman had no problem finding her voice as her curse-laden shouts about the "racist cracker" in the class preceded her attempt to back up her words with action. Her verbal assault prompted the boy to stand and utter terms that offended her race and gender as he turned to confront her.

Fortunately, her attempt to reach the white student was impeded by the furniture, which allowed for an intervention before a physical fight could break out. Her anger gradually subsided, particularly as she realized the price she would have paid for "initiating" any physi-cal contact with a white resident student. A Boston student assaulting a white resident student, even under the most provocative of circumstances, did not offer much hope for a fair resolu-tion. Clearly, racial tensions in those classes necessitated constant vigilance and attention.

The more common class-management issue in those classes, however, involved the lack of motivation that stimulated confrontations focused on class work. One boy in particular had spent the first few days of class basically doing nothing asked of him. All motivational strategies seemed to have no effect, until he was directly confronted about his lack of effort inside and out of class. Feeling personally challenged, he got agitated and found his voice when he loudly exclaimed, "F**k you!"

A follow-up conversation after class resolved the immediate issue when the student realized that his ongoing contract with teachers, leave him alone and he wouldn't be disruptive, would not be tolerated. His surprise at the concept that his education would be non-negotiable led to some grudging acceptance of the idea of joining the class rather than being a "throw-away."

More importantly, this confrontation inspired the first major breakthrough in meeting the diverse needs of these disaffected students. It became clear that the curriculum needed to give voice to their world at school, a world that differed greatly from the high-achieving mainstream of college-bound students. His public profanity spoke for many of his classmates about their marginalization and overall assessment of the formal curriculum. A new project emerged, one that would immediately engage the whole class, and eventually also send a jolt throughout the entire school.

The concept involved the development of an alternative school newspaper, one that reflected their voices rather than the traditional voices of the academic elite. The students immediately jumped at the idea. From that day forward, the history content would be complemented with class time devoted to fleshing out the newspaper. Given ownership of the project, including interview selections, columns, and artwork, the students responded with enthusiasm. In tribute to my former Navajo students and these disaffected Wayland students, the newspaper's cover banner read *Smoke Signals*.

The unanimous selection for the cover was the "King of the Smoking Area." Prominently displayed on the front page, the "king" sat on a bench located in a distant corner of the campus, sporting his leather jacket, holding a cigarette between his spread legs, and rocking a fierce facial expression. The backdrop of the picture featured a graffiti-covered wall and the caption beneath read, "Come on posers!" Unquestionably, this newspaper had arrived with a roar from the belly of the beast!

In the interview that accompanied the picture, the "king" referenced his love for speed metal and, when asked to cite his favorite class, replied, "Definitely shop." In a follow-up response he explained, "I like shop because you can make what you want. You always get a lot of self-satisfaction. You have something to show for your work and you can bring it home." When asked about English and social studies he said, "They're important, but I don't like to do the work. It's a pain in the neck and I don't think that I get anything out of it."

The students who conducted these interviews extracted more interesting content, arguably, than could be found in any interviews printed in the official school paper. The most controversial segment in the paper revealed the "best and worst" of WHS. In the "best" category, the top four answers were "the mirror in the LRT bathroom"; "teachers that let you cut [class]"; "nothing"; and "2:41" (school was dismissed at 2:40!). Most professionals would not be stunned by these responses; however, voicing such heresies so directly and proudly would prove very troubling to the administration.

Actually, the most controversial pieces in the paper never made it into print. As part of the process of soliciting money for publication, the administration previewed the paper and then responded that it would not be allowed on campus. After I emphasized the amount of work the students had done, how writing had previously been anathema to them, how the project had energized the class, and the critical need for these students to feel valued as members of the school community, the paper was allowed to be published, though not without significant concessions.

We reached an agreement that the administration would have the right of final editing. For the most part the paper maintained its integrity, mainly due to student slang that went undetected. The students also won the right to proudly pass out the paper during lunch, rather than leaving them on a side table as the administration wished. Most discouraging, this edition of the newspaper would be the first . . . and last. The class project had to be terminated. In the final analysis, these student voices would be silenced once again.

The project had inspired the students to be creative, improved their writing skills, established some pride, and invigorated their motivation in class . . . but those benefits could not compete with the maintenance of the school's intellectual image. The work it took to get that one edition published left no doubt as to the lack of respect accorded these students—a lesson they, of course, already understood.

Their voices had been inspired and then, once again, silenced. Their educational needs could not compete with administrative needs. Marginalized students would be allowed a brief moment in the mainstream, only to be swept back to the margins.

While the presence of the Cochituate kids faded into history, sporadic outbursts of racial tensions replaced the waning class issues. In one blatantly public incident, a black Boston student and white resident started fighting in an open area between several buildings, prompting scores of students to come pouring out, mostly to observe. This incident would not be confined to the classroom and could not be ignored.

The glaring racial divisions that emerged, as onlookers divided along racial lines, should have prompted some concerns about the state of race relations on the campus. However, even more troubling than the fight were the comments of two highly esteemed, veteran teachers who arrived to help break it up. As the fight unraveled and tempers cooled they could be heard commenting, "That's why these kids [Boston students] don't belong here." They would subsequently deny those words, but firsthand knowledge and conversations among the Boston students confirmed that their words had been heard . . . and understood.

Clearly, two decades after the creation of the Metropolitan Council for Educational Opportunity, Inc. (METCO), the ideals of desegregation had failed to come close to reality. Adults might find such incidents to be isolated and aberrant, but most students felt the daily tensions, and the Boston students in particular felt the paradoxical sting of feeling unwanted in a school system to which they had also developed a fond attachment. Most adults and students could ignore the realities of race at school, but for non-white students no such option existed.

The Boston students faced the hurdles of being non-white in a predominantly white world and urban children in a suburban world, and of generally being perceived as of a lower class than anyone in Wayland. In many ways the interactions between the two populations brought to mind the parallel play seen among preschoolers or teens playing separate video games. The Boston and Wayland students walked in the same halls, ate in the same lunchroom, and sat in the same classes, but, except for a few athletes, generally didn't interact much with each other in any truly meaningful ways.

Hannah, a white resident student, interviewed Natalie, a Boston student, and in her reflection journal Hannah addressed this situation as follows:

As Natalie said in her beautiful analogy, it's supposed to be a two way street, but people get tired of trying and we end up on two parallel highways just passing each other. I realized that I am guilty, just like most Wayland students, of riding on my one way road. I don't feel comfortable going up to someone that I don't know and striking up conversation, but why should METCO students have to come here and then approach people who they feel are constantly judging them?

Hannah and Natalie represented the second generation of this program. METCO was signed into law in 1966 with the stated goals of striving "to provide the opportunity for participating students from Boston (and Springfield) to learn together in an integrated public school setting with students from racially isolated suburban schools," and "to increase the diversity and reduce the racial isolation in the receiving districts so that the students from different backgrounds can learn from each other in meaningful ways."

In 1968, Wayland High School embraced desegregation when the first class of eight freshmen from Boston was bused out to Wayland. A front-page article in the *Campus Crier* extolling the new program chose to open quite auspiciously with a quote from one of the Boston students: "We never had any sports. I can't wait to play basketball." By 1979, the program would no longer be a front-page issue, but rather appeared to be a marginalized program operating in conjunction with, yet very much apart from, the mainstream of the school. It appeared that just providing these children with access to the Wayland schools would somehow fulfill the METCO mission statement.

Two decades later, feedback from both the resident and Boston students indicated the shortcomings in fulfillment of the program's mission. Students spoke often about the huge social gap that strongly affected their lives. The words of white students, in particular, exposed an "ignorance gap" about the mission of the program. Over the years, a cross-section of students were asked about their feelings on METCO. What they revealed proved to be ominously consistent.

In response to the question on student interviews, "Do you believe that white Boston students should be allowed to participate in the METCO program?" Boston students almost unanimously responded with statements such as Toni's: "I strongly believe that white Boston students shouldn't be able to participate in the METCO program because I feel it defeats the whole purpose of the program. Besides, I think there are already enough white students in the Wayland school system as it is." Another Boston student stated, "In a way I say no because the purpose of the program was for mostly blacks and Hispanics in the city—you don't find that many white kids going to school in the city."

This next Boston student supported his fellow Boston students emphatically: "No, because METCO is for diversity. By bringing in white students, it's not really diversifying it from a racial standpoint. If we allowed white students in, it would become all white." Another black student put it this way: "Considering what the METCO program was designed for, like I said for the integration of towns with predominantly white schools . . . I don't know. That would be like defeating the whole purpose."

White-student opinions about METCO highlighted their ignorance about the intent of the program, specifically with regard to desegregation. Coming of age in the "post–civil rights" era, these students placed an emphasis on class rather than race. As one white student noted, "Yes. I think that everyone deserves the same opportunities. Why should only black kids be allowed? I mean I think it should be really focused on the financial situation, not the child's color." White students repeated such assessments routinely.

When white students spoke more openly and honestly about the program, they often opened the door to some authentic parts of the hidden curriculum around METCO and race. Thus emerged a variety of blunt assessments of the program. One stated, "Yes, of course they should [allow whites]. To exclude them would be racist." This person also noted that the program had negatively impacted his attitudes on race: "It has increased my dislike/distrust towards them tenfold."

A white student presented more pointed comments about diversifying the faculty: "My parents worked hard to move out of the city and into a white suburban community, and when minorities, especially minority educators, follow us here . . ." This resentment definitely represented a minority view in the journals, but in class discussions it resonated with a larger part of their audience.

These next quotes fit more into that uncensored category, including the initial reluctance to speak:

"They stick to themselves and don't speak in classes, [and] they're always looking really intimidating, almost like they want you to stay away from them."
"Wayland just wanted to look better. Like 'Oh hey, look at us, we don't discriminate!'"
"In all honesty, I don't feel like they even like being here. I feel like they are given this opportunity, and most of them just do badly in classes."

Hari, an Indian American resident who proved to be one of the most academically talented and sophisticated students at the high school, delivered a very nuanced perspective on METCO, one that distinguished between facade and reality:

> I think the stated intent of the METCO program is to provide access to educational resources that dedicated students would not have in the Boston public school system. Another stated intent is to engender a reciprocal relationship between the Boston and Wayland students—a relationship of mutual understanding and learning through friendship. Considering the realities of the program, however, I think there are some more insidious intents. The most overarching of these, I would say, is a general sense of external appeasement and self-assurance on the part of the Wayland system. In other words, they commit to the program because it makes them look good to the outside world, and it helps them to feel better about themselves without taking any radical steps towards beneficial educational change.

All of these students had traveled side by side in the halls, had sometimes sat together in the same classroom, had eaten lunch in the same space, and yet they harbored little or no understanding of what had brought them together.

A white student summed up the whole issue with a most unfortunate, but very meaningful, observation when he stated, "I feel like we're never told what it [METCO] is. Maybe it's not important." As evidenced in so many journals, this program may have been ignored in the school's curriculum, but students were still doing their own learning about race through their exposure to METCO.

The incredible lack of understanding about the desegregation program strongly revealed the need for direct attention from the administration, or students' education on this important issue would be consistently relegated to the hidden curriculum.

When Nina reflected on the racial curriculum she had learned at the high school, she was far removed from the overt racial tensions that had flared on campus decades earlier. Those volatile years had gradually been forgotten, though racial tensions persisted. The school and community had emerged as a prototype for the research presented by Eduardo Bonilla-Silva years later in *Racism without Racists* (Rowman and Littlefield, 2003). Bonilla-Silva explained the emergence of subtle racism in the post civil rights generation:

> Color-blind racism emerged as a new racial ideology in the late1960s, concomitantly with the crystallization of the "new racism" as America's new racial structure. Because the social practices and mechanisms to reproduce racial privilege acquired a new, subtle, and apparently nonracial character, new rationalizations emerged to justify the new racial order. (15)

In Wayland, this transformation into the "new racism" was probably aided by the ascendance of "politically correct" speech in the 1990s, which essentially limited the acceptable language with which to discuss race without offending anyone. The movement of white people, who were increasingly afraid of sounding racist, toward "acceptable" language meant that honest and meaningful interracial dialogues would rarely occur.

Ultimately, "PC" speech among affluent white students, along with the history of silencing the voices of marginalized students, gradually transitioned into the silencing of most of the school's black and Latino population. Given the near extinction of overt racial hostilities, the adults could readily come to the conclusion that all was well on the race-relations front. In their journals, however, students continued to tell a very different story.

The reluctance of most teachers and administrators to directly address race issues stifled some of the most potent learning experiences desired by students. Instead of experiencing racial healing, the students internalized ignorance, misunderstandings, and racial stereotypes.

Stan epitomized this post civil rights generation when he wrote about a summer civil-rights course offered at an Ivy League college in which, as a white person, he didn't feel "worthy" in the midst of what he perceived as empowered black people:

> Because I was one of the only white kids and felt unqualified to even be discussing racial inequalities because I was white and had never really been denied anything because of my race. . . . I feel intimidated because I don't feel as though I have experiences enough to share and show that I have learned not to be racist or I have been the victim of racist people, etc. I also am terrified of saying something in class that may be interpreted as being racist, and not even know it. My worst fear is that people will see me as racist and that one day I will realize that I am racist. I don't think that will happen, but nonetheless, it is my worst fear and often keeps me from saying what's really on my mind in class because I don't want to be seen in that light by anyone, even fellow whites. . . . I feel that just because I am white, I cannot debate with a minority about whether what I said was racist or not, because that may even be taken as racist. I feel as though I am kind of trapped in a limbo where all I can do is try not to say anything to any extreme and just stay in the middle so that I don't get accused of anything. It's very frustrating to me.

Zack also understood the fear of addressing race issues, but he framed it very honestly and forthrightly as a privilege he enjoyed. For him, dealing with race was an option, one not shared by his non-white classmates. In this journal passage he succinctly portrays the privilege of being white and the allure of racial denial:

> The apathy of the privileged, the ability to ignore racism without instant repercussions, causes racism to be pushed under the carpet until someone gets into bed and trips over it. At Wayland, we are given and often take full advantage of this luxury, and I am grateful to have someone flip that rug over for me, to show me just what it looks like to look at the world without the suburban filter. . . . As it is my option to take off my filter or to leave it on, I can understand why it would be easy to fall back into my original routine and ignore the racial atmospheres around me. Similarly, I can see why the stresses of considering every possible encounter is [*sic*] tiresome even for me when my senses are alerted.

Adam provided his own analysis of white avoidance. Consistently an honest voice in class, Adam wrote his trenchant opinion in response to interviewing fellow students:

In Wayland it is unpopular to be racist, and therefore most people are not openly. There are obviously some racists anywhere you go, and I compare these people today to the ones that were lynching people in 1960. . . . In 1960 it was easier to just go along with the racism to avoid getting on the bad side of racist whites. Today, in the town of Wayland for example, open racism is not accepted so most people are not openly racist. But many people are not openly racist, not because they are strongly opposed to racism, but because it is the easier thing to do—not being racist avoids punishment. This leads me to wonder, if you took the people from the town of Wayland and put them in the South in 1960, how many would conform to the racist society to make their own lives easier? I believe many would, and I'm sure everyone in Wayland would claim this to be untrue, but my guess is that most people don't care about the race issue enough to put their own privilege in jeopardy.

The Boston students simply did not have the privilege or luxury of avoiding the topic of race in their lives. Yet they also had to be constantly aware that honest talk about race was not acceptable discourse around school, an expectation that did not exist in their home communities. Whereas the white kids could "forget" that race was an issue and find comfort in their school culture, the Boston students often found just the opposite. And when given the opportunity, many of these students spoke very forthrightly, comfortably, and passionately about their world.

Melinda, a proud Latina student, depicted an array of sentiments that surfaced fairly often among the Boston students, particularly the female ones, who generally felt more isolated than their male counterparts. Melinda could be counted on to address race issues with a forthrightness and passion that would captivate a classroom. Her response to a student inquiry as to why she called herself a Latina rather than Hispanic provided one of those lasting memories of powerful student voices unleashed. In this passage, she took issue with the education she had received:

> When you come out here it is very hard not to feel alone and unwelcome, especially here at the high school. So without that sense of belonging or having a place to go and congregate, so to speak, it is a wonder how we have made it this far. This school prides itself on being the best, but the truth is there are so many wrongs it's hard to even think that we believe that it is. Granted we do have some of the most talented teachers and students here, but if the curriculum is not well rounded we only have a bias [*sic*] and closed minded view of things. That is not an education that is sufficient, and it's hurtful to know that because I'm the minority here I can't expect to know who I am, or have others know where I come from.

Shatara, a very strong black student with a very courageous voice, often spoke about situations that she encountered, only to find herself more isolated from the mainstream. Eventually she chose to fight fewer battles, but she never lost her edge until the day she graduated. She gave the following response to a white student who conducted one of the most honest and insightful interracial dialogues turned in over the years. In this particular segment, Shatara responded to a question about white students:

> I don't think the students are bad at all or anything like that. Some people are just spoiled, yeah, some people are spoiled, and I think a lot of students are just living in a bubble right now. And that a lot of people are going to wake up when they have an experience that's really gonna force them to see what's going on. Because, I mean, I've been in a class, I forget what class it was, . . . and I guess a student had said that they didn't believe there were social classes, like a lower social class, as far as money wise, the minorities being poor and you know? And he said that he believed that if everyone just worked hard they could get into that position where they can have whatever they want. And it's something that just totally blew my mind. . . . And the thing is, people don't understand that there are other obstacles for minorities to get over before they can get to where

they want to be, and still when they're there, there are still obstacles they have to get over to stay in that position . . . a lot of Wayland students are ignorant . . . because they'll always be in their comfort zone. 'Cause I know a lot of Wayland students don't want to be outside of their comfort zone. And it's like me and other minorities, basically, a lot of times we're outside of our comfort zones and just have to deal with that.

A succinct comment summed up a consistent underlying message throughout the many journals of all races that addressed the silence on race issues at the high school. A white resident wrote, "Talking about race is not a comfortable thing, but it is something that needs to be done in order for anything to change and for America to become a country where everyone is comfortable and loving with each other. Talking is vital to our country's future."

If the racial issues that continue to divide the United States are to be overcome they must be addressed early in life, and the public schools should welcome the challenge.

What started out with admirable intentions, the voluntary desegregation of the Wayland schools, had clearly failed to bridge the two worlds brought together under the METCO program. For the most part, the resident and Boston students remained isolated from each other, both physically and emotionally. Meanwhile, the white students became further entrenched in their ignorance, and the non-white students internalized their anger and inferior status. The abandonment of suburban education leaders in fulfilling the full mission of the program had left students to fill the void with their own experiences.

Sadly, part of this hidden curriculum had taught many whites to perceive this program as a charity bestowed on "poor black kids" who otherwise would be confined to horrible ghetto schools. Others found themselves reinforcing some of the most egregious stereotypes, especially that of black intellectual inferiority. Given the disproportionate number of Boston students in the "dumb" classes and the dearth of Boston students in honors or advanced-placement classes, this conclusion seemed quite reasonable.

Instead of barriers and stereotypes breaking down, for all intents and purposes, a form of "quasi-segregation" had emerged, producing horribly unintended consequences.

Meanwhile, many resident students agonized privately over their ignorance, or developed resentments toward these "strangers" in *their* school. The decrease in overt racial tensions may have further isolated the profile of the Boston kids, but their presence still fostered the process by which white students internalized conflicted and troubling racial views of these non-white children and their world. This hidden curriculum continued to inform students such as Morgan, who wrote very insightfully about how she processed this world in the 1980s:

As a student at Wayland High School, almost all of my day-to-day interactions are with people identified as "white." I would have agreed that I was Caucasian, but I didn't really think of myself as white, and I didn't *like* to think of myself as white. It felt bland and boring and privileged. "Caucasian" felt only slightly better, with less emotional charge to it: it carried with it much of the same response. I felt intimidated to some degree by people identified as minorities . . . I felt they knew more than I did about life and about suffering. I imagined they all resented me and that they felt I was beneath them. I believed their lives must be more difficult than mine. [That] they must feel more like outsiders, that opportunities must be fewer for them, and that they must be stronger and also more resentful as a result. I felt more confident approaching white people than non-white people, all else being the same. . . . For the most part, I felt separate from people who were not white. I did not know how to talk to them or approach them. I believed that they did not really want to talk to me or be friends with me. . . . I did not see much of them in my classes and I did not see them much on my athletic teams. I did see them getting off and onto their buses. . . . While a part of me would have liked very much to meet more of them and develop friendships with them, I felt distant and not confident enough to approach them.

The school's failure to effectively address the problems inherent in such a complex undertaking as desegregation could be seen as a direct result of the leadership's inability or unwillingness to solicit the voices of children in the schools.

Sitting in committee meetings that continued to talk and failed to act on issues of diversity eventually led to an insight intended to break through the logjam. The epiphany came one day when the most obvious of realizations crystallized. For years, students had been asking for a forum in which their voices would be the focal point. What they needed was a time and space in which they could talk primarily about race, but also about other issues for which they possessed no outlet. After sketching out some ideas, I presented the concept to Manuel Fernandez, the METCO director and a close friend.

This proposal to create a mechanism for all students to attend cofacilitated lunchtime discussions on race had to overcome some strong concerns from Superintendent Bill Zimmerman, but he signed on. The high school leadership, including the head of the social studies department, presented numerous obstacles, but fortunately "Dr. Z.'s" willingness to listen to alternative voices and take a risk won out.

In the spring of 1989, a vote of students identified as the core group resulted in the name Students United for Racial Equality (SURE). The original mission statement for the group established the following objectives: "To create a forum to provide a racially and culturally diverse group of students the opportunity to explore the causes of racial, social, gender, and ethnic discrimination and employ pro-active strategies to raise community consciousness and reduce discrimination in the greater school community. "

Of course, having the superintendent's support paved the way, since little change occurs in schools without consent at the top.

The group gained immediate recognition from the Massachusetts Department of Education in the form of a Multicultural Recognition Award. Other awards came in the form of a Goldin Foundation Award for Excellence in Education and then a World of Difference Institute incentive award. The local media, including the *Middlesex News* and the *Boston Globe*, ran articles on SURE, while the major local television stations brought reporters and cameras to WHS during lunchtime meetings.

A major objection to this initiative had cited the certainty that opening up talk about race would lead to increased racial tensions. However, that perception received a jolt in 1995 at the time of the O. J. Simpson trial. The day after the verdict was announced, race-relations meetings were relocated to a faculty space that could squeeze in up to a hundred people. Many students were turned away, in three successive lunches. It looked like race relations had arrived . . . and those concerns about this dialogue being the catalyst for racial tensions had been misguided.

The ascendance of student voices as evidenced in use of that faculty space owed a debt to the students who had found their voices over the years. Some of those students would not reap the benefits of their advocacy, but their efforts should not be forgotten. Sameer had articulated the issue two years earlier in the student newspaper, the *Last Word* (December 1993). He addressed the growing frustration of the student body in a compelling commentary on the necessity for some student power:

> Many advisory committees and councils have been formed. The time has come to give students a real voice, a voice that will sit as a voting member on our school committee. I believe the faculty should also be given a voting position on our school committee. It is the teachers and students together who make up the school. . . . They [the school committee] simply can't understand the student population without being exposed to it on a daily basis. Thus to deny the voices speaking

silently every day is to deny the chance to make a great system even better. . . . Together we are the ingredients that give this school life, and thus we know best how to better educate the students that pass through the system.

As the new millennium approached, however, Sameer's words still searched for the power they had envisioned. The large turnout after the Simpson verdict could have been a catalyst for further acknowledgment of student voices, but new administrators chose to restore the status quo. Many students still longed for their voices to be heard, though the comfort of the norm seduced most students into silence and conformity, with the expectation of student compliance.

Despite outright resistance or apathy from most adults, some students continued to find their voices. Tucked into that same edition of the *Last Word*, Lisa courageously presented to the school committee a proposal on behalf of a new mandatory course at the high school to be modeled after the "free-ranging discussions that take place in the Race Relations group [SURE]." Lisa's efforts proved to be the first step in a process that would take a few years and a lot of strategizing before finally achieving success.

Advocacy for this course, however, produced more than the usual opposition. Attacks on Lisa's proposal came from high-school administration, as expected, but they also rallied many faculty and some students to oppose the course. Rather than rejecting the importance of racial issues, their approach declared that the school's formal curriculum already dealt admirably with race and racism issues.

This perspective was reflected in the seemingly standard language in teacher evaluations. Teachers shared comments from their evaluations indicating that a standard comment on the "Respect for Diversity and Promotion of Equity" criterion included a reference to how all social-studies teachers dealt with these issues every day in all aspects of their teaching. Teachers would be praised for presenting a wide range of points of view from different cultural perspectives.

Education leaders based their evaluations on the written curriculum and various classroom observations, indicating total ignorance of the real world of the students and the hidden curriculum it spawned.

Indeed, scores of *student* evaluations over the years suggested that the formal curriculum had failed miserably in addressing race issues. Portia summed up this perspective in this rather raw and honest assessment:

> "MY ASS!!! Excuse me, I mean, yeah, right. There was not an ounce of racism, not even a milligram of it, discussed in [College World Cultures]. . . . The notion that one could place the complex and frustrating issue of racism into a category of typical Wayland education is absurd. These critics are trying way too hard to make racism a neutral issue, and I think they are biased, too. What do they know? They are not the ones taking the classes. If anything, they should ask the students, including those in college level classes.

The CWC course that Portia cited was intended to set the foundation for four years in which race and racism would find their way in as subject matter when deemed appropriate. Certainly that would be expected in a junior course in U.S. history. Yet student feedback indicated some quite surprising and unexpected lessons from that curriculum.

While we must acknowledge the presence of some adolescent hyperbole for effect, we can see that students expressed exasperation and exhaustion with the constant emphasis on slavery and Martin Luther King, Jr. (MLK), as their "race education" from elementary school onward. The following comments represent the fundamental ways that students had processed their learning of slavery:

"I felt like all we did was talk about slavery over and over again."

"Slavery was huge and awful but the way we just talked about it over and over kind of just took away the horror of it and just made it repetitive."

"We read and watched movies and stuff. It was mostly about the black race and how racism was bad. Like I said, they drilled it into our heads."

The slavery outcome might seem pretty mundane, but the perceptions of MLK proved rather shocking. By the time they encountered U.S. history in their junior year, many students actually began to express outright resentment for MLK. The ways that white kids had processed this part of their formal education should be appalling to most Americans: "They started doing nothing except quoting MLK, Jr., for days on end." For far too many students, the constant repetition of his words and achievements had obliterated King's fundamental messages, leaving only the memory of "another boring history guy that we're forced to hear about all the time."

Any inspiration from King's life and work had been reduced to huge doses of white guilt that stifled any benefits that would have accrued from a healthy probing of his work and words. A number of white students wrote and spoke about how the constant attention to MLK had exhausted them and made them feel guilty. One student added this comment to that thread: "Year after year all we talked about were the mistakes we white people made and how we are still supposed to apologize today."

In many ways, the students were finding their race education to be no different from much of the curriculum, which simply lacked any important connection to their world at school or in the larger society. One student summed up the feelings expressed often about their overall experience while specifically addressing the teaching of race issues, "We were conditioned in those other classes to distance our own experiences from the racial topics discussed."

Consistently, students would ask to see the curriculum in light of their everyday experiences; otherwise, at best, the curriculum resonated as both terribly boring and entirely devoid of educational value. Given that disconnect, students generated their own lessons, which often failed to reflect the school's mission.

The eventual acceptance of the race and racism course would ultimately lead to the most raw, honest, and provocative student voices on the most controversial issues in their world. But the process would not be easy. It would take some work at freeing their voices, given the strongly conditioned silence of the white students, especially in the presence of non-whites. This challenge received an insightful analysis from Matthew:

> It's like all of [the] white suburban kids are in on a secret, we're part of the club, the cult, and it's okay to fight inside the club, because even if you let something slip, maybe part of the secret, no one will find out because you are just talking to other members of the club. Mike isn't part of the club. So when he left, we all, subconsciously, knew it was OK to talk then. When Mike is there, well, that's obviously a different story. Part of it is that no one wants to offend the one black kid, but there is another aspect. It feels like he's coming from such a different angle, that renders us all ignorant, that it would be simply disrespectful to discuss race in his presence if he had nothing to say.

Over the course of two decades, the reality of Wayland and its celebrated schools presented a complex portrait of a modern suburban American Dream. It rightfully prided itself on being a community relatively safe from violent crime, with spacious open lands and a school system that consistently ranked with the top public schools in the state. Experience had also revealed a community replete with many remarkably friendly, well-intentioned, and supportive adults.

For the most part, resident students generally recognized their privileges. However, in their private lives at school and in the community, they understood that their reality also belied the image of the idyllic suburban community. They also recognized the need for an education that connected with the world of the students bused in from Boston. Bringing these students together in a course devoted to exploring the real issues of race and racism at WHS presented both great challenges and great rewards.

POSTSCRIPT

In the spring of 1992, I was standing in the midst of the junior prom when Dr. Zimmerman approached me. He said something to the effect of, "You were right. I think that we might have had a bad situation at the high school the day of the O. J. verdict if there had been no race-relations classes." The superintendent had initially opposed the program, but now had the humility to acknowledge his mistake. It was a remarkable moment of vindication. School administrators willing to take risks can clearly effect changes that benefit students on issues that might seem impossible to remediate.

Sameer's impassioned opinion piece on behalf of empowering students failed to generate any substantive interest from the high school's administration or those at the highest level of power. However, Sameer eventually found his passions rewarded with a much larger audience. Currently, Sameer writes a blog for Social Media Today and has released a short film, "Have I Shared Too Much?"

LESSONS LEARNED

In the suburban world, school and community image can take precedence over the needs of those students who don't fit the "right" image.

The most disrespected students need their voices respected before learning can ensue.

Failure to provide any means for understanding the desegregation program for which students had been volunteered helped to foster a racial divide and racial misunderstandings in the hidden curriculum.

The public schools present the best place for bridging the racial divide, but they must first be led and staffed by people who are comfortable talking about race.

True, substantive school reform must be supported and modeled by top administration and informed by listening to students.

The students at the top of the academic hierarchy are generally the most compliant with the system since they have the most to lose.

Administrators can evaluate the formal curriculum, but the presence and power of the "hidden curriculum" persists and retains its power despite adult ignorance.

Curriculum detached from the experiences and world of diverse student groups forces students to produce their own lessons, which generally do not reflect the goals of that curriculum.

Administrators need a vision, the self-confidence to accept alternative views, and the integrity to implement their vision on behalf of students.

Chapter 5

White Students Find Their Voices

> As a white male in a wealthy suburban town I have been taught to look down on black people in the inner city slums. It seems weird to me, in all the years that I've known kids like [Boston students] that it took this long, almost until I graduated high school, to have a real conversation about race with an African-American student.
>
> —Joe

To be white at Wayland High School (WHS) meant having the choice of never having to deal with your racial identity. You simply represented "the norm" upon which all others could be ranked, judged, accepted, rejected, or ignored. These students had found that assiduously avoiding any uncomfortable race talk made race seem to disappear. And to be confronted with racial awareness by non-whites stimulated intense discomfort. Yet race issues had been a major part of their world ever since they first attended a school system that had embraced a desegregation program.

As a result of both the formal and hidden curricula, students had developed some consistent learning about race. Many whites expressed the *guilt* they carried around racial issues, while also revealing their *ignorance* about the world outside of their predominantly affluent, white enclave. Initially, students also presented discomfort with the sense of feeling *race-less* and *culture-less*. Yet they also had come to understand that to embrace a white identity would stigmatize them with the taint of racism, which meant condemnation at all levels of the school.

Ultimately, their freedom to honestly explore racial issues by listening to their non-white peers and engaging in cross-racial dialogues enabled many students to replace their ignorance and guilt with a newfound *sensitivity* and *awakening* that resulted in profound feelings of *admiration* and *respect* for their non-white peers. In some cases, these dialogues produced soul mates across racial lines, but in other cases students felt that the efforts to cross those lines proved too exhausting and difficult. For those students, a return to a "colorblind" world awaited in the future.

The first major barrier for white students typically involved their internalized guilt and ignorance about race. Although they generally revealed a race-less identity, the whites had internalized a lot of guilt about the non-whites in their world. Along with that guilt came a lot of self-proclaimed ignorance; both these elements had been suppressed and enabled by the silence about race in their immediate world. In confronting this barrier, of course, the comfort inherent in this silence would have to be replaced with the discomfort of probing honest feelings about race.

Carolyn exemplified this attitude, shared by many of her white peers, when she expressed rather pointedly, "I feel guilty about my ignorance; I feel guilt regarding the advantages and benefits that I was born into. I feel guilty about my inability to inspire change in others around me. I feel guilty about living in Wayland. Every time I get my allowance I feel guilty."

The white students faced some difficult times when they entered a class where race would be the topic on a daily basis. On the one hand, they needed to feel safe in the class, while also feeling the discomfort of honest race talk. Creating this environment took a lot of trial and error. An early strategy included the opening scene of the movie *The Believer*, in which the Ryan Gossling character, Danny Balint, stalks and beats down an Orthodox Jewish student in the middle of an urban intersection.

Many students expressed surprise, saying that the clip wasn't racial since it involved a confrontation between whites. This common response provided an opportunity for the white students to begin thinking of themselves as "racial beings," which then took the sole burden of race off the shoulders of non-whites. It also allowed the white students to feel more responsible for, and empowered to deal directly with, race issues.

A second goal of this specific clip of harsh, and very modern, anti-Semitism anticipated some physical and emotional discomfort on the part of students as they watched an innocent adolescent get assaulted by a neo-Nazi. The students would begin to understand that the initial discomfort would hopefully be the first of many similar feelings throughout the course, since dealing with racism has to involve some uncomfortable feelings if explored properly.

The tone in the class transformed dramatically when that clip was followed up with excerpts from Dave Chappelle's comedy show, which enabled all the students to bond over shared laughter about race. However, assessing the pain behind a black man's comedic approach to racism brought the class back to the mission of the class—always moving into the discomfort. So students might be laughing one minute about racial profiling and then exploring how that issue had brought humiliation to one of their non-white peers in the class.

That first day also included my offer to respond to any questions about race. The students needed to feel confident that a white person could take risks in talking about race in a diverse group, as well as model the discomfort that often comes with discussing race. Encouraging them to make the teacher sweat was intended to inspire as much uncensored speech as possible. And they did stimulate some serious sweat.

As expected, white guilt certainly played a major inhibiting role in the classroom. Oftentimes a reading could spark hidden feelings of guilt, as displayed in this comment: "I did feel some empathy with [a character] on her guilty feelings at being born white . . . you try to forget racial issues that make you feel so guilty, and that doesn't help at all…"

Jonathan Kozol's *Amazing Grace* prompted this statement: "Reading this book makes me feel guilty that I was born with all the opportunities and advantages possible." Another student wrote about feeling like an "entitled white girl" who felt guilt about "not thinking of those less privileged" and for having "judged people's intellect by their word choice."

Some students brought their individual experiences into the classroom, offering circumstances that brought the discussion to much deeper levels. This journal passage offers some insight into Jenny's unique situation with white guilt:

> It's weird, because even though I am technically 25 percent Hispanic, I don't feel like I deserve to call myself Hispanic. I have been raised with a French and American culture, I don't speak Spanish, and I have been raised in a white suburb. I'm very proud of being Hispanic and I'd much rather call myself Hispanic though than white, because I feel guilty being white. I know there's nothing wrong with being white, and there are plenty of nice white people, but still I just feel bad

because of all the terrible racist things white people have done to people of other races. But I guess because I'm 75 percent white, I'm just going to have to live with it. I can just try to be a white person who's aware of the racial injustices.

Getting past internalized feelings of white guilt, while also dealing with "new guilt" in the process, also proved to be a daunting task. An effective way to address that guilt was to suggest that they were too young to take ownership of how they had come to internalize guilt as children. However, as adolescents becoming aware of how race impacted the world around them, they could no longer claim ignorance and would have to accept any new guilt that might materialize. This talk enabled most students to deal with their past "failures" and ignorance, without disabling their ability to move forward in educating themselves for the future.

Jenny's last sentence evidenced her own attempt to deal with past guilt and come to some resolution about what to do with her recent awakening. She also raised an important point that became essential to the class, the belief that there are "plenty of nice white people." Although all the students had been exposed to "great black leaders," their education had not explicitly provided them with whites who had also led the fight against racism. Nor could they generally identify such people in their immediate world.

This significant gap in the formal curriculum, if left unaddressed, will reinforce the feeling among whites that the fight for racial equity is a non-white issue.

Unfortunately, for most whites, feelings of guilt had been a major factor in their distancing themselves from any connection to "whiteness." Embracing white racial pride had come to symbolize overt racist beliefs usually associated with extremists such as the Klan or skinheads. It was acceptable to be a proud Italian or Irish American, but not a proud white person. Overwhelmingly, being associated with overt racism ranked at the top of unacceptable attitudes among white students.

The reluctance to embrace whiteness could be understood from the responses to an interview question asking for immediate word association. The most common responses to "white people" were: *rich, conceited, power, normal, extremely unaware, privileged, selfish, pathetic, assholes, arrogant, cocky, uptight, well-educated,* and *egotistical.* This heavy baggage, which came from mostly white students, may not have been learned at school, but it likely hadn't been addressed at school either.

Surfacing feelings of guilt and looking to move forward produced an interesting pushback. Now students accustomed to operating within the acceptable attitudes endorsed by the suburban facade had to confront the betrayals of that world and replace them with a new reality. However, the "new reality" might actually be a refashioned facade. In the following journal passage, Matthew insightfully, poignantly, and cynically presented the skepticism that might result when well-meaning white students moved "beyond" ignorance and guilt:

WHS student reads the article. The student fails to understand the true meaning, and is able to do nothing more than remember a few especially loaded sentences, statistics, etc. Then, he will proceed to employ these choice phrases as conversation fodder, something to throw out into the arena in an attempt to appear erudite (sort of similar to how I just used erudite instead of intelligent, well-read, scholarly, etc. Did it work? Do you think I'm smarter? I hope not). Or maybe, the student might drop one of those statistics at a fancy dinner, hoping to wow the stratosphere of the Wayland socio-economic atmosphere. That's one scenario. Here is the next: The student reads and understands the article. However, the student doesn't *fully* understand because the student quite simply cannot and will not, through no fault of the student's own, because they have not experienced anything even on the same planet as what the article describes. Yet, when the student goes to the class discussion the next day, the student will feign outrage, empathy, sympathy, and everything else they think that they should feel. They know that they are lying, but who cares about the truth anyways. Those are the two most common, at least from my view. So where do I fit in? Like the second student, I understand but I don't *really* understand. So should I fake it? Yea, those bastards how could they have done that! The ignorance! They were despicable, and so is anyone who is racist! Is that what you want? I feel sad for what they did, guilt at what I haven't done and what I can't feel. That's it.

Essentially, having lived a bright suburban life that ignored all the discordant racial issues had left racial baggage that needed to be addressed, in a safe environment that also allowed for the discomfort of honest race talk.

Stef did a fine job of expressing the struggle of whites grappling with racial ignorance, while also evidencing a positive lesson for her future development:

> If I were to choose one thing that summed up what I learned this year I think it would be my ignorance . . . and I'm so glad that is what I learned because I now have the power to change it. While I'm still definitely ignorant on many counts, I have also diminished a load of ignorance that once clouded my judgments. I really never thought about the true power white people have, the lack of power women have and the struggles that exist everyday [in] living as a minority. . . . I am not in a place of power, yet I act like I am every day. . . . I've learned that everyone has a voice, and that hearing diverse voices can be the best sound out there.

The first unit in the course was also structured to combine the discomfort of honest race talk with a relatively "safe" topic. An initial focus on American Indians served these purposes, while also "leveling" the classroom. Addressing race through the experiences of American Indians created a common bond of ignorance. Whites did not have to feel a distinct disadvantage. Also, this provided a unique opportunity to honor the voices of former Navajo students and friends, especially given the intensity of race issues in their world.

Finally, past experiences with any curriculum on American Indians had generally been very "safe" since they weren't generally viewed in a racial context and students had been conditioned to "honor and respect" Indian people. Basically, students could learn to talk about race safely because those people either "no longer existed," which generated feelings of sadness, or "lived elsewhere" and were held in high regard, consistent with the historical concept of the "noble savage."

Overwhelmingly, student feedback expressed strong support for this unit because they had fully anticipated a course about black-white relations and were pleasantly surprised to be talking about American Indians. And for those students who believed that Indians were extinct, partially because of U.S.-history instruction that ignored American Indians after the nineteenth century, this unit proved very enlightening. Bringing this story up to date also brought attention to the complex issues confronting the country's most marginalized people.

Alex H. stated his amazement at the story of Indian people in this journal passage:

> They seem to be a race that has been completely neglected by Americans and the government. I mean not in the respect that they aren't accounted for . . . but I feel like they have been neglected as a race and an issue for years upon years, and have been overlooked during racial turmoils [*sic*] with blacks, Jews, and Asians in which they should have been included. So, I feel like American Indians have been put on the back burner—I mean you never see any issues on the news regarding Indians. I mean I haven't, but maybe I've just been ignorant to [*sic*] them this whole time, but I feel like I haven't done that on purpose, but that it's been brought upon me from my education and upbringing.

James wrote, "I can honestly say that when talking about discrimination or civil rights I have never really thought about American Indians. . . . For the first time it made me aware of this 'new' minority group." Nina added, "I used to think, like many people, that American Indians were all but dead besides small fringe tribes in the Southwest that I visited when I was younger." Jane got angry about her education and declared, "We never read a reading just about the feelings or the culture of the tribe[s]. I feel cheated, like America is purposely preventing me from reading its true history."

Natalie added her voice to the "newness" of this topic: "Until this year I never gave thought to the struggles that American Indians have in this day and age. . . . In school I have learned about their trials throughout the history of the United States, but that's it, we never looked at the adverse effects."

After two or three weeks on the status of American Indians in the twenty-first century, the class clearly had become relatively comfortable talking about race. Perhaps most importantly, hearing stories from Navajo Nation, reading contemporary articles, and viewing the first "all-Indian" film, *Smoke Signals*, white students began to understand that their "whiteness" played a major role in the world of non-whites.

Exploration into modern American Indian culture and the struggle to maintain Indian cultural identity unexpectedly led to the surfacing of another nagging issue—the students' lack of feeling culturally grounded. This proved very challenging given how many of them had already expressed the feeling of being race-less or being ashamed of being white.

What usually was revealed was the feeling among the students that, unlike non-whites, whites had no culture. The concept of Europeans "becoming white" can be found in David Roediger's *Working towards Whiteness*. When prompted to brainstorm a "Wayland Culture Day" as modeled on urban Caribbean festivals or the Navajo Tribal Fair, the best they could come up with included some booths promoting SAT tutorials and college admissions, along with some sports exhibits and cheerleaders. This exercise generally resulted in laughter and then some envy for those who had a "real culture."

This perception of Wayland as a "bland and boring" place was consistent with the concept of the "bubble." Melanie exemplified this sense of a "culture-less" banality in her own identity and the greater community around her:

> Being white I feel like I have no race, no identity. I've always felt boring. white, middle class, American, only speak English. I've always wanted to be, well, interesting. . . . I also saw how easy it is for white people to live and not have to worry about race. I wonder what it would be like to be a different race. I talked in the beginning on how I felt like I was boring but it is also easy.

Carolyn placed a different spin on this subject by suggesting that the blandness of being white provided her with a level of comfort that seemed unfair:

> I hardly ever think about race in my life—it just isn't something that I concern myself with. I go to a primarily white school and most of my friends are white, so thoughts about race never really occur to me. I can't imagine having this constant weight that comes with being a different race than those around you. Constantly noticing when someone makes a racist comment and constantly trying to figure out their motives or intentions is a burden that no one deserves. If anyone should have to worry about what others are implying with their words or thinking during interactions, then everyone should have to worry about it. But that isn't the way it is—like I said I never notice race in my life.

These discussions usually spawned some greater understanding of urban white ethnic enclaves, especially since some students had attended Italian festivals in the North End of Boston or Greek festivals in Central Square in Cambridge. In many cases these discussions sparked some renewed interest in the students' own ethnic roots, though most students found few ethnic cultural remnants in their lives. Cindy discussed the complexities of whiteness and ethnicity, as she delved into what she perceived as a direct consequence of these discussions about white ethnic culture:

> Something that I thought was interesting . . . was how people began to play down their "whiteness." I know that between my friends, we would have jokes about how they were part Hispanic, or Japanese, and not white. If someone was undeniably white, they could play up their specific ethnicity, which was better than being just plain white. For example, for me being Irish was somehow better than being just white, because there really seems to be no pride in being white, unless you enjoy following in the footsteps of Hitler.

The realization among whites that they were racial beings brought both positive and negative effects, but for the larger purposes of the class this realization enabled them to deal a little more forthrightly and comfortably with their next unit: blacks and Latinos.

Moving into a unit on blacks and Latinos immediately amped up the discomfort in the room. Starting with an excerpt from David Shipler's *A Country of Strangers*, the students were forced to grapple with the challenge of determining the line that often divided people when determining whether a comment was "innocent" or racist. The "interpretation line" often placed whites and blacks on opposite sides of the "gray" zone. A student cited this dilemma: "I have always felt confused by the fine line between being racist or not. . . . In some ways I feel that anyone could perceive any comment as racist if they wanted to."

Over time, however, enhanced listening skills led to greater sensitivity. Students began to write and talk about their enhanced listening skills and greater sensitivity to the realities of the racial world in which they lived.

The discussions about how the races could very differently interpret the same event really helped with the idea of really *listening* to the other voices in the room. With white students becoming more attuned to the subtle nuances of race in their world, in some ways it became like a competition—as whites excitedly brought to class some experiences that previously would have gone unnoticed.

A prime example occurred after an early class exercise that asked students to pair off and exchange a story about race in their lives. On this particular day, an administrator was observing and served as a participant with a white student, who later remarked how it had been clear that the administrator was very uncomfortable in telling a racial story. Clearly, students were finding that even a few weeks' exposure to honest race talk had advanced them beyond some adults in their world.

This revelation spoke keenly to the racial awakening of many white students. In the following passage, Logan talked about his trepidation in taking a course on race before evidencing his newly acquired ability to observe more carefully how racism might play out in the real world:

> I had an uneasy feeling in my stomach about taking race because of what the class required. I though that I would be afraid to speak about race because as we all know, we are raised to "pretend" like nothing's going on. I will be the first one to admit that in our society and especially our town, we pretend like nothing's happening and avoid it at all costs. . . . I work in Boston and valet park for [various] parking lots. When I am working with a couple of my friends (who are all white), and my two other colleagues who are [black] and are higher above than me on the

hierarchy, the racism towards them is shocking. Almost every night we will get one person who asks to speak to the "white guy." Clearly, they don't trust my associate workers with their cars and would rather have a white person take it.

Alex G. captured the essence of what it was like for some of the white students to step into that "gray zone" of interracial interactions. He vividly detailed the struggles of a white student attempting to have a "normal" conversation with a black peer, while also not avoiding the racial nuances of which he had become aware:

> From this article I started to think about my own interactions with other races, blacks in particular. Obviously in a school like Wayland, there is limited opportunity for such a thing; however, I know that I do interact at least with Lasonta [a black student] and Idora [a black student] in race class every day. An example from talking with Idora yesterday in math class goes as follows. I wasn't sure if we had any race homework, so I went up to her and said: "Idora, did we have any race homework?" This was a seemingly neutral question to pose. However, the first thing that Idora said was: "Are you asking me because I'm black?" I can see how Idora much like some of the other blacks in the reading are [*sic*] constantly thinking about race in their lives. From there I responded with, "No, it's because you are the only one here who is in my race class." However, this was not the case. [A white student] was in the room as well. . . . It is possible that either Idora or I were [*sic*] reading into this interaction way too much, but in the end I responded with a joking, "You should be glad that I'm breaking down stereotypes in believing you as a black woman to be responsible." From this, we both laughed somewhat, but I know that Idora did not buy what I said. She somewhat mumbled something about it possibly being for a completely different reason that I cannot remember. It was not a huge confrontation, but I do think that it is a good example of some unconscious interaction between races.

Without question, the goal of producing better listening between students was best achieved through the interview project. These interviews managed to engage students more quickly and deeply in ways that were very surprising. The journal writing, along with class discussions, helped alleviate some of the fear about speaking honestly, but the students still really didn't understand the racial realities of the students sitting around them. In order to access those stories the students had to interact with each other, much like Alex G. wrote about.

In order to better understand the depth of this racial disconnect, some specific aspects of the Metropolitan Council for Educational Opportunity (METCO) program need to be understood. The incredible stress of desegregating white classrooms had led to the creation of a METCO room, where Boston students could decompress together free from the pressures they endured throughout the school day. Essentially it provided a place to chill, let their guards down, and simply "be themselves." Whites were encouraged to visit this room to afford themselves the experience of being part of the racial minority, but very few did so.

In order to complete the interview project, like the one that stimulated Alex G.'s journal, some students felt inspired, for the first time, to make the bold plunge into entering the METCO room, the "foreign world" of the Boston students. The following journal entries, written by two otherwise self-assured and accomplished white seniors near the very end of their years in the Wayland public schools, should provide some fascinating insights into the trepidation evoked in crossing that racial threshold. Magda wrote:

> To be honest . . . I was pretty nervous for this interview. I was so surprised because I go over to random [lunchroom] tables all the time for other class projects or if I'm talking to a friend from another social group, but this time I felt nervous. It made me feel so pathetic but I couldn't help it—it was instinctive. I went over to the table that's right outside the METCO room and it was filled with METCO students, and [I] just sat down at an empty seat in the middle of it. They all kind of looked at me . . . I started to shake a little bit. I said hi and introduced myself because they

all don't know me. I explained to them that I was doing this project for history. . . . Then I said I wanted to interview someone . . . and I asked the girl sitting across from me . . . she said no and then looked down. Alex was sitting next to me and raised her hand enthusiastically and said, "I'll do it!" The shaking stopped. . . .

Later on that day, I realized that I had asked her what would happen if I went into the METCO room, but I never actually went in. I was pretty inspired after the interview because Alex really blew me away, so I decided I would go in . . . I would do it for her. I felt extremely pathetic because I was shaking again. I wanted to get a picture of the inside of the METCO room for this project as well, because I don't think the majority of the white kids at our school have ever seen the inside. The door was closed and I could see [Roland] inside . . . I really like [Roland] so it made me feel a little better. I didn't take a deep breath or anything . . . I just plunged through the door.

And there I was. The whole room looked at me. There were kids at all the tables and the computers. . . . They were just studying, it seemed like. I stood around there for a few moments looking around. I noticed there was a Che poster on the back wall . . . the same one that I had in my room at home. I felt connected at the moment and finally took my picture. I said, "Thank you very much, see you later!" and left. A group of underclassmen saw that I had just come out of that room and looked at me for a second . . . they were confused. I walked down the rest of the commons feeling like I had just gotten off an amusement-park ride. I can't really describe how I felt, but it felt good—really good.

Ailsa described her experience in a similar fashion:

Wow, I didn't think I would be this nervous. It is Thursday, March 19th, and today after school I went over to the commons because I wanted to ask one of the METCO students if I could interview them. I didn't think it would be that hard for me to muster up the courage to ask them for an interview. I kept sitting there, looking at my planner and pretending to do work, and at the same time trying to see if there was someone around I could ask. I finally got up the courage to walk over to the girl doing homework at a table by [the] METCO room. I asked her if she would be willing to do an interview and she said she had a lot of work, so I went into the METCO room. Only two people were in there, both seniors, and both busy. I must say I left the commons pretty upset with myself. I was mad that it took me so long to even ask, and then I was disappointed I hadn't found anyone to interview. . . . What got to me the most, though, was the fact that I was so scared to approach the METCO room. I felt like I didn't really belong there, that the METCO students would look at me with questioning looks, like "What are YOU doing here?" and mostly I felt guilty. I feel like, WOW, this is my fourth year at the high school and this is only the third or fourth time I am approaching the METCO room, because I have to do a homework assignment. A homework assignment. That seems so pathetic to me. Now obviously that's not the only reason I am approaching the METCO room; I honestly want to know what the METCO students think and feel, what their day is like, etc. But in their eyes, it doesn't look like that. It looks like a white girl needs to get her project done, and that's when she approaches the METCO room. Now I guess you could argue better late than never. At least I am approaching the METCO students now, senior year, [rather] than not ever approaching them. I just really wish I had approached them earlier, become better friends with them, and become more comfortable and less intimidated. It's unfortunate because I feel like if students took this class freshman year, a lot more white kids would be in the METCO room and hanging out with METCO students.

The METCO room offered an excellent opportunity to fulfill the two-way street intended by this desegregation program. Sadly, the school's failure to educate white students had fostered separation rather than interracial communication on campus.

White students needed to feel comfortable in honestly confronting their racial beliefs, in order to have the courage to step into a predominantly non-white environment.

Class discussions about the reluctance of whites to enter the METCO room brought immediate responses from the Boston students. In fact, they could *name* the less than one percent of the white student body who ventured across that threshold. They cited fear and intimidation on the part of whites. The results with regard to faculty members proved to be around 4 percent. Once again, the students cited fear and intimidation. So over 95 percent of the white people at the high school had never visited the Boston students at their home base on campus, out of fear—even though whites were on *their own turf.* Desegregation had a long way to go.

For students, this racial divide generally appeared during their elementary-school experiences and most often remained intact until they graduated. The interviews, as indicated, proved even more powerful than the readings in provoking whites to reevaluate their world. Most notably, many whites initially expressed a sense of a "nonracial" world as young children. When probed during the interviews, however, many of them recaptured memories that they had been conditioned to suppress.

For most whites, the elementary-school years represented a nonracial world where kids simply played with any kid who shared common interests. Yet the perception of those "innocent years" often crumbled when non-white classmates shared their experiences. Sometimes, however, those recollections emerged from white students who had forgotten some of their earliest experiences. The following excerpts provide some enlightening insights into how white students processed their early racial experiences:

> It was my first day of school. . . . When I walked into the classroom I saw two Indian kids. They were amongst the few colored people I had ever seen. I was confused, I couldn't tell if they were "black" so I waited for other clues before concluding their race.

> It was second grade when I had at least one black kid in my class. I felt a little sorry for him being black, and actually pitied him for that. I thought that other kids were nice to him for the same reasons, out of pity.

> I had some arguments with this black girl . . . not because she was black, [but] that is what made me feel guilty and wrong.

> I met a black girl in second grade . . . I really liked her but I was always wary of her home life. I had this preconceived idea that she lived in a poor and violent environment.

When stories like these were shared in class, more white students began to recall their own early experiences with race. The students also became more motivated to address these memories, since they seemed to satisfy a growing need to fill in the missing pieces of their racial past. In many ways, the new *awakening* and the "racial discoveries" from the past tended to provide them with a more realistic racial narrative, one more consistent with the experiences of their non-white peers.

During their middle-school years, students experienced a remarkable change with regard to race, both in and out of the classroom. And, for the most part, the white students expressed feelings of guilt, anger, confusion, and frustration.

During middle school, most whites ignored or denied their own racial identities and race issues at the very time when their non-white peers often evidenced a heightened awareness of their racial identity. This transformation is detailed in Beverley Daniel Tatum's *Why Are All the Black Kids Sitting Together in the Cafeteria?* Obviously, white students experienced a great deal of discomfort in formulating their thoughts and feelings about children they had been taught to respect, as sort of a mandate in their suburban world. Yet their informal race education had also brought them much confusion.

Thus, in their private lives, students dealt with their discomfort in ways that challenged "what they had been told" with other perspectives that they had internalized in the hidden curriculum. On occasion, these "unacceptable" perspectives surfaced in the public domain, creating quite a stir. As one student recalled, "In middle school we had a speech given to us because someone wrote 'nigger' on a book." Others evidently began acting out their racial feelings in more overt ways as well.

Students also reported incidents where some white kids pretended to be members of the KKK, actually walking around expressing a hatred for "niggers." Also, it was not uncommon for students to recall the many racist jokes that made the rounds in their early school years, though they generally also professed to have not known what the jokes really meant.

Routinely, both white and non-white students expressed dissatisfaction with how the school officials dealt with these public situations. White students generally felt reprimanded and guilty, but no better informed or equipped to process race in their world. For the most part, however, students remembered the segregation that existed. Sometimes this entered as part of the curriculum, such as having students racially divided when debriefing the movie *Amistad*.

In the cafeteria, however, the racial segregation tended to be less evident . . . and a lot more complex. The racial dynamic at lunch differed mainly for the athletically successful black and Latino boys, who found themselves sought after by whites of both genders for their "cool-ness." A situation in the middle-school lunchroom later surfaced in the race and racism class as one of the most intriguing events to be processed across racial lines.

The story first emerged through the voices of a group of very-high-status white senior girls. It began when some of the most popular middle-school white boys chose to sit at the "black table" in order to chill with the male Boston athletes. Evidently, the most popular white girls decided to follow the same urge, and they took the remaining seats at the table. When the Boston girls arrived, they found "their seats" occupied by these white girls. That prompted some animosities, including one white girl being pulled off her seat by her hair.

Eventually, the Boston girls were told by the lunch monitors to find other seats, since seating was based on a "first come" basis. The white girls who first revealed the story in an after-class discussion indicated how fearful the whole incident had made them when they were only trying to socialize at lunch. Their memories combined the innocence of sitting with friends in the lunchroom and a fear of some black girls that had persisted until their last years in high school.

Of course, the Boston girls also had a very strong memory of the lunch-seating controversy, one that revealed a very different perspective. The major factual difference involved the identity of the Boston girl who had pulled the hair. The victimized white identified the most "intimidating" of the black girls in her current class as the culprit. However, in a subsequent discussion with the Boston girls, a far less vocal and intimidating Latina took absolute ownership of having been the perpetrator. She laughed at the very thought that she intimidated anyone. She and her friends then provided their perspective on the story.

The Boston girls did not focus on the "innocence" of kids just sitting with other kids, but rather on the racial implications of being physically ostracized from "the METCO table" without any "safe haven" in the cafeteria. The Boston boys weren't about to reject the attention of these popular white girls, so the Boston girls took it upon themselves to right the situation. "Their boys" were being taken over by the white girls.

Stigmatized by the altercation and unable to beat the white girls to the table, the Boston girls embarked on a nomadic search for a place to eat. They took up residence in various classrooms and the METCO room until finally settling into a space of their own at lunch. This "resolution" had left both groups of girls with bitter racial memories of middle-school life.

The administration apparently dealt with the problem as a typical "kid issue," without attention paid to the racial aspects involved. In this particular case, ignoring race left a vital educational opportunity unresolved, with long-lasting, unhealthy consequences. The lesson learned by the white girls as part of their hidden curriculum included these intimidating, scary black girls having inexplicably and inexcusably attacked them.

The Boston girls learned that they had been wrong in trying to hold on to their safe place in the cafeteria, which had resulted in rejection and eventual isolation in the cafeteria. One white girl summed up the legacy for all: "Like, I remember in middle school, there was a 'black girl' table, and we didn't go near it. We were scared of it."

By the time they left middle school, whatever their cross-racial peer relationships, most white kids had learned to distance themselves even further from race talk. Yet their high school journals indicated that they had been hoping for an opportunity to explore some of the confusing thoughts and feelings about the non-white people around them.

High-school experiences tended to perpetuate the racial lines drawn in middle school. As evidenced by the avoidance of the METCO room, white ignorance about the intent of METCO, and the negative outcomes of race at the middle school, the white students tended to ignore race. The interviews, however, would provide the single most significant stimulus to the white students' ability to grasp the racial realities that had been ignored or denied throughout their lives.

The most common outcome of these journals proved to be a racial *awakening*, marked mainly by strong feelings of *empathy* and *respect*, *amazement* and *sadness*. It appeared that white students managed to reconstruct a new racial narrative that enabled them to engage their non-white peers in mutual understanding of how race worked in their lives. Most often, their increased empathy overlapped with respect for the people who shared their stories, especially the raw honesty with which they spoke.

At their best, the interviews spawned some new interracial friendships. Nearly all the journals expressed a sense of amazement at how effortlessly, honestly, and profoundly the non-white students responded to their questions. For white students who had spent a lifetime avoiding race discussions, this forthrightness proved to be an eye-opening experience. The manner in which non-white students addressed these "tough" questions alone served to confirm that these topics had truly been contemplated over the course of a lifetime.

A student succinctly summed up the importance of the interview project when he stated, "It took me out of my comfort zone, but the information and opinions I gleaned from the interviews was [sic] invaluable. It forced me to talk to people I never would have talked to before."

A short excerpt of exchanges between Stef, a white resident student, and Franchesca, a Boston student, epitomize both the simplicity and profoundness of the interview process. When Stef asked Franchesca if she felt like the white kids looked down on her, she responded with, "Yes, you can tell that someone feels better than you . . . like you're not as smart." Stef, to her credit, then asked, "Do you think I've done that?" In a display of blunt honesty that routinely shocked the white students who had been conditioned to avoid honest race talk, Franchesca replied, "To be honest, yes."

Another white resident remarked on her interview experience with a non-white with phrases such as "amazed [at her] eagerness to talk" and "I expected her to be apprehensive . . . with a total stranger." The white girl spoke about her astonishment at the lack of apprehension on the part of her black peer, who declared, "I've been aware of race ever since I walked in the door."

Some white students expressed a sense of sadness at what had been missed in those difficult adolescent years when they struggled to find a good friend, especially when a potential soul mate had been right within their grasp—yet miles away, due to a racial-desegregation program that had put them in close physical proximity, yet left them emotionally segregated.

The intent of the interview was to produce an honest exchange of thoughts and feelings, while also bringing racial understanding and empathy to the white students. Essentially, the hidden curriculum intersected with the formal curriculum, only now the students possessed new cognitive ways to assess both.

Indeed, many interviews exhibited honest learning experiences that transcended the persistent racial barriers that existed even during a long-term interracial friendship. David perfectly illustrated this outcome. One of the most popular Boston students to walk the halls of WHS, David maintained consistently amiable relationships with both resident students and faculty. He spoke with a resident friend whom he had known since kindergarten, in an interview that would only further generate respect, given his willingness to speak honestly about his life as a young black male.

David addressed the troubling nature of being followed around in stores, in a way that made this form of racial profiling take on a new light in a very personal way. It was one thing to know it existed, another to know that it happened to David. He also addressed the realities of Wayland's professed progressivism in dealing with race issues. David offered some praise for Wayland's attempts to deal with race, but his interviewer also reported, "Dave also shed light on what Wayland is actually like."

David's honest and forthright assessment of his racial realities brought the admiration so often expressed by resident students: "He was really cool about answering some of my tougher or more intrusive questions." Once again, a white student felt that a large missing piece of an interracial friendship had been exposed, creating a new bond that felt a lot more real. An assignment that a white student "wasn't feeling too excited about doing" transformed into a discussion "I wish we weren't forced to stop (it was late and we both needed sleep)."

Melvin didn't possess the broad appeal of David, mostly due to a more reserved personality. As expressed in an interview, Melvin had been around in elementary school, walked the halls of the middle school among white students, stood next to them in the snack line at the high school, and even sat next to white students in the race class. Yet beyond an occasional wave or smile, he was a mystery. During the interview, however, the mystery gradually dissipated and produced some enlightenment.

A section of the interview asks the subject to respond in a word-association format to racial groups. When asked to say the first thing that came to mind when he heard black people, Mel quickly respond with, "Me. I think of life when I think of black. I think of my life, period." For most white students, such a response brought an immediate awareness of the racial world that they had been oblivious to. On a very personal level, a white student became bluntly confronted with the reality that race defined the world of a non-white friend in ways that it never defined his.

This interview also ended with a newfound sense of respect for a young man who was found to be "so deep, so powerful, and so strong." And Mel would leave a lasting memory when he presented his perspective on dealing with people and circumstances that challenged his own life experiences. Mel stated, "I don't like to be afraid of anything, so when something is new and different, I try to understand it, so I wouldn't [sic] have to fear it." Mel may have been a mystery to most of his classmates, but he proved to be a very insightful and inspiring young man when given the opportunity to access his voice.

Hannah expressed some similar thoughts and feelings after her interview with Natalie. In this case, these two young women, both bright and sensitive, had traveled very different paths through Wayland High School. In fact, they could serve as symbols for the racial achievement gap, given their final standing in the academic pecking order of the high school. In the "better late than never" category, here they met on common ground, opening a discussion between two strong and fine young women:

> My interview with Natalie was far more successful than I had predicted. I chose to interview her because she moved to my elementary school in fifth grade and was the only METCO student in the grade. . . . Natalie talked about how she was the "token black girl," something that I had never thought about before. Wayland parents would call her mom to invite her over, but children would never invite her directly. Intending to be kind, since it was difficult for Natalie to make last minute plans and get a ride back to Boston, parents saw inviting Natalie over as a contribution rather than as a play-date. Understanding her earlier experiences also helped me to understand the situation of METCO students. They are not treated as individuals; people tend to see them as the "token blacks," just like in elementary school. This interview has totally changed the way I think about the METCO program and the students from Boston. At the very least, Wayland students need to appreciate the dedication that Boston students show every time they walk onto the Wayland High School campus.

This sense of opportunities missed, an awakening to a new racial world, and newfound respect for the Boston students reached its pinnacle in several extraordinary interviews. Some exceptional white kids welcomed the challenge of interviewing the Boston student deemed most "intimidating," with the hope that their courage might enable them to cross over the great racial divide. Their courage would not go unrewarded. In fact, their interviews provided racial insights that no books, teacher lectures, or class discussions could ever expect to achieve.

Alex took this bold step in an effort to maximize his racial education. This popular and athletic young man possessed a quiet strength that clearly resonated with all audiences. In a soft-spoken manner, he could publicly address male sexist behaviors, or acknowledge his racial ignorance without apparent insecurity. When the former occurred in the classroom you could see the awe in the eyes of the female students, especially with Alex's willingness to break ranks with the alpha males. His explanation for his choice in the interview process speaks for itself:

> I chose to interview Michaela for a couple of reasons. To be plain, she has been in the most of my classes of any of the black or Latino METCO kids over the course of the past four years. More importantly though is the way that I have viewed Michaela has [*sic*] changed over those four years. As a freshman and sophomore, to me M. was the overly proud, sharp, sassy black girl. I thought she saw racism in everything, where most times there was actually nothing. And I remember last year she was in my history class and we were learning about some event that happened involving blacks, and she was making remarks about how racist and horrible it was and it bothered me. I would sit there wanting her to just be quiet already.
>
> Recently I came to realize and understand who Michaela is in a completely different light. I now see that I was bothered by her comments in history class about race because I would deny the fact that there was racism involved, because I wasn't comfortable talking about it. After having the interview, I honestly think Michaela is a special person with a strong sense and understanding about race and the world around her.
>
> During the interview she talked about how ever since a young age she was aware of her race and [that of] those around her. This made me wonder what it is really that makes a child or person aware of their race, because I know as I was growing up I was never concerned or thought about race.

During the interview I actually felt somewhat taken back [*sic*] and unprepared, not because I didn't have the sheet of questions or some of my own personal questions, but because when we started to converse into deeper and more complex situations and topics I found that I had never really formed an opinion or thought about many of the situations. I could tell that Michaela had well formed and articulated thoughts and ideas about every question that I asked.

Alex went on to express his empathy for Michaela after she asked him how he would feel being the only white kid in a class full of black kids. Alex responded, "I would feel extremely intimidated and afraid to speak my mind and say everything I felt." He ended his journal with a clear understanding "that people on all sides of the race issue just need to talk. Talk and listen and understand. So many negative images, ideas, and stereotypes are formed in the imagination of our minds because we have no real information to base them on."

Alex's journal illustrates the remarkable bridging of the wide racial divide in just an hour's time, when students speak honestly about their world.

Alex R. also interviewed Michaela. This young man came from a very different place from that of his namesake, though he also possessed a good deal of self-confidence. Alex R., who brought an alternative, artsy persona to the class, displayed his strength more through his choosing, in appearance and attitude, to reject the mainstream "jock culture." These two young men probably had significantly different life experiences, but they both found that Michaela had the "most incredible experiences to share," as Alex R. expressed in this journal entry:

I found out that she is such a strong person, resilient, and outspoken, and consistently, from what I learned about her past experiences, people have found her unapproachable or intimidating because of this. They have been unable to see the hilarious, happy, intelligent, and great person that she is. Michaela and I talked a lot about division between the METCO students at the high school and the Wayland students. She told me that it basically started in middle school. Things like the black boys being followed by white girls and the black girls being opposed by white girls and the white girls being intimidated by the black girls carried over from the middle school. . . . I am upset that I have never really talked to Michaela to find out who she is until this year. I am upset that most people at Wayland High School aren't able to approach other black people at our school as they don't approach Michaela. Myself and other people have followed the gossip, the fear, and the instilled estrangement for too long.

Michaela possessed the self-confidence and pride that would not be silenced by her peers or school staff. She displayed a keen awareness of racism and often addressed it, as noted by Alex. Yet to defend your integrity meant punishing consequences for the Boston students, since they were almost always deemed to be the problem. Thus, students such as Michaela received rebuke in both the public domain and private domain—because she found her voice in defense of her dignity.

A positive lesson that emerged from such interviews happened to coincide nicely with a key objective of the course, based on the principle that *the only way to get comfortable talking about race was to simply talk about it, no matter how uncomfortable this was at first.* What also emerged, from both the interviews and class discussions, was the awareness, perhaps for the first time, that the Boston students seemed so much smarter and more mature than the white students.

Give students the opportunity to talk about something they live, in their real world, and they sure can shine.

Carson chose to explore a very different racial angle by interviewing two black female students, one resident and one from Boston, simultaneously, hoping to understand how their lives compared, not just in being female, but also with regard to their experiences in Wayland. His findings included most of the themes in this chapter. Here's some of what he found, as described in his reflection journal:

> They feel that the standards they must live up to in order to gain access to a white school system is [*sic*] ridiculous. They believed that it is almost like people are "constantly watching them," waiting for them to mess up, and that "people don't want them here." They know that they cannot get into fights or misbehave in ways that many white students can get away with. They said this forces them to be confidant [*sic*] and independent, and they know they must be able to hold on [*sic*] emotions. The Wayland girl even explained how she views herself as a "connector" between [METCO] kids and Wayland kids. Both explained how this continues outside of school in the Wayland community. They feel that they have to be "more than polite" because Wayland parents are expecting the [worst]. I thought about this and realized that my mom always says that my black friends are the most polite—the more I thought about it the more I realized this to be true. They compliment my mom's meal, speak politely, say please and thank you and address my mom as Mrs. [H.]. I also thought about how often my mom complains about my other friends' lack of manners, I wonder how she would respond to an impolite [METCO] kid. They also claimed they find it difficult to "blend in," and since they stick out so much they become a lightening [*sic*] rod for criticism. Therefore, unlike white kids, they need to be polite in order to save their reputation. When we talked about where racism is more prevalent they could not decide. They said in the city racism is obvious with all the segregation, but in the suburbs people will smile to your face and act accepting, but be viciously racist deep down. . . . They both agreed that in order for a black girl to get a white guy they need to be perfect. They claimed that white guys hold black women up to impossible standards that white women are not held up to. Being a white guy I began to think more about this. I find plenty of black women attractive, but most are in music videos and celebrities. I cannot decide whether I too hold up black women to impossible standards, or if I am yet to meet one face to face that I am really attracted to. . . . To my surprise they both wanted to marry white guys (although they claim they look for "hot black guys" first). When I asked them why they explained it was in order to have light skinned children. Personally I never knew that the shade of your skin color was so important. They felt that light skinned blacks have a greater opportunity in education, jobs, etc.

Grace found her first interview so enlightening she decided to conduct a more complicated one by interviewing a combination of both black resident and Boston female students, which resulted in some other exciting and interesting outcomes:

> I learned so much from Lasonta, [Idora], Shalona, and Denyse in just an hour, and I really enjoyed talking to them. I brought up the suggestion of asking you, Mr. Frio, if we could try to set up the same lunch meetings that were held for the purpose of discussing race that were at WHS a few years ago. [Denyse] said she had also been thinking about it, and I'm really grateful that they let me interview them, because they were so honest and strong, which I really admired. I want there to be more discussion about race, and I wish that everyone were as open as the people I talked to about it were. I think that I learned a lot about them, and they realized how much I didn't know, which made for quite an interesting and easy discussion. At the end of the conversation, Sammi came over with her guitar singing about how most guys were jerks, and we all started singing along. . . . I know that every discussion about race doesn't end on such a positive note, but I felt so accomplished and more knowledgeable after talking to these girls. I am not naïve, I realize that we all have our differences (I make it sound so simple. It's not, I know), many of which are attributed to our racial backgrounds, yet I love it how we can all come together and talk openly as friends and end our conversation in a song about how we all agree that boys can be jerks. From now on, maybe, we won't have to talk about such things because of an assignment, but rather because we want to.

A student's desire to spend more time on a class subject outside the classroom certainly makes all teachers feel validated. The other outcome, agreeing that all boys are jerks, doesn't carry the same positive message; however, it did speak to an important connection made that day, one between girls. Having experienced a sense of powerlessness with regard to males enabled the young white women to gain empathy not only with respect to the racial experiences of the Boston students, but more specifically with respect to the issues faced by the female Boston students. Such realizations provided rich opportunities for expanding learning.

This gender connection served as the foremost means of getting white girls to empathize with their non-white peers.

Nina also sought to engage a student known to possess strong opinions about racial issues in her world. In the following journal passage, Nina poignantly and trenchantly took on the stereotype of inferior intelligence from an extraordinarily rewarding cross-racial interview discussion. Nina wrote:

> I decided to interview [Theresa] because she has always been one of my more outspoken and fascinating friends. We met in sixth grade and bonded over our shared British heritage and a love for Xena the Warrior Princess. . . . I wouldn't say that our conversations before now had been superficial, but that we never touched on anything so personal as race before now. . . . I could have cut down the interview quite a bit, but I couldn't find the heart to water down her insightful observations or pick out which opinions of hers I found more thought-provoking. I instead found every point she made to be illuminating, shocking and at times heart-wrenching, but evidently by the length of this essay not too concise. The constant humor we sprinkled in was our way (or certainly my way) of coping with an issue that is rooted in pain and frustration. One of my goals in this interview was to be as candid and to shed my usual discomfort when dealing with race. . . . I have always been too uncomfortable to talk about the prominence of a "black kid table" or the separation of different races into different levels of classes. Now I'm starting to realize, and [Theresa's] opinions have confirmed, that by not having any (or very little [*sic*]) classmates of different races (except for Asian students) I have developed subconsciously an opinion about the intellectual capacity of these students. By closing off white students from the few black or Latino students that our school has I think a latent view of these kids is formed—we start to believe (though we would never say it out loud) that non-white or non-Asian students don't have the intellectual capacity to do well in our honors classes. Now, I can begin to see how preposterous this is, and that our current system of dividing students into classes is deeply flawed and arbitrary. . . . Thus, now I am trying to recognize that subconscious prejudice I have of black and Latino kids not being "up to" the skill level required for my classes, and I'm transferring these negative opinions to the system that has kept me apart from these students. . . . I agree with [Theresa] that something in the structure of the educational system here must be changed. However, I am cynical about this happening rapidly based on how unwilling white educators are to talk openly about race.

Although Nina's observations infrequently appeared in print or class discussions, they certainly persisted over the years. As evidenced so well by Nina, even the most sensitive, socially aware, and brightest white students had internalized one of the worst racial stereotypes. Widespread belief in this perspective emerged consistently in class when resident students were asked if they felt intellectually challenged by their black and Latino peers. They routinely responded like it was a trick question.

One of the primary lessons being internalized by the white students in the hidden curriculum included an expectation of black and Latino intellectual inferiority.

Beyond the readings, journals, and interviews, white students also had many opportunities to "go public" and explore their opinions and observations in class discussions. Overwhelmingly, however, most showed a reluctance to speak honestly about race in front of black and Latino students. Without question, this proved to be the most difficult hurdle in the classroom. As expected, writing in private proved far easier than speaking publicly.

Fortunately, some classes contained at least a few white students willing to break the "club's" code of loyalty and silence (as coined by Matthew). They often stimulated others to speak more honestly about race. Sometimes their honesty disturbed the sensibilities of their classmates, which then precipitated even more truth, no matter how "politically incorrect." Otherwise, these most unacceptable perspectives were taken from student journals and anonymously introduced into class discussions.

For example, a statement such as "I do not hate [blacks] anymore, but I still don't think they are as good as whites" could be expected to generate some agreement from other whites, prompting a very productive discussion.

The following passage from Victor's journal would spark productive discussions since it spoke to an issue no doubt relevant to many whites. Here he reflected on his interview with a black male student:

> Nothing would make me happier [than] to see black people turn into white people. I would [like] their culture to break and for them to act exactly like us. With my authentic black friends . . . there is only so much I can take of them. . . . I openly told him that I prefer white girls. When he said white girls I wasn't surprised but I was annoyed. Like a lot of white males, it kind of annoys and angers me when I see a big black guy with a white girl. I don't care if they're with trashy white girls but when they're with a respectable white girl it annoys me. I don't really know why. Maybe I feel that black guys are grimy I don't know. I know a lot of people think that way . . . I guess it's a form of prejudice but whatever. I may have some prejudices towards blacks but I don't really care because I'm not racist.

The depth and breadth of such "unacceptable" public views and racial stereotypes emerged from the word-association segment of the interview. The most common responses to "black" included: *rap, hip-hop, gangs, drugs, angry, braided hair, self-hatred, gold jewelry, athletic,* and *intimidating*. To "Latino/a" the responses most commonly included *large families, big butts, dancing, pretty girls, clubs, souped-up cars, tough guys, skanky girls, gangsters,* and *sexy*. The prevalence of such stereotypes within the hidden curriculum clearly indicated the need for public discussion.

Instead, by keeping a low profile, both at school and in the greater community, the METCO program could function without any negative attention. However, stereotypes associated with urban children of color, mostly very negative, persisted within the hidden curriculum as a detriment to the education of all children at the school. For the white students, left unaddressed, it meant an uncomfortable sense of ignorance and guilt. They deserved better.

A sign posted in the front of their classroom posited, "Silence is the voice of complicity." Were the vast majority of white students, in their hearts, complicit with the racial situation at their school? Their journals and voices in class clearly indicated they were not. Unfortunately, finding their voices had not been a priority in their education, and speaking about race had been virtually ignored. As one student put it, "These kids I think have been failed by the system."

Ryan's responses were typical of those generated by senior exit evaluations and journals on the nature of education at the high school: "Words and phrases like 'open expression,' 'risk-taking,' and 'free association' . . . none of those words could describe anything that goes on very often at Wayland High School." Katie stated, "WHS has been wholly unhelpful . . . in providing me with real world knowledge or courage to tackle problems facing America."

In lieu of risk-taking open expression, far too many students reported thoughts similar to what another student wrote at length about, regarding what she perceived as the enduring nature of her learning. At the end she concluded with, "I just sat there, another obedient student who was taught to do just that: obey."

Thrust into an interracial world constructed by adults—a world in which they served as the experimental pawns—these white students had been deserted and left, for the most part, to create their own lessons about race. Their formal education, with its focus on some past factual aspects of the history of race and racism, left students to struggle in ignorance with the racial reverberations in their immediate world. Essentially, each day these students entered a world that brought them in contact with non-white students, a strange world that, at best, remained a silent mystery until their final year of education.

Indeed, through years of detached engagement or total disengagement from these "foreigners" in their midst, white students had internalized some age-old stereotypes that produced a wealth of guilt and shame. Finding their voices on race enabled many white students to gain respect and empathy for their Boston peers, along with a desire to do something about the racial injustices in their world. Yet they also acknowledged the difficulties in confronting the power of a system that had silenced them for so long.

Some vowed to continue their journey to racial understanding, while others recognized that their commitment to justice might be fleeting. They had come to understand the discomfort that came from true interracial discourse and the benefits accorded them from a system that ignored racial injustices. A few simply found dealing with race too exhausting, and bluntly declared no desire to pursue any further race education. How all of this affected the non-white students can be found in the voices of those students. It's time for them to be heard.

POSTSCRIPT

Zack came to class each day with a willingness to listen, to consider, and to test out his thoughts in class. During the race and racism class, Zack began to see his world differently, especially with regard to the racial injustices that had previously escaped his vision. Like many of his white classmates, he felt empowered to continue his growth in racial awareness, and as it turned out he kept his commitment:

> One time, back in race/crime/psych, you mentioned that in college the likelihood that any of us would come to interact with many black people or the black community as a whole is [*sic*] unlikely. Because we have the option not to, and because we are naturally inclined towards our biases, then we would go with what was comfortable. Four years later, I can say that this statement made a profound impact in my life. One of the first classes I decided to take at [college] was intro to African American studies. I took it because I enjoyed your class and because I knew that what you said was true; if I never stepped outside of my comfort zone I never would've had a chance to meet some incredible people. Day One of class, I met my best friend at [college]. Since then I have lived with all black kids, while maintaining membership in a mostly white fraternity. The black community is small at [the college], about 4 percent, so I've had the chance to meet virtually

everyone in it. Integrating was not easy, it took being uncomfortable, time, and learning to just be myself no matter what. This has been an incredible life experience and I can honestly trace it back to what you said in class. I want to thank you for that.

LESSONS LEARNED

The hidden curriculum on race produces some of the most unfortunate and unhealthy learning within the school.

Whites deserve to be better educated about whites who have fought for racial equality, in order to have more positive role models in discussing race issues.

In dealing with race, enhanced listening skills led to greater sensitivity to the realities of the racial world in which the students lived.

White students tend to suppress much resentment against the institutions that function to create a "cultural wasteland" in the suburbs.

Honest race *talk* begins with enhanced *listening* skills.

White students must be honest in confronting their racial beliefs before they can feel comfortable entering spaces that are overwhelmingly non-white.

Middle-school white children tend to internalize a lot of guilt, anger, confusion, and frustration as their non-white peers experience their racial identity development.

By talking and listening to each other in the interview process, students were able to assess the intersection of the formal and hidden curricula.

Allowing students to bring their life experiences to the classroom allows them to shine in ways often absent in the formal curriculum.

Cross-racial empathy can be attained through mutual understanding of powerlessness—such as that expressed by female students.

The hidden curriculum contained a lesson expressly antithetical to the goals of desegregation—that of black and Latino intellectual inferiority.

Chapter 6

Black and Latino Students Speak Their Minds

I don't mean to sound harsh, but we are capable and we do have the ability to succeed if you give us the chance to.

—Melinda

I feel like people are in denial and our generations are focused on living happy, no drama, lives. They don't want [to] nor will they focus on the poverty and crime because it ties into race.

—Lasonta

Standing outside the METCO room amid the chaos of the commons, a black girl who didn't look at all familiar passionately engaged another student in conversation. An introduction later, Michelle revealed that she had just moved from the South to Boston, and now found herself in the METCO program. Of course her former history class entered the conversation, which led to the discovery that this clearly engaging and very bright junior's transcript contained an A at the honors level in her previous school—yet she'd found herself enrolled in a lower-level class at Wayland High School (WHS).

About two weeks prior to my meeting Michelle, a white student from a neighboring school system, without a transcript, had moved into the honors-level class. Physically, Saul had integrated seamlessly into the class, but he seemed very lost in the course and not quite motivated to get himself in gear. Something didn't seem right. The explanation indicated that this white student's parents, short of a transcript, had told the school that he was an honors student, and their word was sufficient to gain him entry. Despite Michelle's expressed desire to be at the honors level, her fate seemed to be settled.

Fortunately, there existed some alternative methods for circumventing the usual protocol for moving students, so Michelle came into the honors level through the back door. Michelle managed to outperform Saul, though that honestly didn't represent much of a challenge. But more importantly, Michelle helped to totally transform the nature of that class. Remarkably, a small switch for her managed to generate some huge lessons for her classmates and teacher.

Dally sat bent over an open book in the METCO room, struggling with a homework assignment. An hour after school had ended, her attention remained riveted on her studies. An attempt to help her with calculus problems proved useless. So the conversation turned to history class, as I figured any student doing this math must be at the honors level. Instead, Dally spoke about bombing in a college-level history class. This placement just didn't sound right.

A meeting was arranged at the departmental level, where her current teacher provided information with regard to Dally's poor record in his class that clearly indicated she did not belong at the honors level. That part of the story was already known. The department head remained unconvinced, so the case was then transferred to the principal for a final decision. The request was rejected since the handbook clearly stated she had missed the deadline for level changes. Dally was disappointed, but the case had been closed.

Subsequently, Mr. Griffin, Dally's guidance counselor, noticed a document on the principal's desk affirming a white resident student's move into honors English . . . dated past the deadline. Confronted with the discrepancy, the principal authorized Dally's transfer. Justice had been served. This story certainly possessed a strong racial subtext, though some plausible deniability could always be claimed. Dally would prove to be one of the most insightful and courageous students over the next two years, despite the extra burden of speaking English as a second language.

Michelle's and Dally's stories illustrate one of the many issues confronting the Boston students when they journeyed to Wayland as part of the process of desegregating the schools. Their class placement evidenced the murky area in the racial divide, the one that brought racism into the picture for some, mostly non-whites, but not for most white students and adults. This so-called postracial world championed by whites in the late twentieth century had shifted attention away from race, making it extremely difficult for non-whites to publicly confront racism in their lives.

Since overt acts of racism occurred very sporadically, these questionable cases of subtle racism would provide the most prevalent nagging issue for many Boston students throughout their schooling.

Beyond subtle racism, these students faced numerous challenges, beginning with the long commute out of the city to the upper-middle-class, white, suburban world of Wayland. They shared little if any life experiences with their predominantly white hosts, with whom many would spend twelve years during their most formative time of life. Ultimately, most Boston students would express some level of appreciation for the education they received, though it did not come without some significant intellectual, social, and emotional costs.

It is difficult to fathom the world of the Boston students. Start with the social stresses of normal teenagers, compounded by the complicated racial-identity aspects of desegregating a school populated by mostly indifferent whites. Add to the mix a heavy dose of internalized intellectual inferiority—and, finally, consider the main task of competing with their "intellectual superiors" *on their turf* in a high-stakes, high-pressure, high-stress academic environment.

To ratchet up the stress, they faced the highest of expectations from their home community, and often the lowest of expectations in their adopted community. When you factor in some random messages of hatred and rejection occasionally received from their resident peers, some staff members, and the greater community . . . it's much too exhausting to contemplate.

The Boston students' journals covered all these issues, but most often they addressed the burden of "*representing*" their race, coping with white *ignorance* of racial matters, *internalizing* the pains of racism, grappling with their *racial identities* while living in "*two worlds*," dealing with issues of *accommodation* and *assimilation*, managing a *curriculum* that often felt unbending to their needs, and *contending with educators* who possessed little or no experience dealing with race issues.

As much as they might want to be just students and kids dealing with typical adolescent problems, the Boston students could not avoid the very difficult and often painful complications and complexities of desegregating a white suburban community.

The schools also included a handful of seemingly well-adjusted black and Latino *resident* students, who would lend their own complexity to the world of race at school. Not only did they have to deal with complicated issues of race in their predominantly white neighborhoods, but they also had to navigate the chasm between their white peers and those students who arrived each day from Boston. Yet these residents often were provided a semblance of acceptance among their peers not accorded the "foreigners" who arrived from Boston.

The Boston students' initial experiences in Wayland contained a lot of immediate and very strong racial content, unlike the memories retained by white students, which were routinely devoid of racial content. Typically, that first contact sounded much like this student expressed it: "When I got off the bus the first day of school and saw so many white kids walking around . . . I mean I had seen white people in Boston before, but never talked to them. I was scared at first because there were more white people than people my color." Toni recalled:

> I do remember my first encounter with a white kid when I first came to Wayland. I remember when I first walked into my third grade class and all the kids were white except for about one student . . . I don't think I really remember the kid's name but I recall being introduced. . . . He just kind of looked at me with somewhat [*sic*] confusion, like he didn't understand why I looked the way I did or why my skin was a lot darker than his.

Another Boston student cited a key aspect of the METCO experience: "Uh, race has always been there, like, it's always been present, and I've felt it ever since I first walked in the door." That first entrance into a classroom proved quite memorable for Shatara as well:

> The first contact I had with students of another race was when I had first came [*sic*] to Wayland, and I entered my class late on the first day of school. When I walked into the room all the kids stared at me strangely. I felt so uncomfortable because I had never [seen] that many white students together in my life. I had just come from an all black Boston public school.

This Boston girl summed up her earliest years in Wayland with a strong reference to how she felt at the time: "From first to third grade I wore ribbons in my hair (a Haitian custom). I was always complimented on them, but when it came to learning about other cultures and people of color I always felt my inferiority." Those early years certainly contained some harsh moments for the Boston students, enough for Miriam to recall, "Growing up as a Haitian-American female I learned early on that facing discrimination would occur as often, and be as painful, as facing my own reflection."

By middle school the racial issues surfaced in a major way (see Beverley Daniel Tatum). Even Justin, who had once been perceived as a "dark white kid" and managed to cruise through elementary school, had a very different story to tell about these difficult years. His recollections reflected those of his peers, who noticed racism far more than was reported by their white peers:

> Middle school was the worst time for racism. Kids began to be aware of the fact that we were different than other kids. Black kids were the "cool kids" that everyone wanted to chill with, but we were also the first to be blamed for something. Like with the iPods over the last few years, everyone thinks it's the METCO kids who steal. Yeah, some METCO kids have stolen stuff, but I know that the kids who do will usually get white kids to steal it for them.

Mel experienced a situation that placed all the students in the program under suspicion of criminal activity, indicating the failure of adults in processing race issues:

Someone stole a credit card, and I remember all the METCO kids in the entire middle school going down to the office during the morning announcements. They weren't even casual about saying the individual names; they said all METCO kids to [assistant principal's] office. It was very embarrassing, because all the white kids looked at you very funny, and had that "Oh I wonder what they did now" look.

This incident helped to provide some race education for all the students involved, as would a couple of other racial incidents recalled by students. One student recalled a sixth-grade activity where the students passed the ball to each other while saying names, in order to learn the names of classmates. One particular group contained a few Boston students among a white majority. The Boston students passed to each other since they only knew each other, until a white boy screamed out loud, "'Why are the blacks passing only to the blacks?' The way it was said it made everyone upset of [*sic*] what he had just said."

Why are the blacks only passing to the blacks? A pretty simple question coming from a kid, except that it dealt directly with race. A pretty simple solution might have been to ask the boys, in a nonjudgmental manner, why they did so. Provide them with an opportunity to speak and you might find this situation de-escalated and resolved . . . and then some healthy education can take place.

Yet, when race is the issue, most educators seem to do their best to avoid any possibility that they might get caught in the middle of a "racial situation." Instead, racial misunderstandings end up escalating and festering, rather than being preempted or resolved . . . always to the detriment of all students and adults involved.

The mess that resulted from the white girls and Boston girls fighting over seats in the middle-school lunchroom illustrated the difficulties confronted by the Boston girls as they struggled to find their place in the social groupings. This next story addresses an incident reported by the senior girls, one that sullied what the girls perceived as the highlight of their middle-school years.

In the eighth grade, in preparation for the annual Martin Luther King dinner, the Boston girls were practicing a tradition that each class eagerly anticipated. During their last year of middle school these girls looked forward to performing a step dance on center stage at the MLK dinner and assembly. In this particular case, some white girls asked to join in during the practices that were already up and running. Although the timing seemed to be the immediate issue, the Boston girls felt most aggrieved when their refusal was construed to be racist.

Essentially, the formal intent of the MLK dinner, to bring the races together in an evening of fun and harmony, resulted in some very unintended, and very negative, consequences for a number of students. Meanwhile, this incident exacerbated the hard feelings that had ensued from the cafeteria incident.

If the socializing of Boston boys and white resident girls in the cafeteria had served to marginalize the Boston girls, this dance situation, unfortunately, would further debilitate the increasingly difficult lives of these girls. It only exacerbated the lack of positive attention paid to the Boston girls as academic achievers or social desirables. Almost totally ignored by the white boys, intimidating to most white girls and adults, and often deserted by the Boston boys, these Boston girls lived through a much tougher time socializing at the middle school.

During a time in their lives when physical appearance and social flirting were of supreme importance, many of the Boston girls expressed anger at how they were generally disrespected on both fronts. Miriam stated it very bluntly in response to a question about dating white boys: "Nothing is wrong with me, my skin might be a different color, but so what? Why is it so hard for them to be attracted to me?"

A biracial student who identified "half black and half white" wrote about the disrespect shown black women and how it had led her to believe that blacks were not as beautiful as whites. She attributed this to the movies, which she thought glorified the beauty of white women and excluded black women from glamorous roles. These views may have some exceptions, but the Boston girls could express very specifically the realities in their everyday lives.

Given their feelings of rejection, the Boston girls faced extraordinarily difficult circumstances. Obviously they longed for ways to build their self-esteem . . . and the step dance happened to be their best opportunity. From their perspective, they organized this group, choreographed the dances, and practiced diligently—only to find *they* were being accused of being racists! Ultimately, a white girl participated, but the Boston girls internalized their resentment over the next few years.

Consider how the white girls and their families must have perceived this incident. These white girls, in the spirit of MLK, were attempting to show their solidarity with the Boston girls, while their parents probably felt great pride in their children's courage in joining this dance performance . . . only to have their commendable efforts at interracial bonding rejected!

A traditional event greatly anticipated by the Boston girls had gone horribly awry. Instead of enjoying an evening in which the girls had expected to showcase their racial pride, they had been called racist. The whole situation had become a racial mess. As one girl stated, "It turned into a big thing when all we were trying to do was keep one thing for ourselves that we could be proud of in this all white environment." Everyone ended up angry, frustrated, and probably utterly confused by each other's motives.

If the Boston girls' voices had had a history of being heard, and their difficult circumstances understood, this whole situation could have been avoided. Despite whatever the leadership personnel felt about the outcome of this incident, both the Boston and resident girls clearly had internalized cross-racial animosities.

Beyond the ignorance about the struggles faced by the Boston girls, the step dance debacle also illustrated the most stressful and debilitating issue that separated the Boston students totally from their white peers—the pressure of "representing." The girls had hoped to take ownership of how they would be represented, but instead that had been hijacked. Instead of shining on stage in their big moment, the girls had to be burdened with being called racists.

This phenomenon operated every minute the Boston students spent within the community, whether in the classroom, at sporting events, in the halls, sleeping over at resident homes, standing in line at a local Dunkin' Donuts . . . or attending prom. Carrying the weight of representing the totality of "their people" by acting "appropriately" every day brought approbation from the white community, whereas "bad" behaviors reinforced the negative stereotypes internalized by whites—the kind that led some to suggest that they "didn't belong out here."

"Representing" also referred to situations in the classroom where the students might be asked to speak authoritatively on subjects connected to "their race." A Boston girl found herself in the spotlight as the "go to" person in her class on all things African or "black." For her, "representing" really had nothing to do with her, but mostly with the need to satisfy white audiences.

A boy wrote, "I remember feeling singled out a lot in order to confirm teachers' statements or defending the reality of my life. . . . I remember the need to prove my blackness not only to the METCO students, but to the whites too. Somehow my answers didn't always satisfy people's beliefs of [*sic*] me and other blacks." Lasonta prided herself on "telling it how it is," which she did when she stated, "People expect you to be all ghetto, but when they hear strength, independence, and intelligence come out of my mouth, they are shocked, and I like it."

Keanna cited a more nuanced version of "representing" when asked in an interview if she felt good or bad about taking on the role of educating her white peers about racial issues. She stated, "Both, I mean I am glad to have a chance to educate people, but it is also kind of a lot of responsibility. Like, I'm always worried if I get a bad grade that people will think all black people are stupid."

That spotlight of "representing" shone most brightly everywhere but inside the METCO office. Step outside that office, and you needed to be on your best behavior, because the stakes were very high for you and every other black and Latino student at the school. And, like most racial experiences, they generally appeared very randomly, making appropriate responses very difficult. Grace, a white girl, interviewed Keanna about just such an incident, one with a teacher who unmistakably reinforced the expectations of "representing":

> Going along with this whole theme was an instance earlier this year when Keanna and a few friends were laughing at a joke in the commons and a teacher came up and said something to the effect of, "Don't you know everyone is staring at you and do you know what they're thinking? You have to set a better example." I found this REALLY surprising that a teacher would go up and say that. She said that they all reacted kind of politely but as soon as the teacher left they said to each other, "What was that?!" I was mostly struck by what a burden it must be to feel like everyone else and to feel afraid to get one bad grade because you might have tainted someone's view of an entire race.

The negative and unfair burden of "representing" took on a much more sinister feature in that many white students and teachers held very clear opinions on what *kind* of "black behavior" would be deemed acceptable. Essentially, the Boston students were being instructed in what behaviors were expected by the white community. In the throes of figuring out the complexities of their individual racial identities, it had to be exceptionally frustrating and confusing to be held to so many variations of other people's expectations as well.

Shatara framed not only the problem, but also a potentially awful consequence:

> Like sometimes, you feel like you can't be yourself. And I feel like I have to represent. Whatever I do is like I'm representing all the METCO kids, like if I do something bad, I'm risking putting the METCO kids' name on the line, basically. There's been many incidents where people have done something and they look at the Boston kids like, "Oh they're acting up, they shouldn't be out here."

As mentioned earlier, Michelle's presence in an honors-level class was transformative. First of all, it brought out a positive aspect of "representing." Within the first quarter the class self-divided into opposing positions for a debate on the protection of slavery and the slave trade in the Constitution. Their reading of Derrick Bell's *And We Are Not Saved: The Elusive Quest for Racial Justice* had provided them with compelling arguments on both sides, so each year the debate proved to be passionate and complex. However, Michelle's presence in the classroom completely altered the tone and nature of the debate.

Students who felt convinced by the practical, financial, and political arguments that favored the slave system found themselves arguing their case in the presence of this friendly and articulate black girl. She put a face on the *people* they were committing to a life of enslavement. This was no longer an intellectual debate devoid of humanity. And since Michelle had the combination of a warm personality and the willingness to speak her mind, the white students were forced to more deeply consider their options before determining "Michelle's fate." Unlike the Founding Fathers, these students would not have the comfort to argue the fate of people who had no representation in the room.

Second, Michelle's presence modeled how a desegregated classroom could work. To the credit of the resident students, they continued to argue their convictions, though their judgments had taken on a more measured tone, one that reflected and respected the humanity in that room. The key involved trusting the students to freely discuss difficult racial issues, and then employing a debriefing process that enabled the students to express how Michelle's presence might have impacted their discussion and final conclusions.

Through this concluding activity, students would be able to identify the "silent" power of race in the classroom and how heterogeneity promotes deeper thinking and understanding through different life experiences and perspectives.

Clearly, when race directly entered the curriculum, the issue of "representing" brought much greater challenges. Most students understood the danger in challenging a teacher's beliefs or content—a danger that certainly magnified when layered with race. With the heightened level of sensitivity, the Boston students often found themselves flooded with apprehension about "speaking for their race." Since white adults and students were often ill equipped to deal with unexpected racial comments, the stakes in such a conversation were very high.

This racial dynamic associated with "representing," based on student reports, mostly evidenced the racial ignorance in the typical classroom. For example, a non-white student might express vocal indignation at a student's or teacher's public attempt to "hear a black person's opinion." Or a non-white student's attempt at "keepin' it real" would most likely result in a very uncomfortable and ultimately unresolved interaction. All students would learn that even the powerful adults either felt powerless to address race issues or lacked the skills to adequately resolve racial issues.

Race issues and the tensions they created most often boiled beneath the surface, in that zone of subtle racism. As David Shipler's research confirmed, whites were far less likely to perceive subtle racism than non-whites. For whites, only the most egregious and obvious cases of racism warranted attention. Therefore, the vast majority of whites routinely ignored all other situations that non-white students felt as racial attacks on their dignity.

Most white students had certainly learned to avoid any public conversations about race, both in public and private. But this did not necessarily apply to all white students in their private world. In 1992, most adults were probably shocked to read the *Middlesex News* (May 15), which published a front-page story on Students United for Racial Equality, with the following lead: "Nicole Newton, a black METCO student at Wayland High School, recalled with resentment the times students have call her 'nigger.'"

Nicole certainly wasn't the first Boston student, or the last, to have this experience. Yet many white people would continue to react with surprise, mainly due to ignorance about the reality of race issues on campus. The dearth of any authentic racial connections between students, consistently referenced in student writing, fueled racial misunderstandings and ultimately resulted in a lot of unresolved resentments.

The article exposed the persistence of a racism that most whites might have conveniently denied or ignored, mainly because it operated within the private world of the students. Overt, public forms of racism, from the Simpson verdict to the killing of Trayvon Martin, would typically produce a public outcry and calls for more interracial dialogue and healing. However, like President Obama's call for a "teachable moment" in his "beer summit," such "moments" tend to quickly fade. Administrators, like the media, move on rather quickly.

No real education would actually take place since each event would be attributed to individual aberrations, rather than the conspicuous signs of deeper, systemic problems.

At Wayland High School, administrators typically responded with the formation of committees and initiatives intended to promote tolerance and equity. Over the years, some strides were made in dealing with race issues, in the form of mentoring programs, after-school tutoring for Boston students, the lunchtime race-relations meetings, and eventually the race and racism course.

Despite all of these efforts, however, the racial achievement gap persisted, racist graffiti continued to randomly appear, the American Indian symbols faded and then returned, and non-white students continued to suffer assaults on their dignity. White people could return to the primary tasks of educating students in the formal curriculum, leaving non-white students to deal with the pain left in the wake of failed antiracism efforts.

Since school efforts to promote antiracism lacked an understanding of the real-world issues in the school community, they were doomed to failure. The adults needed to be listening to students, but the approaches to race problems mostly promoted student silence.

When adult efforts failed, students paid the biggest price. Non-white students in particular learned that their situation appeared intractable in the short term and unimportant in the long term. Simultaneously, it placed the burden of calling attention to racism on the shoulders of the Boston students and METCO staff, both of which groups rarely felt comfortable exposing their vulnerability. To do so would have brought the kind of attention that METCO couldn't really afford.

With the program tacitly viewed as a "privilege" given to non-whites rather than an educational and cultural bridge between two communities, the Boston participants were very reluctant to bring negative attention to the program. To bring public attention to racial issues would have disturbed the strong facade that allowed the community and school officials to feel comfortable with the interracial harmony associated with METCO.

This image depended upon the silence of non-white students about the ongoing realities of their world. Students learned to be silent in public and to internalize their pain, but the journal entries of the Boston students continued to convey the deleterious effects of maintaining their dignity under such difficult circumstances. In her senior year, Toni summed up how she coped:

> I don't think I really have relationships with people that are white outside of school. Maybe some Hispanic, but hardly any white or even Asian. I think that everyone has changed since middle school and elementary, including myself. All the people that used to be friends at one particular time aren't anymore, and I think that is due to the fact that people grow apart and aware of their differences and are too scared to address them, so we don't. And we continue to let it build up inside and move on with our lives without even taking a look back.

This coping through silent internalization, however, continually impacted race relations. One Boston student placed the burden mainly on the shoulders of the white students when responding to the interview question, "Do you think you have built up unconsciously anger towards white people?" Her response cited the "fake" way that Boston students were treated and how troubling it was that "people have to feel like they have to try so hard to make an effort to talk."

This dialogue brought up the issues of the complexity of racial desegregation and the role of accommodation. Journals often addressed a number of accommodations that had been crafted in order to succeed at school, despite the lack of reciprocity on the part of white students. Boston students who couldn't or wouldn't make accommodations generally either left the program or severely underperformed. Students who made significant accommodations faced the dilemma of harsh judgment from their Boston peers along with greater acceptance from white students and faculty.

Denyse, a young black woman with a warm smile for everyone, always tried her best to bridge the "two worlds" and managed to do so for many years. Denyse seemed to represent the Boston girls who managed to associate very easily with white kids during school hours, though never feeling like a real, deep connection had been made. She certainly felt that she could connect with them in some very normal teenage ways, yet she felt that too often her white peers could not see past their stereotypes.

For Denyse, the racial bonds, though strained, managed to hold steady as she sought to establish her individual identity in the midst of transcending the two worlds in which she traveled. Denyse wrote about fond memories of visiting a white friend's home in elementary school and maintaining white friendships in middle school. However, she noted that those friendships were limited to the schoolhouse, where she also remained tight with the other Boston girls. Here's Denyse's take on the high-school years:

> In the high school it's hard to balance being in METCO with being a girl in Wayland. There are some Wayland girls who haven't done anything to me directly, but everyone considers themselves in their groups. Sometimes, I feel forced into being a METCO person. Sometimes, I do really wish I could feel comfortable going to the popular table, but it would be unnatural. I feel like we wouldn't talk about the same things, but then there are some times when I can relate to what they're talking about. Like with TV shows. I love *Project Runway* and *Laguna Beach*, but sometimes girls will give me looks like why would I watch those shows? Why am I not supposed to? It's just hard. I wish I could socialize more like the boys. It's just not as easy for the girls. The guys say it's the sports thing, but it shouldn't be about sports. If I'm your friend—let's hang out! I'm an artsy person. I always wanted to do a play.

Denyse's journal illustrates the variety of major issues faced by the Boston students, with a specific emphasis on missed opportunities at interracial friendships. In the larger context, her story also exhibits the exceptionally challenging task of dealing with accommodation and assimilation. Students wrote about feeling like a minority throughout the school day, yet going home and finding the role reversed. The expectations of the two communities added a great deal of stress into the lives of these adolescents.

One student voiced frustration at the transition experienced each day, especially the feeling that only the Boston students could "fully and completely feel who I am." The inability to connect with the Wayland students proved to be most troubling, and led to this conclusion: "And it's sad to say because I bet that there is some white person that's out there that knows what I'm talking about. Too bad it's not in Wayland."

Undoubtedly, that white student existed, but the racial barrier between students prevented that connection from ever forming. For some boys, especially the star athletes, accommodating to the "Wayland world" proved to be relatively easy. As evidenced in that middle-school-cafeteria seating episode, the popular Boston boys attracted massive attention from the popular white boys . . . and girls. These Boston boys seemed to serve as "cool trophies," since being associated with them in public or in the Wayland community established a "cool" status for white students that could not be duplicated.

However, the consequence of the increased socializing between some Boston boys and white resident girls reverberated in the METCO room, on the bus, and eventually in the classroom. Basically, the boys were fitting in, while the girls were feeling ostracized. What the boys viewed as an ideal social situation constituted a social disaster for the Boston girls. To see the flirtatious interactions and hear the boys talk about their experiences with white girls hurt many of the Boston girls deeply. These tensions illustrated the larger issue that lurked beneath the surface across the years.

That issue can best be stated in one word: assimilation. Just how many and what sorts of accommodations were acceptable? When did accommodations cross the line to assimilation? Was assimilation acceptable? Each individual student could answer these questions, but their answers could and often would be judged by their peers and adults alike. In simple terms, students might be accused of "selling out" or assimilating in order to gain acceptance.

This incredibly daunting and emotional issue played out in class one day when some Boston girls directly confronted a Boston boy as a "sellout." The catalyst for this confrontation initially occurred in the wake of the middle-school discussions of *A Long Walk*—how the Boston boys were allowing Wayland boys to disrespect them by using the "N word." Needless to say, it provoked a heated discussion. Idora addressed this specific issue directly in this journal passage:

> I've given the METCO boys (football players especially) a little bit of slack. I've always wondered why they allowed themselves to accept the blatant racial jokes I know are thrown at them. They, OK, some of them, are at the total denial end of the spectrum. It must be a lot easier to pretend that the underlying problems don't exist. But there is a limit to my understanding. Although I understand why the boys prefer not to acknowledge the possibility of racist attitudes (the energy I spend trying to figure out whether a comment was or wasn't racially charged would/could be spent on something more productive), I just don't understand them NOT reacting to obviously racist comments. A lot of the kids that the boys deal with seem to think telling a "black" joke in front of a black person is OK because a black person is present. If a person reacts, then the joke teller shrugs it off and is like "I'm sorry, I didn't think it bothered you" or "I didn't mean to be racist." They can't seem to face their own prejudices. It's really frustrating to sit and talk to these kids (Wayland kids and METCO guys) who are so far from me on the [social] spectrum.

When this heated discussion entered the classroom, the white resident students pretty much took a backseat, as it quickly became apparent, based on the Boston students' body language, that they weren't even in the room. The goal of students talking directly to other students, and not primarily through the teacher, reached its fullest potential that day. This was serious business.

The male student under attack defended his actions, while his accusers refused to let him dodge. The one item that generated the most emotion focused on the use of the word "nigga," an issue that dated back to middle school. Evidently, the Boston football players had allowed the white players to use the term as a form of "football bonding." Eventually the boy agreed that it was out of line and that it had been terminated. However, the girls responded that they had overhead other, very similar, terms being used to replace that word—terms that carried the same connotation.

Both parties agreed to further work on that issue, but there would be no agreement on the larger question, one that really couldn't be unanimously resolved: how does one maintain an "authentic" racial identity while also managing to ignore or address white racial prejudices? Of course, there is no such absolute construct as an "authentic" racial or ethnic identity, but that certainly hasn't prevented people from establishing some guidelines. Otherwise, how do you explain terms such as "whitewashed," "bananas" (Asian Americans), "apples" (American Indians), or "oreo?"

The accommodation/assimilation issue most often appeared in journals when Boston students reported high levels of stress from trying to fit into two worlds: being part of the "new world" of Wayland, while also coping with life in their "other world," in their Boston neighborhoods. Some students found themselves dealing with long bouts of isolation at the most social time in their lives. Meanwhile, the most important social bonds, those forged with each other, though often sustaining, would constantly be frayed as individual students found either acceptance or rejection in the Wayland community.

Making accommodations to survive in both worlds would dramatically impact the most intense identity-development years. The Boston students would find themselves dealing with the daunting and complex racial aspects of what it meant to be black or Latino, while being immersed in the highly competitive academic world of white suburban kids.

Living in two worlds while trying to please both, being true to themselves, and meeting high academic expectations would fuel much of the angst heard in their voices. Ultimately, this struggle often negatively impacted their academic, social, and emotional development.

Even those students who seemed most comfortable with their accommodations and their ability to manage both worlds, primarily athletic male students, walked a very thin line. Sadly, those students accorded a "privileged" acceptance into the white community might face some appalling consequences. For those Boston students who found themselves a home in Wayland, their acceptance could prove to be quite ephemeral when their "blackness" quite unexpectedly perforated a veneer of "color blindness."

Kadeem managed to make a lot of friendships in Wayland, and ended up spending much time in his host community. In many ways, he became very comfortable in this dual life. Along with having an exceptionally engaging personality, Kadeem played sports, caused no trouble, acted politely, and posed no academic challenge to the resident students. In other words, he had "represented" his people well. But he would find that those years of relatively "good representing" could dissipate in a flash.

The starting point for a particularly long journal stemmed from the context of his strong relationships with white residents. As he wrote, "Because Wayland is predominantly white, most of my friends are white. Sometimes I am invited over to stay the night and to hang out. Sometimes I have to ask to stay because I have events on weekends that I have to make." His feelings of being welcome in town changed dramatically one day when money was stolen from a resident home. The situation quickly focused on Kadeem and Mike, a fellow Boston student.

The tensions heightened, and then escalated dramatically when the use of "nigger" entered into the fray. The crossing of that racial threshold prompted this journal passage:

> This is where I get very upset. Because I have been going to [this] house for the longest time, being nice to them twenty-four seven. I would clean dishes after dinner and make up the bed when I left. I thought this family was a family that I could depend on when I needed it the most, but I guess not. . . . It took a little bit of money to go missing so they could live up their stereotypes that black people steal. The world is a crazy place to live in when you're a minority because you have to shape yourself to be white to fit in. The METCO kids that I see do well with Wayland families are the ones who act whiter. I feel like Obama in a way. I tried to hide the fact that I was black in this society and make people see me as a person, and as soon as something that makes me look black like stolen money [arises] I am kicked out and not wanted. This is what I thought my final [journal] should be on, for you to see my struggle and use it in your future race classes.

Mike also wrote his perspective on the same incident. Over the years, Mike, a proud young man, had struggled mightily with the stresses of maintaining his racial integrity in the midst of a white suburban world. During a class discussion on how the METCO program had impacted both the Boston and resident students, Mike highlighted the direction his life had taken, away from the lure of the streets and toward college. He credited the value placed on academics by the majority of students at WHS with having enabled him to flow with a much healthier mainstream than the anti-education, violent behaviors he perceived in the city.

Mike further asserted that the person he had become fit his values and dreams in ways that the city might not have served him. Being in Wayland had cost him some "street cred," which contributed to his identity struggle, but that was a price he felt worth paying. With ease and clarity, Mike articulated how he had managed to develop his individual identity after navigating the waters of two worlds for nearly twelve years.

As an athletic star Mike had gained entry into the Wayland community, and "the incident" seemed to shake to the core all the goodwill he had accumulated over the years. Like Kadeem, Mike had made accommodations that felt right for him, only to find himself defined by the racial stereotypes he had neither created nor contributed to. Mike's journal captures the raw emotions of racism, along with the strength of a young man who refused to be defined by it:

> My first thought was "Na" this can't be true. It was and I couldn't believe my ears. This whole time I have treated [these people] with respect, and gratitude. I never even thought about stealing a cookie . . . why would I take 160 bills? I have a job, I go to school, and I'm best friends with their son. I can't believe his parents would think such a thing . . . calling me a nigger. I honestly wish I could bring my girl cousin up to Wayland and have her kick her little ass and show her a nigger. But I was raised better than that. I was raised to use my voice, and not my actions . . . I wish they could see who actually stole the money, and their faces when they realize they are just a bunch of racist bastards. It's not their fault though. I cannot blame somebody for who they are. [It's] the way they were brought up to believe. All black people steal, right? I mean it's hard enough to study for [a] test, and write these essay papers for school, but now I have to realize that every time I step foot into one of my white friend's house and something goes missing the finger is [pointed] straight towards me. I might have been born in Boston, and raised to be hard, rough, and ghetto, but I'm going to make a difference in this world. Nobody, I don't care if you are white, blue or brown is smarter or better than me. . . . I am going to shine brighter than the sun. I am going to blow up, and I don't give a damn if you white people like it or NOT.

Mike's loss of trust in white people as a response to this specific incident exhibited a frustrating aspect of racism and stereotypes—how a few random experiences in life can reinforce and expand their power, especially if those experiences are left unprocessed. Mike had encountered, and would continue to encounter, many trustworthy and honorable white people, but those whites would be totally overshadowed, probably for an extended period of time, by the strong emotions evoked in this incident.

In schools that listen to student voices and allow students to process these events, students like Mike, along with his peers, can gain some peace, and perspective, and move forward with more confidence in their power to deal with tough issues.

Examples such as Mike and Kadeem's could occur randomly, sometimes in a very timely fashion. One such incident involved the local police. Allowing students some input into the curriculum and the willingness to process events in a timely fashion all coalesced when a female Boston student walked into class a little bit late and very agitated. She immediately raised her hand and asked to tell why she was so upset. Just before class, her boyfriend had dropped her off at school, only to be pulled over by the Wayland police. The discovery of an outstanding warrant led to an arrest and a trip to Framingham District Court.

The girl felt that her boyfriend had been pulled over because of racial profiling. That statement provoked immediate debate within the class. The incident, fraught with hearsay and opinions, needed much clarification. This was a "real-world" topic and the class deserved a "real-world" dialogue. The class responded very positively to bringing in an officer to provide the police's side of the story (several were on campus due to some anticipated year-end antics from a rival high school). Within minutes an officer stood in front of the room explaining the sequence of events.

Upon his arrival, Raesia, a young woman with a strong voice and the courage to question authority, positioned her chair in the middle of the open space, right in front of the officer. The officer explained the situation as being a result of a standard procedure by which officers randomly ran plates as they entered school grounds. He responded to several questions rather easily, reiterating the randomness of the procedure. Yet he wasn't able to shake Raesia. She repeated several times something along the lines of, "With all due respect I'm not buying it." This girl was on a mission.

After the officer left, several white students offered stories that raised significant doubts about his explanation. Their stories involved bringing unregistered cars to school or driving with revoked licenses all year, without ever having been flagged—stories that they obviously had not chosen to share with the officer. The outpouring of stories indicated the law of probability supporting Raesia's position. The raging debate prompted the need for a firmer resolution.

I was directed by the first officer to the man who actually ran the plate quite unexpectedly led to the real story. He initially presented the warrant as sufficient to validate his actions, but he continued to make a more convincing case for probable cause by mentioning cornrows and lots of bling hanging off this guy's neck, like the plate check was a no-brainer. The Boston students, and those who seemed convinced that this had been a case of racial profiling, had been vindicated. Unfortunately, one officer's actions can sometimes overshadow the overall performance of a whole department.

Had this event not been processed immediately, had there been no outlet for student voices, tensions would have built throughout the day. Students would have left class, and perhaps school, with a lot of frustration and anger. All kinds of rumors would have spread across campus. The educational process would have been disrupted throughout the day. Tensions would likely have persisted for days or weeks. There would have been a lot of lessons lost rather than lessons gained.

When hot topics like the racial-profiling incident entered the classroom, the many racial nuances that lay just beneath the surface emerged in a way that exemplified the real-life complexities of dealing with race, particularly for non-whites. White students had come to understand that they could continue to avoid dealing with racial issues—a privilege generally not accorded their non-white peers. The incident in the parking lot, along with the interviews, elucidated the situations that presented internal conflicts that were often confronted by the non-white students. In search of empathy, Denyse wrote:

> I want to be able to [take] someone in this class so that they can feel like what it is to be in my shoes as a black student. And what it is that I go through every day not only in transporting there and back to the city, but the thought process that I live with every day of my life. Because I know in some ways it is similar but I also know in many ways it is different. I know for everyone life can be hard and difficult as it is enough, but also being another race that is a minority adds another weight on your shoulders.

Denyse did her best to navigate her two worlds, and her appeal for empathy certainly fit into the mission of the school. Yet for the vast majority of white students the solution seemed rather simple—just look and act like white people. Assimilation, for non-white students, however, proved generally unacceptable and clearly more complicated. Since most administrators and teachers had not processed this extremely significant aspect of desegregation, the students were generally left to work through these muddied waters on their own. For the Boston students this added one more nuance to all of the fundamental identity issues faced by teens without regard to race.

For those boys who did not gain the acceptance accorded Mike and Kadeem, the result could lead to the opposite end of the spectrum—segregation. Justin represented that group of students. Justin presented as a hardworking student who took every opportunity to boost his grades and make the best of his academic experience in Wayland.

As a senior, Justin was provided with the opportunity to opt for the honors-level curriculum, for which he had never been recommended at the high school. Humorous, polite, and soft-spoken, Justin appeared eminently likable, yet his journals revealed the deeper thoughts and feelings of a young man struggling with the complexities of a social life at Wayland High School:

> But being able to have friends and be somewhat smart is impossible. Maybe not impossible to a Wayland kid who lives out in Wayland, but as a Boston student who doesn't live out in Wayland it's very difficult. When I come out to Wayland and hang around kids, I feel like such an outcast. Kids out in Wayland treat Boston kids like foreigners. I have been friends with a majority of kids in my grade for some time and yet I still feel the same way. The worst is sometimes a group of my friends make me feel like a lingerer. Like I don't belong there and that sucks because not having companionship is hard to live with. Ever since my best friend got kicked out of Wayland, I basically [have] had no friends. He set the standard, when he was here kids were afraid of me. He and I had all the power. Wayland kids had no power compared to us two together. No one stood up to us, no one bothered us. The only letdown is Wayland kids always came to us when their shit went missing, thinking we stole it. We had our own money we didn't need snobby rich Wayland kids' money.

Like most adolescent issues, having reliable friends has no racial bounds. Yet unspoken or unresolved racial issues, as addressed by Justin, effectively place one more barrier between people of any age. Unquestionably, entering the gulf between segregation and assimilation proved quite treacherous.

Boston students could usually find some solace in the bonding they found through language as a means of racial identity. While most ethnic Europeans had become comfortable shedding any remnants of "foreignness" in order to fit into the mainstream, the Boston students often felt a need to maintain a language that "protected" against assimilation. This student explained the situation in stark terms: "I use slang because we created it, black people, to be different and . . . if you don't talk black what do you talk, white?"

Keanna lent her perspective on language as well. Her journal dealt with the many complexities with regard to language, especially with regard to gender and the two worlds in which these students traveled:

> Yeah some people do say, "Oh you talk like a white girl" or "You go to a white school," but I kind of laugh and shrug it off because this is who I am, I'm not going to change that.
> I've been going to Wayland since second grade and you know . . . maybe it's true. Well I think it can be harder for the boys because there's this thing that they have to be tough you know, to be providers. So when they come to Wayland and it's, I guess, soft? Is that the right word? Boston is a lot harsher so coming to Wayland where it's softer they still feel like they need to be hard. But I'm just who I am, you know, [and] like I said, I'm not changing that.

Language provided one measure for judging one's racial identity. Becoming "who you really are" presented many choices, which in the world of the Boston students became increasingly complicated as they traveled through two different worlds. Miriam, in her usual, deeply self-reflective, way, found herself grappling with the reality of what it felt like to have perhaps accommodated too much. In response to a question about black Boston girls, she responded:

> I don't feel black enough around them. . . . Like at the METCO prom, it was awkward for me because when I party, it's with white kids, so me dancing might impress the Wayland kids with no rhythm, but to the other METCO kids, it's kind of pathetic.

Miriam's comfortableness with Wayland whites, however, also led her to ruminate about what she might have lost:

> Like there are all these classic reggae songs that as a West Indian I should know and as a young urban black female I should know, but I don't. Like I'm detached from my roots—some might say being white is better, you know, stereotypically more sophisticated and whatnot, but I feel that I'm not connected and that I've missed out and am in the dark about a lot of things expected of me being a young urban Haitian-American black female.

Extremely bright, motivated, academically very successful, Miriam was a student whose detachment from her West Indian roots represented the prototype generally rewarded at Wayland High School. Teachers and administrators alike respected her immensely. She kept about the business of making the most of her educational opportunity, while also appearing to navigate seamlessly between the Boston students and her white peers. Yet, as her journals indicate, there was much more to the story.

One day, late in her senior year, while talking in the commons after school, Miriam spoke at length on her METCO experience, in very blunt and scathing terms. It seemed like the "loss of roots" and the "keeping silent about her real identity" all came together, and she expressed a burning desire to leave Wayland behind. The pain in her words, so often kept under wraps, revealed the need to speak honestly and to be heard. Her firm declaration that her children would not travel a similar path revealed the depth of her angst over the high price she had paid.

Negotiating "proper behavior" in Wayland had to be balanced with the need to survive in the city. Returning to their urban neighborhoods, some students had to cope with identity issues in other profound ways. What passed muster in Wayland for the "right amount of blackness" might not suit their city neighborhoods. Being able to "present properly" in both worlds seemed to produce two separate and yet authentic personas. A lapse, or failure to accommodate, could present some problems.

An urban coping mechanism that is termed the "cool pose," with its intimidation intent (and that is explored in *Cool Pose*, by Richard Majors) followed many Boston students who traveled out to Wayland. However, what functioned well in urban neighborhoods could prove disabling or dangerous out in the suburbs. It certainly could impact one's educational achievement.

A faculty member once commented on how scary he found a Boston student who had mastered the cool pose. This young man, however, could also be found singing tunes from *The Lion King* in an empty classroom. Certainly each of these personae could elicit very different responses from teachers and ultimately impact his educational achievement. It would not be surprising that his public demeanor might bring lower academic expectations.

For those students who exhibited strong racial pride and a willingness to break the code about racism, the school could be quite unforgiving. Jilvonya arguably presented the school's worst METCO prototype, a physically and personally imposing black girl who routinely expressed her voice in very strong fashion. Her accommodations, like Michaela's, would be minimal. When Jilvonya perceived racism, unlike most of her peers, she had a tendency to directly confront it. Her unwillingness to just "let it go" seemed to scare most of the students and staff.

A couple of Jilvonya stories will help set the context for understanding her voice. Jilvonya made her reputation in the span of her first few months at the high school. The most powerful seniors at WHS conducted a "rite of passage" that involved setting up the rug at the entrance to the commons in order to trip underclassmen, particularly freshmen. On this particular day they tripped a male Boston student.

Jilvonya, also a freshman, had neither gender nor racial unity with the perpetrators. She also had a propensity for confronting any situation that suggested disrespect for fellow Boston students. So she headed over to the seniors, with a couple of other Boston girls in tow, and called those boys out. The boys backed off, and the confrontation was defused when an administrator escorted Jilvonya out of the lunchroom. The boys who perpetrated and witnessed this incident brought it to class immediately after lunch, and it became the day's lesson.

When challenged to process the racial aspects of the confrontation, they claimed race was not an issue, but rather it was a case where boys respected girls by not getting aggressive. Follow-up questions revealed that they had not laughed at, mimicked, or toyed with Jilvonya. They didn't immediately see the significance; so then they were confronted with what would have transpired if the freshmen girls had been white. There was no way some freshmen white girls would have been treated the same way.

Of course it was about race. They knew that disrespecting Jilvonya would have brought a confrontation for which they had no preparation . . . and no desire. By the end of class, the racial nature of the event in the commons had clearly emerged, and the students could see the nature of what had *really happened.* For Jilvonya, however, this early incident at the high school only served to put adults on high alert about her as a "problem child."

In her junior year, Jilvonya engaged in a public shouting match with a fellow Boston girl. The altercation ended up with Jilvonya being escorted into the backseat of a police car and taken off campus. Jilvonya suffered the humiliation of being taken into custody on school grounds, and the whole school got to see a racial scene usually viewed on the nightly news. The rumors about that day had a life of their own. Nothing reflected well on the Boston students, and it was all quite unnecessary. The lessons that day could not have been worse.

Meanwhile, Jilvonya never presented a problem in class. In fact, she could always be counted on to contribute her personal perspective on any given topic. Clearly, she was listening, processing, thinking, and speaking her mind—a student actually fulfilling the expectations of the school's professed mission statement. In print, she also exhibited her usual passion, as displayed in this excerpt from Jilvonya's journal about her reaction to the book *Our America,* by LeAlan Jones and Lloyd Newman:

> While reading this book I felt like I was seeing my life, or the lives of many that I know. I heard them use the slang I use every day, [and] the streets in the book even resemble streets I've walked on with my two feet. In this book we witnessed the ghetto lifestyles of two boys from the projects undergoing the everyday struggles of life as I know it. People in Wayland that are not of color may read this book and take it as a surprise, or find themselves in shock at these things, but when I read it I was like yup, yup that's how it be. . . . It's how the world is and will continue to be until better comes. I've grown up to get used to this life, and to use what I know as a black educated girl with

opportunity to get around and away from this life. I have my education and of course my drive to be something in life, and with that I believe I will get far. Traveling to Wayland every day can sometimes be hard because you witness people that just have everything layed [*sic*] out for them and made easy, when in the back of my mind I know that when I go back home I will witness my people struggling and working their asses off for the same opportunity, that they rarely ever get. It's like living in two worlds. A part of me wants the Wayland life of having everything easy, but my heart will always stay in the ghetto because my people lay in the ghetto.

Jilvonya's refusal to make many accommodations to her "second world" put her at risk in ways that most Boston students studiously avoided. Yet, as Mike the star athlete found out, acceptance based on extensive accommodations could disappear in a flash. The "stealing" incident during his senior year certainly damaged his perspective on his carefully crafted relationships.

The following journal excerpt was written after the stealing accusation and refers to the character Mookie from Spike Lee's *Do The Right Thing*, a character the white students felt comfortable with . . . until he threw the trash can through Sal's window. Instead of a trash can, here Mike uses words in his own attempt to be heard:

It's wrong how America always hides the fact that racism still exists, and won't do anything to help prevent it. Their way of preventing racism is not to talk about it at all, and it's wrong. It's not asking much of them to listen, and do something about it. Although I'm a student at Wayland High School I still understand that there are many people who don't think I have the right to be a part of that community or hate me because I'm black. So every day I have to live with the fact people hate me because of my skin color, and any mistake I make affects the rest of my life; while my friends are doing drugs, and it only acts as a slap on the wrist. I'll play my role as Mookie, but I will understand that I'm only doing it to prove that I'm better than any form or shape society wants to make of me. I have the power to be intelligent, hard working, and strong. I too have the right to be looked at as a man, and not anything lower. I'm black and proud of [who] I am no matter what people say. It's time to wake up, and listen!

Mike understood his situation and the complexities of what it took to maintain his balance, achieve his educational goals, play sports, and remain an "acceptable" black member of the school community. However, he never lost touch with the constant stress of managing so many complicated expectations and situations as he maneuvered his way through these two worlds. Once again, here's an excerpt from a lengthy journal:

I'm a typical black young man that plays sports like all the rest and the only reason that I have [white] friends is because of that reason. Playing sports is just a way of America hiding the fact that it's a white world. I mean it gives blacks the chance to change many lives if they become famous, but is it really worth our souls? . . . I've seen a lot of horrible things in the Ghetto, and it's crazy to think these Wayland kids have no idea what really goes down. I mean sure they read books about MLK and all but I feel like they just don't really take it into consideration. . . . I wish they would listen to our cries for justice. I mean I think the world would be a much better place if we had no ghettos, and everybody was equal. I doubt anything like that would ever happen though just because of the simple fact that white people are way too far ahead of everyone else [so] it's impossible to catch up. . . . It's sad to think that I'm literally born with a disability to be dumb. So I have to work every day of my life to prove white people wrong, and catch up. . . . I see the [Wayland] kids looking at me different, and watching what they say. I see the teachers giving me different grades just because of what they assume, and not correcting me on my knowledge. It sucks to go to school every single day and notice that you're out numbered. I have to be extra careful for my actions because one slip up can ruin my whole life.

Here was a young man who had the courage to battle it out on a football field, and managed to spend twelve years struggling with all the difficult issues his voice has expressed on these pages, and yet he just couldn't speak his truth in class. He had learned well to keep his silence. As Mike said, "I didn't even have the courage to speak my mind to a class of white students." If the school and community needed to believe in their fantasy of racial harmony, Mike's silence helped sell the dream.

Despite all these complex issues of "representing," coping with the racial ignorance of their hosts, managing issues of accommodation and assimilation, handling racial-identity development while living in two worlds, and internalizing the pain of racism, the Boston students still had to keep their eyes on the prize. On a daily basis they were expected to focus on competing academically at one of the most high-powered high schools in Massachusetts, essentially without any adjustments to the school's curriculum.

Constantly reminded of the importance of their educational opportunities at Wayland High School, the Boston students found themselves also constantly confronting all the other demons in their world. To properly "represent" their people they had to do well academically. Yet, to do too well academically meant probable estrangement from their Boston peers. On the other hand, to do poorly served to reinforce some of the worst stereotypes that they had already internalized.

Mastering a curriculum that barely acknowledged any of their needs, and with teachers who lacked any leadership that might help them better meet those needs, these students often found themselves frustrated in an uphill battle that appeared totally overwhelming.

Desire for relevant curriculum, connection to teachers, fair treatment by administrators, and affirmation of their identities entered their journals on a routine basis. Beyond the normal academic stresses, the Boston students cited a curriculum that failed to address them as urban students of color and teachers who expected less of them, along with teachers and administrators who either ignored their issues or disciplined them differently than they did the resident students.

A desegregation program, by nature, should be expected to confront the realities of race. Ignoring race hindered the social growth of all students while doing more harm academically to the black and Latino students. No doubt some Boston students took the curriculum at face value, as did many resident students. However, those Boston students who spoke and wrote about their education often cited the school's failure to meet the interests and needs of its nonwhite students.

Melinda wrote arguably the most passionate assessment of her education at WHS. Much of this journal can be attributed to her work with social-change awareness programs outside of school and her work in the race and racism course:

> A lot of the things that have stopped me from achieving is [sic] the way the curriculum at Wayland High School is set up as well as the faculty. When a child has no one to look up to that they can identify with that child will go about life just trying to get by as opposed to [striving] to be great. . . . I do appreciate the quality of education yet I still feel as though it is missing something very important. The curriculum didn't address who I was and who my people were, it didn't celebrate my ancestors as well as heroes today. It certainly doesn't address the social change and progress that this school needs to go through. It's like if we say we [can't] see it then it's not there. It was frustrating going through American history and only hearing that my people were in chains and were freed. It is a shame that we even call the course American history when all we study is European, white history in this community. . . . This school prides itself on being the best, but the truth is there are so many wrongs [it's] hard to even think that we believe that it is. Granted we do have some of the most talented teachers and students here, but if the curriculum is not well rounded we only have a bias [sic] and close minded [sic] view of things. That is not an education

that is sufficient and it's hurtful to know that because I'm a minority here I can't expect to know who I am, or have others know where I come from. . . . Some teachers have this mind set that because we are METCO we can't be as smart and as capable as Wayland students. Therefore, they expect less and treat us differently. "We are incapable of turning in papers on time, and if we do it's not normal," according to some teachers' thoughts. If we get a 100 on a test it just couldn't be possible so therefore we must have cheated.

This next student quoted presented her individual struggle with "her" history as part of a larger vision of the power of education. As Idora expressed it:

There are instances when I attempt to "just be" that I grant myself temporary amnesia from my past. The sad part is that it never works 100 percent. I can never divorce myself entirely from the discrimination of my history. It frustrates me because when I learn about "my" history it seemed inundated with sorrow, and freckled with moments of pride and happiness. So it leads me to worry, is that what I have to look forward to? I often feel that there is an unspoken obligation to exist as an angry individual among the ignorant, and regard their attempts at self-education as excuses. I would prefer to educate myself and those around me so that the level of respect can someday reach equilibrium. Education and experience are the only tools that I can think of that can eradicate the problem of miscommunication.

Students generally had a lot more to say about teachers than the curriculum. In general, they expressed respect for their teachers, yet, like Melinda said, specific attention to the Boston students and their various cultures would have greatly enhanced the valuable connections between students and teachers. Without administrative leadership, however, teachers possessed little incentive to pursue what many perceived as a treacherous course.

This lack of adaptation on the part of education leaders could be seen as a persistent form of subtle racism. Faculty members routinely take their cues from administrators, and incentives for curriculum adjustments had very little advocacy on campus. Therefore, when racial tensions arose randomly in the classroom, teachers certainly faced one of the most challenging situations they might ever have to confront. To do so with no understanding of the dynamics of race at school, no good modeling by administrators, and no professional training provided a prescription for failure. It was not uncommon for Boston students to address this problem.

An incident occurred where a non-white student threw a chair at a boy who told her that she should be happy that white people brought "her people" over on a boat. The Boston student got a reprimand, and the white student's inflammatory remark went unaddressed. The girl wrote about how she would have stopped the class and made it the day's lesson. Of course this would have been a productive use of a class period, but dealing with racial issues intimidated most adults.

Michaela wrote about these situations from her years of direct experience. As noted by her white classmates, she rarely allowed a racially charged incident or remark to go unchallenged, inside or outside of class. What she found were teachers who had no leadership in dealing with race, leaving them perhaps well-intentioned, but also unskilled and unsupported in handling race issues. In this journal passage, she provided some keen insights into teacher attitudes about race in the classroom, along with some suggested remedies:

There are situations that come up; teachers don't even know what to do. I think that's a problem. You know? Like, someone makes a racist comment [and] either (a) they ignore it and act like they didn't hear it, or (b) they'll pull the kid after class and they'll pull the black kid after class, or whoever they made the comment to, or (c) maybe they might speak up, but then they keep going. And it's those types of things where it's like teachers are scared to say something. I feel like, to be a teacher you should be required to have a race class, you have to do a workshop, you have to do something, because if teachers hear this stuff, they don't know what to do, and it's frustrating, like, you want to feel support, but at the same time you don't feel it from the teacher because he or she is scared to say something. I think that's a problem. It's like I offered—I know this because I talked to some of the faculty, teachers are offered to do workshops, they don't do them. And when stuff like this comes up they don't know what to do. It's like they freeze up.

The extent of administrative indifference to the needs of the Boston students could be learned, once again, by listening to the students. For two successive academic years an after-school tutorial program for METCO students met two days a week, from 2:30 until 5:00 pm, in a space one floor up from the administrative offices.

Once, while I was tutoring a student in math, he turned to the publication date in his math book, which proved to be over thirty years old. Since the lowest-level classes contained a disproportionate number of Boston students, he got the message, as he expressed it: "They don't think we're worth new books." Sure, some people might say that the math hadn't changed in thirty years . . . but do you think that rationale had denied the higher-level students the newest textbooks?

Students also learned another lesson. Over the course of *hundreds of hours* in that space, *not once* did any level of administrator or department head make an appearance to help those kids. And to think that all the administrators had to do was take the elevator up one floor. Maybe they believed that no one noticed. The kids did. They constantly paid attention to how people dealt with them—as should be obvious in their journals. Even the smallest detail might not escape their radar.

Every day this lack of attention paid to the Boston students damaged their educational prospects. Every day that their voices went unheard meant not only diminished academic achievement, but also emotional distress that further impeded their academic performance. Furthermore, the public utterances about the system's commitment to educational excellence resulted only in further marginalization within the school.

Administrators might sprinkle their public comments with the proper buzzwords about educational equity, multicultural curriculum, respecting all children, and attacking the racial achievement gap, but those words offered no solace to those children who awoke early each morning to travel an hour and a half to receive their education.

Toni expressed her opinion of administrative actions on tough issues by comparing them to those of the faculty: "Administration is the same way, if not worse, because they try to cover up everything that goes on in this school without really dealing with it." Of course, covering up usually "works" for administrators because those kids with voices will eventually learn silence, and the problems eventually "disappear." Ignore the bullying, and the victims learn that nothing can or will be done, and eventually they stop reporting. Schools really do an excellent job of promoting student silence.

Resident black, Latino, and biracial resident students certainly were not immune to the problems confronted by their Boston peers. In fact, their experiences often mirrored those of their Boston peers, though they also brought some different perspectives to what it meant to be black or Latino and living in Wayland. Again, racial-identity development played a major role in their lives. In many ways, their existence *between* the two worlds experienced by the Boston students provided for some journals rich in complexities beyond the rest of their classmates'.

Maggie wrote the journal excerpted below in response to a history-textbook assignment in her junior year. The reading addressed the role of Hispanics in the West after the United States gained possession, as documented in Rodolfo Acuna's *Occupied America: A History of Chicanos*. However, Maggie found herself responding to the inner identity struggle she lived as a Hispanic in a modern white community:

> I was lucky to live in a beautiful town with no crime and white picket fences. I have food in my stomach and clean clothes on my back. Lately I have been questioning my identity and where I stand, culturally. I am surrounded by white kids who make jokes about Spanish people working at Dunkin' Donuts or Burger King. And I am insulted because those are my people, my blood, my roots. And these snobby white kids are not. But I am a snobby "white" kid. I'm on the upper rung economically, I have a pretty much secure future, I've never had to really struggle through life. Of course I've experienced pain and sorrow, but life has never been a struggle for survival. I used to feel proud to be Costa Rican but now I feel as though being Hispanic is almost a handicap. . . . I sit here at this nice computer with a cup of milk in one hand, my silver bracelet clinking against the desk, and I feel like a traitor. I feel as though I should be out in the "barrios" with all the other "Chicanos." I feel like this isn't my place. I'm supposed to be poor and living in a ghetto with gunshots ringing through the night air and people in the apartment next to us sniffing crack and smoking heroin. . . . But I'm not. I'm here and I have a future and why me and not someone else. . . . I don't care that the majority of Hispanics work in low paying jobs and that they can't speak English. That doesn't make them stupid but it seems as though everyone thinks it does. Because I have white parents and I live in a predominantly white town . . . therefore I am white, and my blood may be Spanish but I have been robbed of my culture. I have been taught to hang my head in shame for the sake of my nationality.

The combination of media stereotypes and the general lack of a curriculum that addressed any of Maggie's concerns didn't necessarily prevent her from gaining excellent success in school; but the issues addressed in this journal certainly prevented her from achieving her full potential as both a student and young woman. Coming to grips with her confused self-perception—especially the part that speaks to her shame for being a privileged suburban girl—complicated all the other stresses of high expectations in a high-stakes education.

Most of the Boston students would graduate with a suburban brand on their résumés, move on to postsecondary education, and eventually gain opportunities to access a greater piece of the economic pie—a process covered in Susan Eaton's *The Other Boston Busing Story*. In hindsight, perhaps much of what they endured would wilt under the weight of time and the power of greater opportunities found. The following journal excerpts, however, capture their voices before the future editing of memory, age, and circumstances.

At the time, there appeared to be a lot of encouraging interracial dialogue and movement across the racial lines; but after rereading these journals from across the years, I had to revise my optimistic memories based on the reality of their actual words. First, some short takes on a "final summing up" of the Boston students' voices:

> "When I have children I really think that I would put them in a Boston public school. The reason why I say this is because I know how it feels to go through school every day, all day feeling uncomfortable. I would not want my kids to feel this way. I think always feeling uncomfortable brings your self-esteem down."

> "[What I will take from Wayland is] the fact that privileged white students will never see eye to eye with me on any issue of race."

> "Although I do not think racism correct, I have to deal with it, because you can't really change the way people are. You can speak out against it, but that doesn't mean that it will make a difference."

"My experience in Wayland has given me a negative attitude towards race and racism. In Wayland, sometimes I just feel that their [*sic*] is no hope."

"The world is a crazy place to live in when you're a minority because you have to shape yourself to be white to fit in. . . . I feel like Obama in [the] way I tried to hide the fact that I was black in this society."

"Overall I think that a lot of students don't think there is a need to even discuss racism because they don't view it as an issue, because it's not something that white people have to deal with, like people of color."

"I want to get out of here as soon as possible. I want to start new life and make new friends, and trust reliable kids."

Talia maintained a positive attitude about life in general and also within the confines of her immediate environment. In fact, her infectious smile would be a lasting memory from the classroom. However, in the final journal excerpted below, she offered a pessimistic view on race issues, despite whatever progress she had observed in the course. Talia recognized the limits of a formal education, given the role of the family and greater society in teaching some powerful lessons about race:

> Race is a major issue in our society today, and I remember one of the topics brought up in class was whether or not people think that racism would end or not, and me personally, I don't think it will end because not enough parents are teaching their children right from wrong when it comes to racism. Some parents are just stuck in a life style from the past. For example, whites think most blacks are criminals or thugs and not good people. And blacks think most whites are snobby, selfish, and need to be hurt because of what they did to blacks in the past.

Some positive statements, of course, also emanated from some Boston students. These next statements represent a fairly common opinion among those who spoke in class discussions, though few expressed these sentiments in print. Mel cited an important lesson he learned from a white girl who made him optimistic about his future dealings with white people:

> [I] found respect for people that are different, especially [Lindsey] who has changed my life with her [relating] of females to minorities—[I'd] never heard of it like that, and she will always be remembered in my heart for it. Makes me understand more, and actually feel like I have more of a link to her, and she actually opens up a bigger door for me to explore with white people to help them understand and vice versa.

Keanna also expressed some benefits she experienced from participating in the METCO program: "I don't think I would have been subjected to a lot of these things, I wouldn't have some of the friendships and the outlooks on life, and perspectives that I do now, if I didn't have this opportunity."

The final words from the Boston students belong to three young people who wrote very honestly and poignantly about the general feelings of gratitude, anger, sadness, frustration, and hope that exemplified the lives of these students, who struggled to find themselves and academic success in a predominantly white environment.

The first of three "final voices" belongs to Brittany. Here she presented her final reflections as she prepared to leave WHS. Her experiences illustrate the sentiments of many of her peers who found some common ground in the white community, but also the persistence of barriers still to overcome. Here are Brittany's concluding remarks:

I mean I feel like they'll never really understand because they don't have to really think about it when you're [*sic*] not of the minority. Most of them will go on and have gained nothing from anything that was said, but there will be a few who are a little more conscious, a little more aware of how the world really works. I feel like right now that's all I can ask for. Maybe that's not asking for a lot but I just feel like I can't force anyone to change their opinions on whether or not they may feel like something is racist, when there's no doubt in my mind that it is. But that also comes from experiencing racism on a daily basis, and no white person could ever even scratch the surface of fully understanding that.

Toni's voice has been heard in this chapter, mostly citing the lack of attention paid to racism by teachers and administrators and the racial gap between girls. Before we hear her parting words, a brief part of Toni's story should prove instructive. Toni entered WHS as an academic star in the making. She immediately established a strong academic record that eventually enabled her to enter an honors-level U.S.-history class during junior year.

In the fall of her senior year, when asked if she might like a college recommendation from me, Toni seemed quite surprised. She bluntly stated that she hadn't asked because she didn't believe that she was smart enough to warrant one! This freshman who had entered the high school brimming with confidence and had then established a strong academic record was graduating with the idea that she did not deserve to be "recommended" like her white peers. Evidently, all of her achievement had been plagued with self-doubt, despite so much contrary evidence.

Toni exemplified the power of internalized intellectual inferiority to persist despite strong academic achievement and positive feedback.

Toni received some words on her behalf back then, and she can share some of her own parting words with you:

Imagine being black and explaining to your young child that they will not be treated as other Americans. They'll never be totally accepted, always regarded warily. What could you possibly tell them to make them understand? How will you respond to the many questions they'll ask, when you yourself don't fully understand? How will I ever be able to explain that life will always be unfair for black people in your daily life? This is very upsetting to me because I know that no matter what I do or say, things will always be twice as difficult for me, as a black female, [as it is for] any other group of people in this country. Knowing that my efforts won't really change how white people see my race in America makes me angry, sad, and disappointed. Knowing this and continuing to learn about the society around me makes me lose all hope and draws me closer to my black race by decreasing my respect, tolerance and interaction with white people. Deep down I know that it is wrong for me to think that way, but it's hard not to when I know that this will always be part of my everyday life. Whenever I walk into a room full of white people or move into a neighborhood that's predominantly white, I will be looked at funny with suspicion or hostility. That is something that will be forever a part of me and I'll never be able to escape.

The final student words encapsulate many of the themes presented by these remarkable students over thirty years at Wayland. Melinda had a definite knack for "keepin' it real" in the classroom, and she didn't fail to deliver as she prepared to embark on her next life challenge. The limitations of her schooling did not keep Melinda from leaving on a positive note:

In leaving Wayland, I would like the teachers to know that I have listened and appreciated the knowledge you have instilled in me, and I know you work hard to get a lot of information to the students. But I would like for you to be aware that in neglecting any one of your students, it becomes a threat to society. We cannot live our lives with our heads in the sand and think that everything will pan out, because they [*sic*] don't. Our parents and our country have trusted you with their prized possessions and it's up to you to make sure you're teaching us how to strive, thrive and drive in the future. . . . When I look back at what has gotten me to this point, it was strongly based on my social justice role in my community. Through my involvement in these programs I have found strength to succeed even when others would like to see me fail. It has given me the drive to educate others of [*sic*] the untold truths and inequalities that this country would like to sweep under the carpet. . . . A lot of the things that stopped me from achieving is [*sic*] the way the curriculum at Wayland High School is set up, as well as the faculty. When a child has no one to look up to that they can identify with, [the] child will go about life just trying to get by as opposed to striving to be great.

POSTSCRIPT

The last time I saw Jilvonya occurred during my final year at WHS, when she came by to visit. At that time she had graduated from Clark Atlanta and was preparing to volunteer at a mental-health clinic in South Africa before returning to graduate school. Most recently, Jilvonya works at Children's Healthcare of Atlanta. She managed to maintain a strong racial identity throughout some very trying experiences at Wayland High School—experiences that brought her to the brink of expulsion. But in the end she maintained her integrity, while her intelligence and motivation allowed her to achieve her goals.

As a Boston student, Dally may have had to "luck" her way into an honors-level history course at Wayland High School after facing an uphill battle from the school's leadership team, but her intelligence and motivation—and her voice—could not be denied. She stated, "The beginning of senior year I felt intimidated by the mostly white classes and I didn't want to stand out more by voicing my opinions. But I did speak out and made the student body aware of the racial differences in our class."

Dally took her newfound confidence and forged remarkable successes in her life. She received a degree from Bentley University and now serves as a senior accountant at Ernst and Young, an international professional-services network and one of the "Big Four" accountancy firms. And her résumé of accounting skills I find no more comprehensible than that calculus homework she eventually mastered.

LESSONS LEARNED

The subtle racism most often confronted by the non-white students mostly evaded the radar of whites.

Desegregating a white school system placed exceptionally difficult burdens on the shoulders of adolescents.

When administrators and teachers avoid the race issue in dealing with students, that may solve the immediate problem, but ultimately the racial tensions fester and grow.

Heterogeneous classrooms need to draw on the varied experiences of students to develop deeper thinking and understanding.

Antiracism efforts usually addressed individual events rather than systemic issues. Rather than listening to students, these approaches tended to silence students in their wake.

Dealing with "two worlds" fueled much angst within the students and ultimately impacted their academic, social, and emotional development.

Schools that listen to students about issues of racism and help them process those issues create a healthier environment for all students.

Competing in a rigorous academic environment lacking any adjustments to the needs of urban children of color, including educators trained to deal with the many academic, social, and emotional needs of these children, proved overwhelming for most students.

Confronting race issues needs strong, sustained, and authentic leadership on the part of administrators.

Internalized intellectual inferiority can persist despite success and positive feedback.

Administrators who can't talk honestly about race cannot lead efforts to eradicate the racial achievement gap.

Chapter 7

Asians ("New Jews") and "Old" Jews

In the back of my mind, I can see a little girl pointing at me. I see that little girl pulling the outer corners of her eyelids into narrow slits. I hear that little girl laughing and saying that I'm Chinese.

—Asian American female student

Whenever there is a situation where Jews can be brought up . . . like if someone is complaining or being cheap . . . there is often twenty minute rants [sic] about Jews.

—Victor

The year was 1993, and this would be the first meeting of the Coalition for Asian Pacific American Youth (CAPAY). This youth-led organization had been founded in response to racist violence against Asians in Boston high schools. Its mission was to provide "culturally-responsive resources, critical education and community-based advocacy/service-learning opportunities to strengthen the voices, leadership, and organizing capacities of Asian American youth within their schools."

Facilitating a morning workshop that included the diverse Asian American communities in eastern Massachusetts proved to be an exceptionally informative experience. Mainly, the students used the time to tell some of their very diverse stories. Debriefing the Wayland attendees after the conference brought immediate exclamations such as, "I never felt so white in my life! Those kids were really Asian!" In fact, that workshop illustrated the tremendous spectrum of color, class, religion, and ethnicity within the Asian American community. Creating a sense of unity would indeed be a challenging task.

For Lisa, a leading organizer, the conference had greatly complicated what it meant to be Asian American and underlined the challenge of generating Asian unity. The conference had underscored the tremendous spectrum of Asian American identities, along with the numerous issues confronting Asian Americans in the greater white society.

On the surface, the Asian American students at Wayland High School (WHS) indeed appeared to be an integral part of the mainstream at the high school. Yet just beneath the surface their voices captured the disconcerting issues confronted by non-whites in a predominantly white community. These issues had a long history, as detailed in Ronald Takaki's *Strangers from a Different Shore.*

The Asian American students wrote often about overt and subtle racism, dealing with the indignities of jokes based on stereotypes, dealing with extraordinary academic expectations, and navigating between two worlds with identity issues centered on assimilation and accommodation. In fact, their identity issues proved to be exceptionally challenging and complex, given the struggle to define themselves both within the Asian community and in the predominantly white mainstream.

For the most part, these students felt very much a part of the Wayland community, yet they also often felt the uneasiness of their racial difference. Eleanor addressed this complicated situation in many of its nuances:

> I usually feel "accepted" in the Wayland community—around my friends, in classes, etc. However, at the same time, there is always a voice in the back of my mind reminding me that I am different. Being a minority, I am especially sensitive to any type of racism. Whenever anything happens, I always wonder if it's because I'm Asian. Like a few weeks ago my house was egged, well at least we found eggshells on our driveway. So, the first thought that came into my head was, "Is it because I'm Asian?" If this happened to a white family they could probably never think of their race as a possible cause. This sensitivity is an everyday occurrence—I am constantly aware of my difference and any seemingly trivial event will set off the trigger. Even in my own home, when I bring over my white friends, I can tell when they feel awkward in my house and around my family and it makes me feel uncomfortable as well. I believe if I brought a METCO kid over [to] my house that METCO kid would feel more comfortable and at ease in my house than most white kids. And it's not because the METCO student is any less different from me; it's just that we understand and can accept differences.

Another student conveyed the fundamental dynamic of life for Wayland's Asian American students—the denial of their racial existence on the outside combined with the interior realities of a racial identity—when she stated, "Sure I am constantly aware that I am different from most of the kids here, but I have learned to live and sometimes repress that relentless nagging in the back of my mind."

This situation led some Asian students to write, "I feel more comfortable around white people than other Asians." Yet, as evidenced in so many journals, Asian students could not escape some of the discomfort associated with being racially different. A fairly common attitude would be expressed in words such as these: "Sure, sometimes I'm proud to be Asian, but more often that not, society makes me feel lesser and embarrassed to be Asian."

What does it mean to be Asian in America? The numerous monikers applied to Asians tell a lot about their very complex story: "new Jews," "honorary whites," "model minority," "perpetual foreigners," "invisible minority," "ABCs," "FOBs," "bananas," "whitewashed," and "twinkies." All of these terms will be evidenced in the students' journals, oftentimes changing over time and circumstances.

Asian American students wrote about becoming "invisible" as they "blended in" with whites, while at other times they felt the harsh pain that comes with racial intolerance in America. Their voices epitomized the fluidity that characterizes the Asian American identity, as it ebbs and flows, with the references to feeling more comfortable with and more "accepted" by whites, while also hearing that constant internal voice of racial difference. These identity issues emerged in the early school years and continued to fluctuate into the college years and beyond.

Darren, a child of Chinese immigrants, remembered his earliest experience with racial difference as a first-grader, when he was being called "Chop Suey." He felt very uncomfortable having it "pointed out" that he wasn't white, though the situation worsened in eighth grade when he became engaged in a war of racial slurs with a white kid. "It got way too serious and it felt really shitty." When asked about interracial friendships, Darren laughed and responded, "Of course! If I didn't I wouldn't have any friends! Since it's a white society I've come to act and live like a white person. People call me 'Twinkie.'"

Emily lived at an extreme end of the spectrum, expressing how she felt a near-total lack of racial tension in her childhood, saying that she didn't even really acknowledge her racial difference when she was young. Her only early racial memory recalled feelings of frustration with people who would "pull back their eyes because Asians have 'squinted' eyes."

Carol found her identity shift dramatically while she was young, after her family moved to Wayland:

> When I moved from the South, which didn't have a large Asian community, I found at Wayland a group of Asians in my grade. I think that's a benefit because in earlier years I thought I was white. My old school didn't have a big Asian crowd and my friends were all white, so back then I didn't consider myself different from the rest of my peers. Coming to Wayland, I learned that there were Asians in my class who I could relate to about family situations. We ate similar foods for dinner and we talked about how protective our parents always were. It was a great feeling to share experiences with someone I knew that understood me.

Arguably, in thirty years at Wayland, the most unique experience faced by an Asian American student involved a student who entered the Wayland schools . . . as a Boston student. Although METCO was open to all non-white students, Asian parents for a variety of reasons had not typically signed their children up. Debbie's participation brought a truly unique perspective to the program, as indicated in her journals:

> It was the first time in my life when I stepped out of my comfort zone. I was really nervous and worried about adjusting to a brand new environment and making new friends. The situation on the METCO bus did not help at all. I felt like an outcast since I was the only Chinese girl on the bus. Not only did I feel isolated, I was also scared of some kids because they seemed very tough. I was a timid and shy girl, who didn't want to cause any trouble. These kids teased me for being Chinese. They asked questions, such as, "What are you doing here?" and made nasty comments, like, "Eww . . . you're Chinese. Your people have accents. . . . Do you talk like that?" I felt unwanted, and I've [sic] never had this kind of feelings before when I was at my old school. I got along well with the black and Hispanic students. Therefore, I thought I wouldn't have problems dealing with the METCO students. My intuition was wrong, though. They were probably not used to seeing Chinese people in the METCO Program, and I thought that they hated me for interfering with their "territory." I naturally sensed that I didn't belong to this program. . . . I was an alien from another planet. I ignored their offensive comments and thought that they were immature. But, deep in my heart, I was extremely hurt. I felt that I didn't belong to this social group because I wasn't black or Hispanic.

Debbie, an outsider to both the Boston and Wayland kids, never quit trying to find a way to fit into both METCO and Wayland, while also working through her own identity issues. Displaying the same determination she showed in pursuing her academics, Debbie eventually managed to provide a social bridge between the Boston and resident students. At first it took some basic kindness on the part of a few Boston students who reached out to Debbie. Then, in her own quiet way, Debbie used her inherent compassion and goodwill as a means toward achieving the fundamental goals of the METCO program:

> Thankfully, some kids were friendly as they reached out to me. They made me feel more comfortable by talking and joking with me. I tried to learn about their beliefs., such as their ideals, their favorite topics, and their chats. Things started to improve, and a barrier seemed to be pulled down in a matter of days. They began to take me in and eventually stopped teasing me. . . . Meanwhile in school, I connected with the Wayland kids easily. I instantly made many friends. They presumed that I was from Wayland since there were some Chinese resident students. Therefore, they were surprised to hear that I was a Boston resident. An awkward silence usually followed, but it didn't

prevent us from making friends with each other. We got along well as they treated me as one of them. . . . I understood their language, enjoyed their jokes, and was involved in their games. Each time when METCO held social events, I invited my Wayland friends to join me, such as [for] the Martin Luther King dinner. It was the first exposure to get the local Wayland students involved in the METCO community.

Debbie's ability to bridge the various worlds in which she traveled, without losing a sense of her own racial identity, was not easily replicated by her resident Asian American peers. By high school an increased number of Asian American students began to "find" their Asian identities, while many continued to "blend" into the white mainstream. This dichotomy produced everything from exceptionally proud and provocative voices to what the Asian students referred to as the most "whitewashed."

The single most riveting public assertion of Asian pride in my thirty years at WHS surfaced quite unexpectedly during an in-school talent-show performance, when Jerome provoked a good portion of the student body and faculty. Choosing to shed all the anger he felt for having previously compromised his racial identity, Jerome delivered a rap in which he put to rhyme an angry and forceful assertion of his Asian pride, throwing all the Asian stereotypes back at his audience while using both sexual references and strong curse words.

Jerome's "coming out" as a proud Asian American would result in some significant social costs. For whites, the Jerome who appeared on that stage was a "foreign" person, not the friend they had always known. One of his best friends expressed feeling blindsided by the strong emotions that emerged on stage. Having no comparable identity struggle, this student couldn't comprehend the sudden transformation. Jerome lost some friends that day, but regained his pride.

A much less jarring assertion of Asian identity occurred rather surprisingly in the midst of class one day, when a full-blooded Asian had an epiphany. With a bemused look on his face, he blurted out to the class, "I just realized, I'm Asian! All this time I thought I was white." This case speaks directly to the fluidity of race, as this student had managed to navigate the world as white until suddenly "discovering" his Asian identity.

For some Asian American students, however, identity might be constantly reinforced, which would sustain that identity, as with most of their black and Latino peers. The following excerpts evidence how any "forgetfulness" in their racial identity could be mitigated suddenly and randomly:

"In the back of my mind, I can see a little girl pointing at me. I see that little girl pulling the outer corners of her eyelids into narrow slits."

"There were so many times I would walk through the halls and hear 'chink.'"

"I can tell when they [whites] feel awkward in my house and around my family and it makes me feel uncomfortable as well."

"I know that I can pull out several stories during which I was the brunt of a joke or tease, originating around the fact that I am Asian, and it . . . hurt."

"People laughed at my different accent and I was touched, got hurt by many Americans."

"As soon as my brothers and I walked onto the playground there, we were bombarded with shouts of, 'Look at them, they're Chinese!'"

"One thing I remember specifically about elementary school was how the other students thought my home-made lunches smelled weird."

"I mean people go 'ching chong cho cho' and stuff like that."

Beyond physical appearance, the language issue tended to permeate the identity issues confronting Asian Americans in ways that recalled first-generation Europeans. For Europeans, the generational loss of their first language often coincided with their movement out of urban poverty, as they shed their "foreignness" and melted into the great pot of suburban whites. Second- and third-generation Asians might "pass" for white, but as the students continually noted, it didn't stop people from expressing surprise at their command of English.

In fact, their command of English often presented a more complex issue within the Asian American community. For Chinese born in America ("ABCs") who did not pick up their parents' native tongue, there awaited some strong identity issues, such as those encountered by many of the suburban kids at CAPAY who found themselves far less fluent than their urban peers.

As with most immigrants, language retention can readily separate those with "cultural credibility" from those who have been "Americanized" or "whitewashed." The language issue and identity surfaced routinely when students returned from trips to Asia, where they were immediately identified as Americans. These students, especially the fluent ones, felt totally estranged from their "mother country" while simultaneously faced with being treated as foreigners in America. Their voices spoke to a strong sense of alienation, a feeling of "being without a country" to truly call home.

The following journal entry from Sherry provides a heartfelt and insightful deconstruction of the larger story of divisions within the greater Chinese American community, even when language fluency isn't the issue:

> What I'm trying to understand is that because I'm not doing everything Chinese 24/7 of my life, I no longer qualify as Chinese in their eyes. They call most American-born Chinese people "juhk sihng" and say they're not entirely Chinese either. I think I'll always be Chinese no matter how little time I spend with my family—I understand that family is a huge part of being Chinese, but that doesn't change the fact that I've grown up with these traditions and that it's part of me and my identity. It's also strange because every time I go into New York with my family, there are kids in Chinatown that don't count my siblings and I [sic] as Chinese. I don't exactly understand why they wouldn't, especially because just like them, our parents emigrated from China, and we speak Cantonese as well as they do—the only difference between us is that my family lives in the suburbs and they live in the city. Just because they spend a good portion of their time in Chinatown, why should they be able to deem themselves more Chinese than we are. . . . Also, it's not like they act entirely Asian themselves—what does acting Asian even mean anyway? I'm Asian because I'm born Asian, not because of a certain way I behave. Something that many of my friends and I have noticed is that maybe some Asians pick up "white" traits when they live in the suburbs, and that Asians in the city (some that I know) pick up the hip-hop lifestyle. So yes, while us suburban Asian kids wear "white people clothing," it's not like Asians in the city are being original either. They're just simply picking up the "hip-hop lifestyle" that some would say is a "black" thing. What do they expect us to do? There really isn't any "stereotypical Asian clothing"—do they expect us to wear kimonos and silk dresses everywhere we go? I just think it's quite hypocritical of them to say that, especially when they're not exactly falling into that "Asian" category 100 percent either.

Ultimately, many suburban Asian Americans chose either to fit into their suburban culture ("honorary whites") by keeping the "Asian thing" under wraps ("bananas" and "twinkies"), or to separate into little pockets, sitting at the "Asian table" in the commons ("perpetual foreigners"). But then, when they were outside of school, these students consistently spoke of the joy in attending Asian-specific cultural camps and centers and family gatherings. Quite frankly, their identity issues seemed endless. Therefore, it was no surprise that so many of their journals dealt with the identity struggle.

On the surface, most Asian American students managed to cope very well in an environment where the overwhelming majority of the students and adults operated in ignorance of their private struggles.

And yet, in many ways, the mask of control mimicked that of many black and Latino peers who presented a "nonracial" persona in the public domain. A comparison could also be made to so many white students who managed to maintain the mask of the ideal suburban adolescent though nearly cracking under the pressure of schoolwork and extracurricular activities. So, for the most part, Asian American students presented an "assimilated face" to their white peers, yet their apparent seamless threading into the Wayland schools and community belied the turmoil faced by many of these teens.

The intensity of their emotional struggle can be vividly heard in the following excerpts. This young woman speaks to the accommodations made by Asians in their attempt to fit it: "When I was a freshman, I was very excited to be in a class with Americans. I came from [Asia] at the end of eighth grade, so everything was new. I wanted to be like an 'American.'"

Despite making many accommodations to fit in, this student found the language barrier to be a major barrier toward making friends. This brought much emotional upheaval, to the point where she exclaimed, "I became one with very low self esteem and self image . . . I hated my life and myself."

Chia-Chia shared this struggle as she sought to find her place at WHS. Born in China and having lived for years in Japan, Chia-Chia came to Wayland High School with an incredibly upbeat attitude and a vibrant, outgoing personality. Stylish and personable, she appeared to approach her new life with confidence. However, reflecting back on her first few years, fitting into this suburban culture would prove far more daunting than she had imagined:

Well, when I first came here, I didn't feel anything. I didn't think there [were] any problems. I felt like I was American. I even felt nationalistic towards America. I put [an] American flag on my Jeep's back window and I wanted to tell people, "Hey look at me, I'm an Asian and I'm driving a car that's made in [the] U.S.A. and I'm proud of it!" I bought a yellow ribbon to put on my Jeep's back window also. I bought earrings to support the U.S. army (few [sic] percent of that [money] would go to them) in the desert. I prayed for them to come home safely. I've always told myself that "UNITED COLOR = UNITED STATES of AMERICA." I've always admired America as being the most international and diverse country in the world, that has worked within a very short of time. Everyone helps and depends on everyone, as in race and nationality background, and lives in peace. Everyone believes in freedom, and I thought this was wonderful. But I don't feel this way anymore. It's a lie. . . . I don't like to be called the Chinese girl—it's just that they assumed that I was, or just anyone who's yellow, they assume that they are Chinese. I don't like that. A freshman girl pissed me off last year. I was talking to [a student] in the girls' bathroom in Mandarin, and that freshman girl (she's white) made fun of me on [sic] my back. I saw it by the mirror and I hate white people [who] just stare at me for whatever reason. They stare at me like, why are you here? Can you speak English? . . . I'm not quiet at all. I just don't like this place and people so I don't express myself in front of them. I'm just a quiet nerd in this place. . . . Lot of people made fun of my name and I couldn't stand it. Sometimes I got really annoyed and I'd say the "F" word. And sometimes I just got sick of it and [would] think they are really immature and I [would] just leave. The worst of all [was when] I got made fun of by a teacher. He sang my name every time he saw me in class. He's a teacher for Christ's sake. A teacher making fun of a kid's name? I mean come on, get real. . . . He repeated it many times and I got sick of it. So I gave him a finger behind him, . . . just to get my anger out without shoving him. . . . The beginning of school this year I took Spanish 2 and we had [homework]. The question was, "Do you like to study, sing, or dance?" [The teacher] asked this Asian American kid, and he said, "I like to sing." Teacher goes, "Oh, you don't like to study?" I was pissed. What did [sic] that supposed to mean? Asian Americans are supposed to like to study? They can't do other things? I was gonna ask her what she meant by that, but I didn't. I should have.

For students with a longer history in the United States, the issues were similar, but presented some different challenges as well. Derrick addressed an identity struggle faced mainly by Asian males as they sought to establish an acceptable level of masculinity, one not usually associated with Asian Americans:

> Banana, twinkie . . . yeah, I've been called all of those before. When people ask me where I'm from I always say "Boston." I don't know what it is that makes me dislike Wayland so much. Maybe it's all the racist remarks I hear from people here, it's actually beginning to become a tangible feeling. At first, I wouldn't think much of it; however, as time went on I've begun [sic] to dislike white teens when I first meet them. I would judge and label all white boys as the same. Ever since I could remember, I've been labeled as a whitewashed Asian, regardless of what I do out of school. One thing that really gets me pissed off is when kids stereotype me from the color of my skin. Making fun of my eyes when I have superior eyesight, or saying I'm amazing at math when more than 75 percent of my friends are horrible at mathematics. Saying that, because I'm Asian, I score high on SATs because I've been tutored for SATs since I was seven (even though most of all my Asian friends scored less than 1500 on the new SAT . . . though many scored 2200). I've always struggled with trying to make people see me . . . well, as me. Not as this smart, slanty-eyed whitewashed Asian kid from the town of Wayland. . . . In middle school I became extremely proud of being Chinese, always saying things like "Asian Pride!" and hanging out with only Asian kids (very few Asians in Wayland so I went to Quincy and Boston a lot). My "Asian Pride" slowly died as I was entering high school. This made me hate Wayland, and I always wished we never moved from [another Massachusetts suburb]. In tenth grade, I began hanging out with Wayland Asians (which are completely different than the one's [sic] who live in Boston). I've experienced an "Asian pride" phase, a gangster/ghetto city Asian phase, and a whitewashed, smart Asian phase. But I feel that where I am now are all those phases integrated into one. I guess I'll have to wait to [sic] until I'm in college to see how I really am. But I already think the people I'm going to be hanging out with the most are the Christian Asians, regardless if they are whitewashed or whatever.

Derrick's struggles traveled many paths without firm resolution before he left high school, a common theme in many identity journals. However, he anticipated finding more certainty later in life.

Karen, a biracial student, felt extremely frustrated with her more complicated identity struggle, without a sense of resolution. The following comes from Karen's self-interview as a senior at WHS:

> For the longest time I never acknowledged the fact that I was bi-racial. I mean everyone knows that I was born in England, lived in Canada and have a Swiss dad and Chinese mom, but I guess no one really knew how I felt about all of it. A lot of people only see me from the outside, [and] they have no idea how I feel and who I really am on the inside. I've never really been [able] to talk about it with friends or family, so I've always kept it inside me. . . . Personally, I've never really experienced any harsh discrimination directed toward me that I can remember, but I have had racial comments thrown around me. Whenever I hear anything racial about a certain group of people it makes me feel very uncomfortable, especially when it's a racial slur about Chinese. I've always laughed off a joke on Canadians or British and never really heard anything on Swiss, but a comment on Asian people really offends me no matter how severe or subtle it may be. . . . A lot of white people really don't understand how different diverse people feel. They've always been protected behind the color of their skin. Never have they had to think twice about if they fit into society, because the color of their skin has always given them an advantage over others. Their concerns remain on gaining money and power. It's actually only been recently that I have been more aware of my bi-racial background. When I was younger I always tried to hide my Asian-ness. I think it was because I was scared of how kids would poke fun of me. . . . Where do I ever fit in? I mean, if I don't always feel entirely comfortable in an all white society or when I go to places like Malaysia and my being half Chinese isn't completely enough to not separate me from everyone,

where [can] I feel 100 percent comfortable?? Even though a lot of people don't really think of me as part Asian, it doesn't help the fact that I don't feel like I am "white enough." In vice versa situations: I felt I wasn't "Asian enough" when I attended a camp over the summer where 85 percent of the kids were Asian. I didn't even speak the language! To tell the truth . . . I don't think I will ever be completely comfortable with who I am. Sometimes I feel privileged, sometimes I feel out of place, sometimes I'm completely neutral . . . I just feel different a lot of the time. I think that's probably the adjective that describes me the best . . . "different." I wish I could explain myself more clearly to people who haven't experienced all of these feelings (whites) so that they may have a better understanding of what it is like for people they so often put down. Understanding something is really hard if you haven't encountered it yourself.

For the Indian Americans at WHS, the identity issue presented another unusual twist to the story of Asian Americans. In 1923, the U.S. Supreme Court decided that Bhagat Singh Thind couldn't be a citizen under the Naturalization Act of 1790, which granted that right only to whites. Prior to this decision, anthropologists had classified immigrants from India as Caucasians, which enabled them to be granted American citizenship. The courts and social scientists can make their pronouncements, but these students operated in the real world where real people trumped any government dictates or classifications.

Experts had their say, but for Indian Americans everyday experiences evidenced a racial ambiguity that proved very disconcerting, especially to their non-Indian peers. This ambiguity contributed greatly to the general avoidance of race discussions in relationships with unambiguously white Americans . . . until the interviews. Heather chose to interview Anita, an Indian American friend, and walked away with these observations:

> When I went over to interview [Anita], I didn't know what to expect, but she had already done a few interviews, and she knew just what to do. Once we dove into it, I found that talking to her about race was really pretty easy. She is one of my best friends and has been since the seventh grade, but we never really discussed race before. I knew that she was Indian, and we talked about her being Indian. I dressed up in saris and other traditional Indian clothes, and I had eaten dinners at her house before. . . . However, before that day we never talked about how she felt about being Indian, or her experiences with racism. Through conducting the interview, I really learned a great deal more than I thought I knew, and I really thought I knew a lot. I never knew, however, that when she was in elementary school, her fellow students just thought she was black. When I think about that, I can't help but laugh.

In another case, a student found herself engaged in a conversation with a white male friend who took exception to her declaration of a non-white identity. In a convoluted way he captured the confusion faced by whites in determining the race of their Indian American friends. His statement, "Okay fine you're not white, but like you're not really not white," pretty much summed up the common assessment. This attempt by a white kid to explain race to an Indian American reflected the response from students when this topic entered the race class. When presented with the Singh case, they quickly realized that the best white minds in American history had utilized thousands of fancy words in an effort to determine the racial status of Indian Americans. Basically, this seemingly inarticulate explanation by a white student captured the essence of several Supreme Court decisions in one sentence. A reading of the Court's decision by Justice George Sutherland surely evidences how convoluted the social construct of race can be.

Viraj, who moved to WHS from out of state, illustrated the best example of how the racial-identity spectrum for Indian Americans could play out in the real world. Viraj spoke of boarding a plane in a Midwestern state, having lived as a "nigger," and about two hours later finding himself in a place where he was accepted as "white." It's very difficult to fathom how adolescents function across the spectrum of these racial constructs.

To make matters even more complicated for the Indian American population, they sometimes found themselves to be outsiders with respect to the rest of the Asian community. This issue proved to be of no small consequence when Indian Americans sought to take leadership roles at CAPAY. One of the most active students in Students United for Racial Quality (SURE), an Indian American, found herself having to defend her inclusion in this pan-Asian organization at the first organizational meeting. That struggle persisted for years and continues to be an issue for pan-Asian groups.

The seeming homogeneity of Asians to many non-Asians masks tremendous diversity within the Asian/Pacific community. Many Asian American students struggled with the social, emotional, and occasional academic consequences of facing these identity issues because their voices were silenced at school.

Feelings of identity confusion and estrangement from the mainstream, as well as the Asian community, could not have been stronger than those expressed by Ahmed, a Muslim student who did his share of fitting in until he found a place far more suitable to his inner values. Ahmed "looked different," and his silence probably only heightened the mystery. In this journal passage, Ahmed profoundly detailed the many paths he traveled before finding himself centered in a way that seemed to foster awe among his peers:

> When I first moved to Wayland [later in my schooling], I instinctively did everything I could to fit in. I mostly hung out with jocks and other kids that thought they were tough or thought they were thugs. I started listening to rap. My language became steadily fouler. One habit that I remember in [particular] was that I would wear my pants very low, so low that my boxers would show. This would cause me to walk with my legs far apart, so that my pants wouldn't fall to the ground. It was basically a strut. Another habit I picked up in order to assimilate was wearing short socks. I not only looked like a fool, talked like a fool, walked like a fool, listened to foolish music, I was a fool. . . . Now that I think about it, I find it comical. I also became distant from my parents. I had not yet acquired the level of disrespect that many Wayland kids had for their parents, but I was on my way there. However, my upbringing still held when it came to treatment of my parents, but I still talked to them less, and gave them less respect than was due to them. Upon my entry into eighth grade, I lost interest in rap, but I still hung out with kids that listened to it, so it still influenced me slightly. I started to listen to rock. Regardless of the genre, both types of music contained the same immorality and had basically the same disgusting content. The people who I considered my friends were mostly on their way to becoming drug users and alcoholics. I think at that point I spent more time polluting my mind with music than doing my homework, or doing any other activity for that matter. I see people like how I used to be all the time. They are so caught up in "fitting in" that they have no real substance. They concern themselves so much in what others will think that they stop being individuals. Their image is more important to them than they are to themselves. When I see people like them, I feel pity, though I must admit, when I see people with low pants like I used to wear them, I smile kind of mockingly. However, I try to remind myself that I have no right to look down on people like this because I used to be like this. When I pray at school, I feel like a stranger. When I am around people when they [are] making crude jokes, and everyone acts like it's normal, I feel like a stranger. When people look at me weird because of how I look, I feel like a stranger. When kids in my class talk about drinking, drugging, and partying, I feel like a stranger. When I hear about and see how they treat their parents, I feel like a stranger. When I go to the airport, I feel like a stranger. When my religion, my ideas, my culture, or my identity are harshly criticized and attacked, directly or indirectly, I feel like a stranger. I know this sounds somewhat troubling, but I don't find this to be a bad thing at all. As a matter of fact, I find

comfort in it. This is because of the last part of the Prophet's (pbuh) prophecy, which was, ". . . so glad tiding to the strangers." The fact that I have affirm [sic] belief in God and his prophet (pbuh) and have different morals makes me strange in this country. The fact that I am Muslim makes me strange in this country. I am not saying that I adhere perfectly to these morals, but the fact that I have them makes me kind of strange. I realize that it may seem that I think that I am different in a way that makes me better than the people around me. This is not what I am trying to say. I don't think I am better than anyone, I simply believe my shortcomings are in different areas.

By senior year, Ahmed served as a model for the "unassimilated" student who managed to carve his own path through the minefield of racial-identity development within and outside the dominant white mainstream. It certainly limited his peer relationships, but anyone who wanted to be a part of his world understood that Ahmed would not be sacrificing or compromising the essential values that he held. Race, ethnicity, and religion would not be ignored.

Indeed, he provided one of those highlight moments in class when a student's voice commanded absolute rapt attention from everyone. It was the day he spoke, for the first time, about his racial and religious identity. And the more he spoke, the more respect you could see building in the classroom. Ahmed managed to assert his authentic voice in a very peaceful, assured manner, yet his words carried much power.

A decade earlier, Jerome had fashioned his Asian pride in a far different manner, on the stage in song and dance, with wit and anger. Both would manage to establish a presence that other students, particularly white students, felt both inspired by and, yet, estranged from.

In the early years of the race-relations course, the attention to Asian issues fluctuated depending on the strength of Asian voices in the class. Eventually the unit expanded and took hold thanks to prodding from a student named Ping-Hong, along with his recommendation of the movie *Better Luck Tomorrow*. A preview of the movie didn't inspire confidence in its classroom use, but respect for Ping-Hong's certainty that students would relate to it and that it would provoke discussion prevailed. In testimony to the importance of student voices . . . feedback after viewing the film confirmed Ping's assessment.

Ailsa certainly spoke for what a number of students reported when she wrote, "*Better Luck Tomorrow* was especially interesting because I had never seen a movie dedicated to Asians, and the problems they deal with on a daily basis."

The film captures the various identity struggles, especially of suburban Asians, with particular attention to the acceptance and rejection of making accommodations with the power of whiteness. Journals often dealt with the theme of accommodating oneself to white culture as the path of least resistance, since it appeared to reduce the potential for any bad feelings with peers and academic problems with teachers. Yet just beneath the surface lurked that constant reminder about the cost of accommodation, and the accompanying desire to resist assimilation.

This dynamic became the focus of an interview in which an Asian student found himself reexamining his own Asian identity and his relationship to white culture. This probing dialogue between two extremely bright and insightful students produced an incredibly rich interview in which the Asian student talked about the desire to make more accommodations to white society, especially with regard to job opportunities. However, he also acknowledged, "I think considering future circumstance like who I meet and where I work, I could possibly want to be more attached to my roots."

These next statements expressed similar feelings about students maintaining their pride while dealing with the discomfort of managing issues of accommodation and assimilation:

"And sadly, I have come to realize that I am more comfortable in an all white community because sometimes it makes me forget about race and I accept everyone as white."

"Unfortunately, I know that no matter how hard I try, I am Chinese and there really is not anything I can do about it. Instead, I just have to live with that fact I am Chinese."

"So no matter how hard we try to assimilate, there will always be that factor of appearance that we cannot control."

"Because I personally do not take pride in being Asian, I have tried to become 'white-washed.'"

"But more often than not, society makes me feel lesser and embarrassed to be Asian."

"Asians just look different than whites. So no matter how hard we try to assimilate, there will always be that factor of appearance that we cannot control."

"In such a complex world of identities, there is only one "main," acceptable one: being straight and white."

"It usually comes as a huge surprise when I open my mouth and speak with no accent. Adding to that surprise is the fact that I talk very much like an American."

"It's really hard to be happy with being different, especially when the difference makes you a less acceptable person in society. But what is even worse . . . is the guilt I feel this way."

The fluidity of identity, within and between racial worlds, could offer some positive outcomes, though not without difficulties, at each part of the spectrum— as indicated in Arthur's voice:

Many times I feel as if I have to act differently in front of my white friends compared to my Asian friends. Although I try my hardest to just treat everyone the same since they are all "friends," it's hard to act yourself when you are afraid others may not understand how you feel. I've never been confused with being white since I've always stuck pretty close to my Asian friends and I guess acted Asian, but recently I've felt the need to just do something new. . . . Over the course of the summer I decided to change the way I dress due to interest in hip-hop/sneaker culture. After coming back to school with a new dress style [it] felt like it was easier to do different things and participate in things I wouldn't have done before.

As with being more diverse I was also fed up with fitting into an Asian stereotype, especially at school. For example I . . . notice that a lot of Asians are less likely to participate or raise their voices and participate in school activities. If they do participate in school activities [they] are always things like math club [and] science club, things like that. At the same time I do feel like I'm leaving out my Asian friends that I used to hang out with at school. But even though it feels like with my white friends I may not be able to reach the type of friendship I have with my Asian friends, it's still worth a try, and the important thing is that I'll be able to try something new.

Arthur's perspective offered the benefits that come with the fluidity of racial identities. By breaking through the boundaries of racial stereotypes, those pressures to conform to certain cultural behaviors and beliefs, Arthur was liberated to pursue his own truly individual identity. Of course, this pursuit came with many challenges. Most often, students faced scorn from their "own racial group" and the pain associated with the jokes and other racist behaviors that would more readily appear outside that group.

The most frequent cause for shame resulted from the silence or laughter that followed the evidently ubiquitous Asian jokes. The constant teasing and jokes focused on the stereotypes associated with academic brilliance, especially in math and science, their penchant for studying, and "language difficulties." Both adults and children often expressed surprise at their command of the English language ("perpetual foreigners"), mimicked the brand of English spoken by those Asians new to America ("FOBs," for "fresh off the boat"), or teased them about their "funny" names.

Much like other students subjected to stereotypes, it was not uncommon for the Asian students to laugh at the jokes or join in the joke telling. As one student expressed it in response to a question about Asian stereotypes, "Well for me it's mostly just like a joking thing, like wow, I just Asian failed that."

In a physics class where students were assigned partners and two Asians were partnered up, Shelia found herself confronted by other students with remarks such as, "No fair, come on, two Asians?" Most Asian American students either ignored or laughed at these jokes. Tom expressed the ways in which he coped with the constancy of attacks on his dignity:

> A lot of times, when somebody is rude, I assume and question whether it is because I'm Asian. I've always had a wall of toughness for defense. I've become used to shrugging it away and disregarding racist comments. I even joke about it sometimes, make fun of other Asians and myself, not sure if I'm doing it in spite. I'm pretty sure I'm comfortable with my Asianness at this point in my life, which allows me to kind of understand the stereotypes that come with being Asian. I realize now the differences of being a minority and the different pressures that I have to deal with.

The jokes, as expected, revolved around Asian stereotypes very much in evidence when students responded to the "first words that come to mind" portion of the interview. Responses from hundreds of interviews were very consistent: *smart, hard-working, good students, karate, Chinese food, math, science, band, very nice,* and *short.* Oftentimes, non-Asian students reacted with incredulity that these stereotypes could be painful since they mostly seemed so "positive."

That discussion routinely roused the voices of Asian students who worked hard only to achieve average grades, particularly those who did poorly in math and science. They tended to focus most of their anger on teachers who held them to "Asian standards" in these subjects. They described such teachers as those who would express concerns that they were neglecting to achieve up to their abilities, while the students felt that they were working as hard as they could.

If the black and Latino students were expected to do poorly in school and the Asian kids were expected to be at the top, it had to be very difficult for those Asian students who struggled academically. The frustration and guilt over a low grade, coupled with a perceived reprimand from the teacher for not working up to their capability placed an enormous stress on such students.

Addressing stereotypes, even the "positive" ones associated with Asians, helps students to understand how they deny individuality and prevent authentic interracial friendships.

Of course children of all races wish to be seen as individuals, but non-whites constantly felt the pressure of negotiating a comfort level with both their individual and "group identities" in the midst of a dominant white peer group. This struggle provided the essential subtext of what Asians referred to as being "whitewashed."

Through a brainstorming exercise where students took off the censors and defined what it meant to be white, Asian, black, Latino, or Jewish, they could appreciate how these attributes exposed the futility of such an exercise. It also provided an appreciation of what it means to be born into an ethnic group or race, and how that shouldn't have the power to limit one's own unique identity.

Yet the real world often put pressure on these kids to embody the stereotypes of their "group identity," while simultaneously pressuring them to reject such attachments. When the black football players allowed whites to call them "niggas," they had allowed for the supremacy of the football-team pride over the disrespect toward their race as voiced by the Boston girls who found that choice abhorrent. For Asian students, those choices occurred regularly, and their reactions covered the whole spectrum from guilt and shame to anger and sadness.

This ebb and flow between the white and Asian worlds constantly created some angst because Asian students, like the Boston students, also found their white peers' racial ignorance so prevalent and frustrating. One young woman expressed her exasperation with the situation; having experienced being call a "chink" at random times and places she exclaimed, "It's definitely harder for white kids to understand how hurtful racism can be . . . I hear white people always talking about feeling bad for the minorities . . . but still . . . do they really know how it feels?"

Ultimately, the unpredictable acts of racism, along with the realization that the white majority remained ignorant or dismissive of these acts, wore down some of the Asian students. One girl expressed her resignation with the sad state of affairs when she declared, "Honestly I used to wish I was white because of how much more opportunities there were for them even if you were a woman." The challenges of navigating the racial worlds could certainly prove overwhelming for many adolescents.

Again, consider the story of Debbie, the Chinese American child from Boston bused out to Wayland as part of the METCO program. Here she was, a Boston resident trying to maintain a connection to her urban neighborhood while also navigating between Wayland whites and Asians on the one side and Boston blacks and Latinos on another. In many ways she may have provided the most complex situation faced by an adolescent attempting to be herself while also fitting into the mainstream.

When she rode the bus on her first day of kindergarten she found herself an outsider in a sea of blacks and Latinos. Upon arrival in Wayland, her Boston peers initially faced isolation while Debbie gained immediate acceptance, since she was perceived to be a Wayland resident. Eventually she befriended her Boston peers, achieved honorary white status in the suburbs, and yet faced problems with peers understanding how to identify her in both communities. These multiple issues had to be exasperating.

Well liked and respected, hardworking, and academically successful, Debbie managed to become a true bridge between students of all races. Yet, her complex identity struggle illustrates the incredible reality of race in the real world. In this final journal, Debbie articulated these racial experiences as she prepared to graduate:

> When my friends found out that I'll be taking accounting classes in college, all they said was, "Wow, that's so Asian." . . . At times I don't feel quite "Asian" at all. I don't belong to any of the aforementioned categories [play violin or piano, score the highest grades in math and science]. At times, I feel out of place because I don't fit the Asian stereotype. Even my Asian friends say that I'm so whitewashed; they think that I have too many white friends, and not enough Asian friends. This race issue gets more complicated because I'm an Asian student in the METCO Program. In the eyes of other METCO students, I act like a "white person." On the other hand, my Wayland resident friends jokingly say to me at times, "Debbie you're so black. Look at you. . . . You even have that Boston accent." I know it's a joke, but it stimulates me to think more deeply about myself. . . . If I'm not that Chinese, then what am I? Mixed? When I first joined the METCO Program, some Asian parents weren't pleased with my parents' decision. They believed that I would be looked down upon by the Wayland community because I'm with the "black people." My parents just ignored their ignorant comments while I was frustrated that they thought this way.

The depiction of Asian Americans as a "model minority," predicated on the stereotype of their educational achievement, hard work, success in business, and desire to not draw attention while also having their issues ignored ("invisible minority") had gained them access to white communities, as "honorary whites." But student journals certainly portrayed the persistent power of the "perpetual foreigner" stereotype in keeping them diligent about their possible marginalization by white America.

In many ways, these stereotypes mimicked those associated with the Jewish population that had preceded them into Wayland. On the surface, the similarities, like all stereotypes, possessed some apparent validation. Indeed, the stories told by Jewish students confirmed some of the same issues, but they also belied those stereotypes. Their experiences of being white, but yet not "really" white, along with the long history of anti-Semitism, contributed to creating a different narrative for these students.

THE "OLD" JEWS

As the video screen scrolled down in the front of the class, the words "kill the Jews" appeared in bold print scrawled against the white background. This public message of hate from a student could not be ignored—every student in the room seemed to be looking, waiting for a reaction. Once the "suspects" had been determined, a discussion would later ensue with two girls in a seminar room. Having developed a foundation of trust with these two girls enabled a casual conversation before broaching the main topic.

Pulling out a wallet picture of a little girl initiated the discussion. Their joyful exclamations of "Your daughter is so cute!" came as anticipated. What they didn't expect were looks of pain and disappointment on their teacher's face, followed by the question, "Why do you think she deserves to be killed?" They needed to know that the message on the screen included this little Jewish girl, their teacher's daughter. They stammered that they would never wish her harm. Of course that had been understood from the beginning, and they deserved to hear that.

The girls clearly needed to understand the very broad and hateful implications of these three words, and making the matter very personal and real helped them rethink what they had learned. The subsequent discussion went well, since the friendly relationship continued and they did truly seem to understand the full import of their actions. This incident proved to be a precursor to the many opportunities to address such common examples of racism and anti-Semitism within the hidden curriculum.

As it turned out, this anti-Semitic incident would prove to be one of many to be encountered over the course of thirty years at Wayland High School. Unfortunately, school leadership would once again prove unwilling or ill equipped to respond, which allowed this part of the hidden curriculum to thrive.

Over the course of three decades, Jewish students wrote sparsely about their experiences, though they were willing to share them in private discussions. For the most part, their stories evidenced a desire for invisibility as a means of gaining acceptance in the mainstream. This "blending in" brought with it a good deal of shame as a consequence of ignoring the persistence of anti-Semitism in their world. Ignoring the jokes and taunts also brought a good deal of internalized self-hatred.

The decade of the eighties in Wayland, a time when many Jewish families moved into town, did produce some very public displays of anti-Semitism. On the evening of Parents' Night in 1986, cars throughout the parking lot had a picture of Ivan Boesky, decorated with anti-Semitic slurs, under a wiper blade. The poster child for corporate corruption at the time, Boesky's high profile apparently also spawned some spray-painting of swastikas on the mailboxes and driveways of presumably Jewish homes in town.

In an informal class discussion about anti-Semitism, some Christian students revealed how everyone knew the Jews all lived up in the "Jewish hills" where some kids drove around during December to call attention to the "lack of Christmas lights." That decade also generated a lot of controversy among the faculty, as the recent influx of Jews brought into question the traditional Christmas displays in the classrooms and public areas. Each piece of Christmas, from Santa to wreaths, had to be painstakingly contested before the school eventually relented on the public display of overt Christian symbols.

The nineties also found some Jewish students finding their voices in addressing the very evident anti-Semitism in town and at their school. Sarah wrote an article entitled "Anti-Semitism: One Student's Experience" (*Last Word*, November 1991), in which she opened with the following anecdote:

> My initial reaction was silence; I was so shocked by what I had heard that I froze, unable to form a response. I was sitting in front of a group of girls during our lacrosse practice; they were all talking together and creating a low hush. I wasn't really paying attention to their conversation until three words exploded in my ears. "F--- the Jew!" commented one of the girls casually. Her friend sitting beside her gave the girl a nudge, saying "Shush she's Jewish," pointing to me.

Sarah went on to explain that she had been exposed to more anti-Semitic remarks than many Jews, because she did not have stereotypical "Jewish" features. In fact, many people made such comments in front of her and then, upon discovering her religion, would admonish her to "lighten up." Many Jewish students did "lighten up" as they learned that speaking out potentially brought them more problems at school.

Perhaps that silence emboldened those individuals who, on a Sunday in August 1992, printed in black marker the phrases "Kill all Jews" and "Hitler could of [sic] used a microwave oven" on the guardrail at Lake Shore Drive in the Dudley Pond neighborhood. This rising wave of public anti-Semitism brought the issue to the race-relations meetings and the classroom, where it became apparent that the ignorance about non-whites clearly extended to the Jewish students as well.

In the nineties, the battle lines were drawn over academic requirements and Jewish holidays. The main issue regarded how teachers approached assignments during the Jewish holidays. Some teachers refused to acknowledge the holidays by holding Jewish students responsible for homework, including one teacher who told the class that they were only exempt from homework "on major holidays, like Christmas and Easter."

The occasional tolerance messages from the administration failed to stem the tide of anti-Semitism, since this decade saw the proliferation of "penny tossing" aimed at Jewish teachers and students. This phenomenon was first revealed to me when I paid a visit to a colleague's classroom. Around this Jewish teacher's desk and in front of the blackboard were strewn an array of pennies. When students were asked about this "game," they reacted with some surprise that teachers weren't aware of this means of calling attention to the "cheapness" of Jews.

Of course, the history of anti-Semitism confirmed that its existence had no boundaries of time or place. A series of public incidents on the South Shore of Boston led to some interviews with Jewish students, who reported the throwing of bagels, athletes being called "Jew boy" or "kike," and the town of Sharon being called "Jewville" (*Patriot Ledger*, February 17–18, 1996).

Reactions from local students and parents brought to the surface troubling, yet understand-able, explanations as to why students had not previously reported these incidents. A couple of statements reflected what students had evidently learned about the tough issues: "What are you going to accomplish by going and telling someone about this?" and "It's not worth the effort or the problems of making a big issue out of it."

Unfortunately, these students were speaking to the realities within most schools and com-munities: they had learned resignation, avoidance, and ultimately silence about tough issues such as anti-Semitism, as modeled by so many adults around them.

These crude forms of anti-Semitism continued into the new century, with the continual litany of jokes, the usual name-calling, occasional swastikas and other graffiti, and the ongo-ing "penny tossing," along with an apparently new "game" where some students at WHS glued money to the floor of the commons and anyone who tried to pick it up was called "Jew." On one sports team the sole Jewish player was termed "the Kike." And in class, both Christian and Jewish students presented numerous insights into the many subtle ways that anti-Semitism had become part of the fabric of their lives.

Though many people seemed stunned at the reports of anti-Semitism, its insertion into the fabric of American history suggested otherwise. Though generally tolerated in the first half century of the Republic, anti-Semitism rose with the immigration of Jews in larger numbers. By the late nineteenth century, Jews faced exclusion from Christian social circles and denial of the vote in some states (until 1877), and in the next century, Jews felt the consequences of everything from America's fear of Bolshevism to the writings of Henry Ford to the Depression attacks from Father Coughlin.

Though never as pernicious as evidenced in other countries, anti-Semitism had become so entrenched in the United States that what most students experienced seemed to be a rather "normal" part of their world. By the twenty-first century, most of Wayland's Jewish students, overwhelmingly members of Reform Judaism, reported their desire to become invisible in the world of Christian whites. However, that process did not come without any costs. Their journals pointed to the creation of their own version of "two worlds": one of apparent assimi-lation at school while maintaining a Jewish identity in their private lives.

To be "overtly" Jewish at WHS never seemed to be a socially acceptable choice for a student, any more than did "acting real Asian" or expressing any overt signs of racial pride. So during the school year they blended in by ignoring the rather constant drone of anti-Semitism they experienced at school and in the community. The rest of the year, whether at Jewish community centers or summer camps, these students could relax, feel safe, and "be them-selves."

Speaking about those outside experiences always brought an excitement to their voices that seemed genuinely founded in the relief that came from the comfort of being able to shed their "secret." It wasn't quite the secret kept by most gay and lesbian students, but Jewish students appeared to avoid being associated with their roots more in an avoidance of shame than a fear of social suicide.

For Melanie, the lack of emphasis on a Jewish identity harkened back to elementary school, when she learned a lesson about being Jewish:

> Being Jewish is the one thing that makes me interesting. White middle class, speak English, oh [sic] Jew, at least I [have] some culture. I remember this time in fourth grade when we took our first MCAS. I think we were practicing how to fill in the bubbles at the beginning of the test. When I got to the section that asked for your racial identity I was looking to fill in Jewish. I didn't see it and raised my hand for the teacher (who was also Jewish, one of the few I had ever had in

elementary school) to come over. I asked her if I could fill in "other" and she asked what I thought I was. I said Jewish and she told me that was not a race or ethnicity and to fill in white. I think that was one of the first times I realized I was "boring."

Given the nature of a small suburban town, Jewish students couldn't totally "hide" their identities, so most Jewish kids simply chose to downplay their "Jewishness" in order to avoid as much negative attention as possible. When confronted with Jewish jokes or other forms of anti-Semitism these students had learned to laugh or ignore. So the Jewish kids played a delicate game in which they denied concerns about the teasing, even sometimes joining in on the "fun." In this manner they acted very much like many non-white students, just trying to "get by" by not standing up.

Naomi expressed this daily reality all too well:

> Being Jewish in a mainly Catholic town, I feel I am constantly dealing with racial jokes and hiding my true identity—laughing rather than sticking up for myself and revealing my religion. I would rather blend in, and pretend I find their jokes funny, then [sic] stick up for myself and reveal my true emotions. I guess I am afraid of what will happen. Will they question me? Will they think of me differently because I care about my religion? Will I spoil the moment and make the situation awkward? I know I will be put under a spotlight—which I like under normal circumstances, but not because of religious differences. . . . I feel violated and disrespected by my peers constantly, and it is no [accident]. They all know that I am Jewish. I guess that's why my closest friends are not from Wayland—they are other Jews whom I identify with and respect. I know that I will never feel truly comfortable with my "friends" from school because they don't fully respect me and they probably won't until I stick up for myself.

Since anti-Semitism would rarely if ever get addressed by adults, students could experience overt acts right up to their last days at the high school. Stef's journal excerpt comes from a very outspoken and strong senior, who wrote about an incident that completely disempowered her:

> Today I was sitting in the commons and [these kids] started making really nasty Jewish comments towards me. In my life I have NEVER been exposed to such anti-Semitism. I know earlier in this journal I said that I would stick up for myself and not let them demean me . . . I was defenseless today. I sat there and took it because I had nothing to say. . . . I felt truly pathetic. These people were supposed to be my friends, yet they had no problem making me feel worthless. They threw pennies at me and said that I should be sharing the wealth, etc. etc. They then continued to call me a "Jew pussy" and talked about how I go to this health club for rich kids and [Jewish] pussies etc. etc. and that I take boxing lessons because a [Jew] pussy needs to learn how to stick up for herself and [Jews] need to learn how to fight. My peers were cracking up as I was ridiculed until I finally had to just walk out of the commons and sit in the language building until the block was over. I have never been so disrespected and I had nothing to say back because I knew they all just wanted to get a rise out of me. From this, I think I've learned to choose my "friends" far more wisely. There wasn't anything I could have said to make them shut up, so I hope they felt stupid enough when I walked away . . . sometimes that's more [effective] than freaking out.

What Stef confronted that day reflected attitudes that simply weren't that uncommon. However, much like other forms of racism, the anti-Semitism much more often appeared as a constant undercurrent rather than loud explosions. The drone could become easily normalized to the point where victims typically became numb to the cumulative emotional impact. Those explosions, however, brought back into stark reality the less overt acts of anti-Semitism that they lived with and carried inside.

Unlike their Asian peers who overwhelmingly recognized that their racial appearance mitigated the potential for blending in, most Jewish students had come to understand that their "white" identities could be preserved for long periods of time . . . and yet dissolve in an instant. And you could never predict when or how these events might occur. Sadly, friends as well as strangers could precipitate them. Bonding together seemed like a good strategy, but that could precipitate the very attention they wished to avoid. For Jewish students it could lead to a name, like the "Jew Crew," which could then bring its own brand of teasing.

The majority of kids who witnessed the incident when Stef was under attack in the commons may have had a desire to speak, as did Stef, but they had little experience in confronting such behavior or seeing adults model such behavior. Later, no doubt some of them told Stef what they wanted to say. Or friends who weren't there probably expressed what they would have said. Yet when Stef looked around in the commons that day searching for potential allies, she found none. This was certainly not surprising given how schools have a history of silencing student voices.

School leaders rarely possessed the skills to forthrightly and effectively address such emotionally charged issues. As leaders learn, those "problems" will disappear because the student victims will learn silence.

As with their Asian American peers, these feelings may not have significantly hampered their academic achievement, but certainly schools aspire to equally important humanistic goals. Since the formal education did not deal with this issue it would be relegated almost totally to the hidden curriculum. That curriculum produced voices such as this student's when he wrote, "I pledged to myself that I wouldn't make any friends with Jews," along with the varied jokes, taunts, and "games" that assaulted the dignity of the Jewish students.

Patrick wrote a very lengthy segment on the level of disrespect accorded the Jewish students, along with a detailed account of the personal experiences that had contributed to his own lack of respect for his Jewish peers:

> I might not hate [Jews] as much as some of my friends but they have not earned my respect yet. . . . In a school filled with [Jews] they do things that ruin their stereotype [sic] rather than help it. Let me tell you about [Jews] in my life from day one. So growing up in COCH [the less affluent part of Wayland] I didn't see many [Jews]—the only [Jewish] family I know is ironically the wealthiest family on my street. I also just heard that North [Wayland] was just extremely wealthy [Jews] that thought they were better than everyone else. At Happy Hollow [Elementary School] there were barely any [Jewish] kids and the few that were, weren't that wealthy and gave [Jews] a pretty good rep. . . . Then we hit middle school. The cool kids were the wealthy [Jewish] kids. They had all the parties in their huge houses and pools and all the girls wanted to hang out with them. The [Jews] had their baztsmitsfas (ya I have no idea how to spell that) and kept to their own [Jewish] crew and didn't really make an effort to hang out with [South Wayland] kids. Then comes high school and the tables turn. The [Jews] still don't have to work. When you see wealthy Jews going out to lunch you see that they just pull out the credit cards their 'rents gave them, when I'm paying for things with money I earned—I have never had [an] allowance. My 'rents don't just give me money—I used to not like it but now I respect that they haven't spoiled me because it has turned me into more of a man. The [Jewish] kids all have nice cars that were just given to them. I [paid] for a large quantity of my car. Things like that aren't big but I notice that and get annoyed seeing things come easier to them than to me. . . . We have more fun and aren't afraid to go crazy, while the [Jewish] kids are scared their parents will get mad at them or they won't get into an Ivy League college even though half of them have connects into top notch colleges.

Earlier, Stef told a story of shame and humiliation during an anti-Semitic incident in the commons when she was unable to find her voice. Patrick observed the incident, and he provided this perspective:

These kids have all this success but yet they are still to big of [sic] pussies to stand up for themselves. A great story is what happened today. [This girl] was talking about how she takes boxing lessons at Bossie (it's a workout facility in North [Wayland] where the very wealthy people go. . .) . . . the wealthy people want to think they're [sic] tough so they take "boxing" lessons at this extremely preppy club. And [this Jewish girl] and this other Jewish boy (the boy is a pretty big kid) don't say anything [to these comments], [they] weren't like trying to intimidate them and start something, but if someone was like "[Ethnic group] people try to be tough but are pussy's [sic]," I don't care if I'm by myself against ten guys I'm still going to say something.

Although such overt situations occurred rarely, the shame associated with being the victim of anti-Semitism routinely surfaced when students spoke about their experiences with Jewish jokes. Much like the Asian American students who learned to ignore the jokes in order to be accepted, Jewish students seemed well versed in this practice. Naomi agonized over the hurt perpetrated by her fellow students and her responses to that hurt:

Being Jewish, I'm ashamed to say that I would rather laugh at the Jewish jokes than stand up for myself. I am one of maybe three Jewish kids in my group of friends, and although I pride myself in trying to differentiate myself from my friends, I still find myself constantly making fun of my religion so I can blend in. The worst is when I meet someone for the first time and they are bickering about one of their friends whose [sic] "SO JEWISH" because they owed someone money. Recently, my brother was at an after-prom party and a hypnotist was hired for entertainment. One of the questions he had asked the kids was, "What would you say to someone who had just stolen your wallet?" and my brother's date replied, "JEW." Although the crowd went silent and recognized the harshness of the statement, I don't think anyone felt the way my brother felt. He usually puts a tough-guy cover [on] to avoid embarrassment, but this public humiliation was unsolvable.

Another student referenced his experiences with anti-Semitism in Wayland, especially the constant Jewish jokes and taunts. Despite the presence of a sizable Jewish community in town, this student concluded, "I still feel as Jews we accept these jokes because we are afraid of what people will think of us if we don't."

Some journals revealed a very personal struggle with internalized self-hatred. Naomi expressed the struggle with self-hatred as evidenced in jokes:

At camp one year, a bunch of my friends (all Jewish) and I were sitting around having a contest to see who knew the worst Jew joke. However, I know for a fact that if I heard anyone other than Jews saying those jokes, I would want to either start sobbing, or slap them across the face! It's a mystery to me as to why it remains OK for minorities to put themselves down, but the second someone outside of their group does the same, it's a hate crime.

Victor also confirmed the rampant anti-Semitism at school, along with his own internalized denial. This journal passage clearly evidences what had become normal for Jewish students:

I am in a group of friends that is entirely anti-Semitic. There is only one kid who is not. I always forget I have Jewish blood in me . . . as do they. Whenever there is a situation where Jews can be brought up . . . like if someone is complaining or being cheap . . . there is often twenty minute rants [sic] about Jews.

This cauldron of tension brewing just beneath the surface—the tension of Jewish kids suppressing their anger and shame at ignoring insults about their identities, and the mostly Christian kids who felt empowered to taunt them—erupted one day in class. Any previous experiences with one-on-one student fights looked inconsequential in the face of what looked like the potential for a fairly large brawl. The animosities dating back at least to middle school, fueled by years of suppressed anger on the part of Jewish students and the disdain from some powerful peers, created a very volatile mix.

Fortunately, the heat dissipated before anyone came to blows. Perhaps all the previous highly charged classes had accustomed them to fighting with their words. Nick wrote about it as follows:

> It was painful to watch the class where [a student] was explaining how Jews disgust him, and how he tests them, and then look over at the line of Jews sitting absolutely silent. James was the only one who spoke up, and the rest just sat there looking at the ground. It was humiliating to watch.

Listening to their words both in class and their journals, it became obvious that the school's curriculum was failing miserably to achieve some of its most important goals. As a reminder, the school's mission statement emphasized the phrases "personal responsibility" and "empathy for others" in the very first sentence. And it ended with the statement, "Our goal is to advance our students' growth into principled, informed, and capable citizens who help guide a democracy that follows humanitarian principles in the global forum, and shape a just society where individuals may reach their full potential."

Not only were most kids not learning these goals, the hidden curriculum had done an excellent job of promoting and reinforcing the exact opposite.

Most of the Jewish students had learned that ignoring anti-Semitism was the safest path for social survival. As a consequence, most of those same students had internalized some amount of self-hatred for allowing their dignity to be compromised. They also learned that most of the adults in their world felt powerless in the face of anti-Semitism. These lessons are no doubt being learned in schools across America, no matter what education leaders might declare for public consumption. Yes, these students have been provided with an excellent intellectual experience, but they deserve much more.

POSTSCRIPT

Lisa faced defeat at the high school, having fought unsuccessfully for the race and racism course . . . but only in the short term. A decade later we would reconnect, at which point she reflected on those challenging times at Wayland High School. After college, she worked for local newspapers in Southern California and Arizona before moving to China, where she worked for a newspaper and TV station as an editor. Later she did investigative reporting at the Center for Public Integrity in Washington, DC, and worked as a reporter for the Sunlight Foundation. She stated, "If it weren't for that lunchtime race-relations forum, I don't think I would have pursued journalism, or worked in China. So thank you." Despite attempts to silence her voice, Lisa has become the model of an active citizen in a democracy.

Stef chose to join a non-Jewish sorority at college and later lived among predominantly Christian roommates, a decision she somewhat regretted, stating,

> Our cultures are very different, and although they are not anti-Semitic, there is a lapse in understanding. . . . I realize what I love about being Jewish is not the religious practice, but the innate culture. . . . Looking back on the confrontation I had in high school, I believe it wasn't meant to be so cruel, as it was a misunderstanding and instance of displaying immaturity. I am comfortable with myself and my identity, and if someone wants to be anti-Semitic towards me, I have come to realize that is simply them wasting their energy rather than truly affecting me.

In the summer of '75, Bob Buchbinder and I left San Francisco in a Jeep, traveling the borders of the continental forty-eight, including El Paso; New Orleans; Miami; New York; Chicago; Milwaukee; Fargo; Bonner's Ferry, Idaho; Vancouver, Canada; and Seattle. Before we left Bob quite bluntly asked me whether I would be one of those Christians who would turn him away or one who would hide him. My first reaction was surprise, but his perspective helped inform what would become a lifetime of understanding the insidiousness of anti-Semitism.

LESSONS LEARNED

On the surface, Asian American students appeared to cope well with their inner identity struggles, a facade that fed into the ignorance of non-Asians in their world.

The identity issues faced by the broad spectrum of Asian Americans brought social, emotional, and sometimes academic costs that resulted from being silenced at school.

Addressing stereotypes in class, even those "positive" ones associated with Asians, helps all students to see how stereotypes deny individuality and prevent students from developing authentic interracial friendships.

Often ignored, Asian and Jewish students face experiences that hinder their healthy emotional/social growth at school—which also harms all other students and adults.

Holding Asian American students to a higher bar of academic success does a disservice to all students, but especially those Asian Americans who struggle with academics just like some of their non-Asian peers.

Persistent anti-Semitism thrived in a culture where students felt silenced and school leadership lacked the will and ability to effectively deal with situations that entered the public domain.

Students learn to model the adults' resignation, avoidance, and silence on the tough issues such as anti-Semitism.

By denying and ignoring issues of racism, education leaders find that the problems will eventually "disappear" and fewer problems will be reported as students learn silence.

Education leaders most often have no training or skills for dealing with race issues—or any important social/emotional issues—and thus they choose to ignore rather than confront them.

Far too many students generally failed to achieve the ideal social/emotional goals of the school's mission statement, but they did learn the exact opposite goals in the hidden curriculum.

Chapter 8

Education Complete, Final Lessons Learned

We take tests to rate our performance in school and for college. It's a business; we take Kaplan courses to boost our scores on the SATs, we have to get good grades so colleges want us . . . what about how passionate we are and who we are; not just our grades.

—Sasha

Student journals throughout this book revealed a world generally kept silent because students had learned that few people in power cared to listen. Their passion, so often tamped down or extinguished, poured out on all sorts of topics but, most importantly, everything imaginable about their education and the nature of their lives at school. Most prominently, students across the racial and class spectrum, at all levels of motivation and achievement, looked for more meaning from their education.

Education can be and should be inspirational, interesting, creative, and meaningful. It simply doesn't have to be a marathon of mundane content, constant drilling, relentless note taking, standardized testing, and pointless homework. This often dreary marathon certainly hasn't worked academically for kids who struggle at school. Even at the top public schools, education falls short of the desires and needs of children. Social and emotional growth, love of learning, and contemporary relevancy may be stated in mission statements, but students clearly expressed having very little fulfillment in these areas.

As education reform places more burdens on teachers with regard to short-term content retention and test-driven skill development, student learning will continue to lag on many of the worthy goals contained in those mission statements. Burdened with more paperwork, more responsibilities, and more focus on standardized-test results, teachers have less time to spend with students outside the classroom and less time for the creative and interactive pedagogy that students consistently cited as the most stimulating parts of their education.

Ultimately, adults who have no experience working with or listening to children in the classroom hold the lives of millions of schoolchildren in the balance. Ignoring those voices will continue to result in high dropout rates, poor achievement in many schools, and unhealthy social/emotional consequences for most children. The nation's children are at risk, and the solutions of more time "on task," more work, harder tests, and more days in school will not address the issues raised by these students.

At even the "best" schools, the drive to increase rigor has placed students on a faster-moving assembly line where their voices have been lost in the hum of an educational system in content overdrive. Unable to keep up with the machine, many students sleepwalk through classes, resort to cheating, succumb to tears, or rely on drugs and alcohol to escape the pain. Modern education reform may bring some benefits to the adults in power, but at high cost to the kids.

As it stands, far too many important lessons have been left to the hidden curriculum where students learn many of the religious, class, and racial stereotypes that last a lifetime. They also learn that educators have nothing to offer in either modeling or teaching about the toughest issues in their world, or the larger society. Ultimately, they learn that schools are predicated on endurance rather than inspiration. The children deserve better.

Students need to be engaged as partners in what will likely be the longest lasting and most important job of their lives. To be afraid of what children have to say, even the damnedest things, only serves to diminish the authenticity and credibility of educators. Students should not be learning some of their most important lessons at school outside the classrooms. If educators resist learning from their students, then students will continue to internalize their own hidden curriculum within the belly of the beast.

Quite simply, schools that truly wished to meet the needs of students would allow for more student input, inspire more student and teacher creativity, and produce a deeper form of learning—yet retain the orderliness that allows all children to learn in a respectful environment. Students aren't looking to run the schools, nor should they, but they do want to be noticed, listened to, and respected for their voices. The best teachers and administrators understand this, even as they are humbled by the difficulty of achieving these goals.

The quotes in this chapter represent the major threads of many student voices when asked, anonymously, to assess their specific courses and school in general. Here are their final notes from school, and it should be no surprise at this point to know that students *want a voice* and the opportunity to *talk with other students*.

"Real life is experiencing and listening—it doesn't matter how many math problems you can do how quickly."

"I feel angry with teachers who wouldn't listen and with people who don't care."

"Writing journals was probably my favorite thing that we did all year. Because I don't like to talk in class, I found that writing journals was allowing me to say what I really wanted to say in class."

"Class discussions started to dip into the areas of my brain that I was trained to shut off during school: the things I read, what I saw on television, what I witnessed all around me, my feelings, and my beliefs."

"Making almost any student speak their mind, making students challenge each other, making every student feel like their opinion has real value . . ."

Students expressed dismay at the conformity of thinking promoted through the content, which also proved to be very disconnected from the real world. Students expressed a strong desire for *content connected to their world*.

"[I expected] everything I learn here would fit nicely, like it always had, into my 'toolbox of school stuff,' right next to the Pythagorean theorem, and that it would exist simply on lines of notebook paper and the backs of flashcards. I was wrong."

"Allowing us, the kids, to choose the topic and discuss things we are curious about and that are important in our life shows that you care what we think, and you want us to engage and be interested."

"I feel that I have learned more things which I can use and draw from in the 'real world' in this class. This is one aspect that I believe our school is lacking."

"Well I feel that is what school is now; kids only worry about what topics will be on the test, nothing else. Kids want to do something useful, fun and experiment, not just sit around."

"In high school (especially here at Wayland), we are forced to think in specific ways— which are dictated by the school (and essentially the country). We look for the right answer—the right answer equals the right grade. Instead of being able to freely roam and think as we please, we are stuck in a box of the same ideas that circulate and bounce until they are lodged in a student's head until the next exam."

"School and the larger system tries [*sic*] to make our lives uniform and our personalities and actions predictable because with that we will be easier to control and [we will] become immersed into the system without question. To question your teachers and your schooling is the best way to educate yourself and those around you."

Students also strongly supported a curriculum that included *an authentic education on race and racism*, particularly since it addressed several of the missing "real-world" elements in their education:

"I think that in this class, it's the first time since I've been in Wayland I actually talked about me and what I've been through as a Latina."

"Since elementary school, I have not looked forward to a class like I would look forward to race. It made me want to learn, it made me want to change."

"The realizations that I have come to and the soul searching which I have done is [*sic*] critical in making me the best person I can be. This class has challenged and rewarded me."

"Race and Racism was the most frustrating topic for me, but that is not necessarily a bad thing. I left almost every class infuriated by something, but even that was good because my anger would keep me thinking the rest of the day."

"At eighteen years old, this was the first time any class or anything forced me to look inside myself and see both the good and the bad."

"This class has opened my eyes to the point where I cannot shut them. This is the kind of stuff that would have helped me as a young black boy growing up."

"I've been dealing with the discomfort of my race, and race in general, since the first grade. I appreciated it more, because the course forced the Wayland kids to be in a similar place as [*sic*] me."

"If Americans can't deal with race in the controlled and educational environment of high school how could they in real life?"

"A lot of what I have been feeling has been relief. I know that sounds weird but I think that I had always on some deep level felt ashamed of myself because I'm not colorblind, I do see different colors when I look at people."

Students consistently advocated for a *more inspiring* education, one *less stressful, less competitive*, and *less grade driven*:

"Our society has made us so competitive with each other that all we care about is if the material is going to be on the test. No one looks to challenge what we're being taught."

"I was never able to do well in school. My parents always put a lot of emphasis on grades and I never lived up to their expectations. Years of failure made me hate the world, leading to destructive behaviors."

"I used to be a smart individual, one who actually cared about learning . . . I truly wish I had the drive to excel in school not because of grades but because I had a passion for learning."

"Many people just do what they need to in order to get the grades they want. They are not driven by passion; they are driven by a desire to get good grades to then go to a 'good' college. Grades are at the forefront of the vast majority of people's minds instead of a genuine interest in subjects."

"For years we have been asked to memorize. Teachers teach, we listen, we memorize, we rewrite, we get graded for reiterating what a teacher already said. After twelve years, it becomes monotonous."

"In school, many personal issues, feelings, beliefs, or ideas must be put aside as they might affect your grade."

"I believe [it] is essential for students to grow a mind of their own, [as] opposed to the growth allowed in a certain box, for many students whose teachers prefer critical thinking, as long as it's on the teacher's terms."

"We are given these endless freedoms, but are they really our choices to make, or are they there just for show? Wayland High School assumes that our natural curiosities and our ingrained desire to please the parents who have pushed us down a path since we were toddlers will create the necessity to achieve no matter the cost."

"Sometimes it just seems like society is getting so out of control, the media is taking over so much, it's as if there are no real people anymore, with real feelings and style and not so mainstream or so competitive and stressed out about every little grade or time specific issues."

This last quote speaks well to the changes in society and school that have evolved over the past half century. Having started elementary school using a fountain pen dipped into a desk inkwell and then retiring with the latest computer technology, it is clear to me that rapid changes in technology will only further change the lives of twenty-first-century children.

The contemporary decline of "community," as presented in Robert Putnam's *Bowling Alone*, can be felt in many ways, but particularly among children who feel the brunt of the "technology weeds" that appear to be inexorably choking out the traditional bonds of human communication. The use of smart phones and iPods, which create a means for solitude in very busy public spaces, have immensely magnified the variety of ways to separate humans from each other.

Indeed, the increase in texting rather than talking has further diminished the opportunities for children to have meaningful conversations. Moving the schools toward more content delivery and standardized testing will eventually eliminate class periods devoted to discussions on significant topics. The most interesting and meaningful learning experiences identified by children will disappear.

If students are *not* allowed to interact with each other in the adult-monitored classroom—if they are *not* able to find their voices in order to feel some control over their lives or to access the guidance of adults—then schools will only continue to reflect the shortcomings of an increasingly alienated society where people speak through machines rather than with people.

Children recognized that they were being socialized in an increasingly complex world with less access to the wisdom and guidance of adults. If modern schools truly wish to serve a far more profound role in this country, they need to seize the opportunity to enhance the fundamental task of academic education by helping children navigate their way through more complex life decisions at younger and younger ages, with decreasing access to parents, grandparents, and other adult relatives.

Public schools are the only places where young men and women of all races, classes, religions, and sexual orientations gather on a regular basis, a captive audience for adults. Children hear about ideals of justice, engaged citizenship, love of learning, empathy, and equity. Schools need to be held accountable for those admirable and enduring ideals.

Children at all levels are already being educated in schools guided by these principles. Children at all ages yearn for a formal education that makes sense in their real world. And all subjects lend themselves to a curriculum that integrates real-life problems. Mathematics is often cited as an exception, yet the work of David Mumford, professor of mathematics at Brown University, and Sol Garfunkel, executive director of the Consortium of Mathematics and its Applications, have both championed such an approach right through high-school math.

Anonymous formal student evaluations certainly offer critical feedback, though students need to know that the teacher has heard the feedback. This channel should allow for a dialogue that would include an action plan toward fulfillment of some student input of value. Less formal but equally valuable feedback can be generated by allowing some homework in a journal format. Of course, students provide constant feedback in every class through their behaviors and performance. Listening on a regular basis promotes a belief in our children, but it also builds a respect for adults who listen. Our children look to adults for support, wisdom, comfort, and guidance—all of which require that we respect their voices.

Chapter 9

Reflections and Recommendations

I don't know that much about the administration.

Administrators turn their backs on [racism] because it doesn't concern them . . . they have the power so why should they care.

ADMINISTRATORS: REFLECTIONS

The two quotes above reflect the major themes to emerge from student voices. Students generally felt disconnected from administrators. Their daily lives brought them into very little, if any, personal contact with most administrators. Administrators entered the lives of students mostly in cases of discipline and at various school-wide assemblies. Most of those public gatherings occurred routinely, such as orientations and ceremonies. The random public gatherings usually resulted from a crisis at school or in the community.

The disconnect between students and administrators appeared as a constant thread over thirty years, but surfaced mostly in students' writing on administrative views on race and their handling of public incidents that brought the administration directly into the students' world. The following were some typical responses to a question about administrators' views on race:

"I don't know."

"I don't really have much contact with administrators."

"I feel that they ignore it a lot. It feels like they act like they don't see it when they really do."

"I have no idea what their attitudes are."

"There [are] a lot of racial tensions, stereotypes and prejudice in this school that the administration ignores and refuses to deal with."

"If there happened to be any sort of big incident at school, you would only hear rumors about it, and not the truth. . . . Any incident involving the administration is covered up."

Clearly, administrators would prefer to diminish the dreadful image presented by public acts of racism, so short-term tamping down of the situation would be appropriate. However, students came to recognize the lack of follow-up with regard to fully addressing the systemic issues as problematic. Marshall expressed his take on a theme that remained fairly consistent among student voices:

125

The administration played the most effective tactic—they would see people getting pissed off, but
they knew if they held out long enough that something else would get the attention of the masses
and this topic would just be dropped. It worked all too well. Teenagers have the attention span of a
goldfish in my opinion. They have just enough muster to carry them through school, but they only
have so much attention left to focus on a few things.

The administrative desire to provide "stability" in these cases, rather than dealing with controversial topics, emerged in a revealing interchange between a principal and a student. Ling-se
uncovered an authentic administrative moment when she asked one about the lack of acknowledgment of black history and race in general: "We don't want to rock the boat." A follow-up
question referencing the importance of such an education in the curriculum elicited the response, "No, it's more important for them [Boston students] to get into college."

Student writing on issues of discipline often addressed what they perceived as a problem
with fairness. Issues of fairness also entered classroom discussions, especially in psychology
when students studied child development. Most often mentioned were more leniency toward
athletes and different standards for the Boston students. Some felt that the Boston students got
unwarranted breaks, while others felt they were dealt with more harshly than resident students.
More importantly, students complained about the overall feeling of lax or inconsistent application of consequences.

The debriefing of a field trip to Madison Park (MP) High School in Boston, during which
the students toured the building and various classrooms, best summed up these themes. When
asked for their impressions of this unique experience, their responses provided some very
interesting feedback. Primarily, they stated with near unanimity how much they liked the
headmaster.

They first encountered the headmaster in the foyer of MP, where this man with an imposing physical appearance and voice greeted the group from the top of a stairwell. He welcomed
the students to his school and then immediately laid out the rules in the building, including no
wearing of caps. All my students were then instructed to remove theirs or be told to leave the
building. They clearly sensed no equivocation and immediately responded as directed.

The headmaster made a number of appearances as the group toured the school, where he
could be seen calling out to students by name, questioning them about an imminent test or
"that biology project due in a week," and welcoming a student back to school after a pro-
longed illness. The Wayland students were amazed. The man absolutely connected to the
students in his building, something the students found incredibly comforting and attractive.

They immediately recognized and admired how he cared about his students as people, in
addition to the business of school. The students also expressed strong support for his clear
rules . . . and his apparent enforcement of them. Their own experiences with overly vague
rules and lax enforcement had made their lives less predictable in a teenage world full of
change and angst. Despite their usual public protestations to the contrary, most of them
recognized that unpredictability was not healthy for them.

The best teachers and administrators understand this, even as they are humbled by the
difficulty of achieving these ideal goals. An orderly school building with defined rules, and
consequences for breaking those rules, may sound fundamental, but all schools struggle in this
endeavor. So a school truly interested in providing an inspirational atmosphere must start with
the voices of children who walk through those doors every day, hoping that the adults will do
right by them. Sometimes that may mean protecting them from themselves, or from their peers
or a teacher.

Reducing physical and emotional stresses on children in order to make them better able to engage in some serious learning requires administrators who are willing and able to connect with students and tackle the tough issues confronting them. The topic of race certainly caused a lot of tension and distress at school, and student interviews surfaced consistent themes regarding how administration dealt with this topic.

At the very least, they needed to know that the adults could be counted on to be caring, stable, consistent, and fair.

Since current reform movements tend to bestow more power on administrators, it is critical for them to listen to and acknowledge the voices of students. Students aren't looking to run the schools, nor should they, but they do want to be noticed, listened to, and respected for their voices. Effective administrators will not be surprised or daunted by the following recommendations.

ADMINISTRATORS: RECOMMENDATIONS

Administrators must be trained to handle the tough issues before they take on leadership roles. The racial achievement gap will not be appropriately addressed or eliminated by administrators who cannot honestly talk about race. Leaders who are afraid to talk about race will not inspire staff to address race issues. Administrators have to be able to model expectations for staff and students.

Administrators need to provide mechanisms for student feedback. Providing all students with an appropriate "evaluative voice" would generate some much-needed feedback. They absolutely should be soliciting anonymous exit surveys from students. Students have already evolved their own methods of evaluating their teachers and administrators through blogging and websites such as RateMyTeachers.com. Providing all students with an appropriate "official voice" would generate some much-needed feedback. Otherwise, all of these administrators operate in a vacuum, while children pay the costs.

Administrators need to have a vision that they can effectively communicate and put into action. Students appreciate a leader with a vision, especially a leader with the fortitude to articulate and maintain the integrity of a vision that keeps the focus squarely on the needs of children. Students are not blind or stupid; they know when an administrator is all talk and no action.

The leading advocate for every child in a school building must be the principal. The hidden curriculum of students included lessons that indicated who had value at school and who didn't. The "smoking area" kids knew they weren't valued, as did the Boston kids (especially the nonathletes), which certainly didn't escape the rest of the student body. There should be no "throwaway kids" in any school building.

Very little will change in schools if administrators don't spend more time in the classroom before and after taking leadership roles. Having more time in the classroom, listening to students, would benefit all administrators. Constant appearances in the halls and classrooms should be a daily routine. Administrators need to put more direct student contact into their world—and not just with their favored groups.

Primary evaluators need to use their power more wisely during the trial period before granting tenure or professional status. Students end up paying the biggest price for poor teachers. A wise superintendent once said that good young teachers rarely become bad teachers. Astute administrators know the power of prevention, and they need to use it more astutely.

Administrators should resist the trend of quantifying all aspects of teaching. Recent trends toward accountability have increasingly moved administrators too far in the direction of the science of teaching and away from the art.

An administrative observation in 2007 contained over two pages of typed notes on a race and relations class, mostly reporting much of the minutiae in the unfolding of any class—who, what, when, and how. This evaluative method was the new rage: jot down as much data as possible and then write a critique at the end that involves some praise and some stimuli to improvement. The "helpful" part of the observation called attention to the following:

> Lastly, Mr. Frio's expectation for students as to how closely they listen and learn from one another? What is "good listening," as he commended his students? How does he know what students have learned: Few students appeared to be taking notes; how might the rich points from this discussion be preserved beyond memory?

An opportunity to respond to this observation would have addressed the real listening—and real learning—that were evidenced in that very class: the learning informed by deeper thoughts and emotions than any notes, the learning that filled the extensive journals that now have significance well beyond that classroom. And the irony of this observation report was that tucked into the data reported in the write-up were quotes from students in which they referenced student comments from previous class meetings.

Even more ironically, the process of "taking notes" had prevented the administrator from really listening to the students and, ultimately, prevented the administrator from learning the lessons imbedded in that day's discussion.

Current trends in evaluation tend to mirror the misguided efforts throughout education. The modern movement toward quantitative assessments of teacher effectiveness might please those outside the classroom, but they fail to address what really happens in a classroom. Teaching is as much art as science. Teaching can't be evaluated in a couple of observations, since the learning dynamic in any classroom evolves over time.

TEACHERS: REFLECTIONS

We are taught to be cogs in a machine but outside of the machine we are made to feel useless.

Teachers overwhelmingly enter the classroom and stay engaged in the classroom because of and on behalf of the children. Most do not seek to become administrators. Teachers do not hire, evaluate, grant tenure to, or supervise other teachers. They teach children. The teachers who respect student feedback know the power and importance of student voices. Other teachers should be encouraged to listen to their students rather than those distant from the classroom. Knowledge of children empowers the ability to better meet their learning needs.

As expected, students had a lot to say about their teachers. Their expectations, again, focused on fairness, leadership, safety, and orderliness—all of which are predicated on respecting student voices. Students being bullied in classrooms receive no solace from adults whom they cannot trust to hear them and keep them safe. Students want to be heard, but they take their cues from the teacher. If their voices are encouraged and respected, students are much more likely to speak their minds.

Most of all, students want to talk with each other. Classrooms provide the opportunity for students to learn from each other on important issues in their lives and the greater society. If the schools don't provide that opportunity, the students will continue to learn some of their most significant lessons within the hidden curriculum.

TEACHERS: RECOMMENDATIONS

Teacher-certification programs need to update their training of teachers for contemporary student populations and rapidly evolving teacher expectations. These programs need to help teachers *connect to the real world of students,* as opposed to the mostly theoretical approach of so many programs. Also, more attention needs to be paid to the affective domain of students. Learning must combine both intellectual and emotional components. Classroom management and social/emotional issues need to be thoroughly explored *before* teachers hit the ground running.

Solicitation and respect for student feedback should be standard practice in classrooms. Unquestionably, students feel that their voices are not heard at school. To listen to those voices and engage them can only help in building a bond of mutual respect in the classroom. Student feedback is critical in assessing whether the curriculum meets the needs of students. Students who have some ownership of the curriculum and classroom expectations will be more invested in the learning within that classroom.

Critical-thinking skills should be the outcome, and content the means to that outcome. Today's students have instant access to infinite amounts of content with the touch of a finger. Memorization of what "everyone should know" makes less sense, except to remember not to let your batteries die. Unlimited access to the Internet and the growth of entertainment technology have transformed learning for students. How students analyze, assess, evaluate, and apply that infinite wealth of content must now take precedence in the classroom.

Bringing some "student curriculum" into the classroom would enhance the skills of both children and teachers. Teachers need to make some efforts to understand how contemporary students are learning outside the domain of the school's formal curriculum. The students' increasing use of technology needs to be addressed. Teachers should help students critically analyze not only the academic, but also the social and entertainment sites that students increasingly access. Thus teachers can help students develop a deeper understanding of their increasingly complex world if they allow that world into the classroom.

Effective and respected teachers convey the relevance of their subject, along with a passion for teaching it. It should be no surprise that students consistently expressed an interest in classes where a teacher exhibited a passion for the subject. This desire transcended pedagogy, since students could enjoy a lecture as much as a full-class discussion. A subject that doesn't excite the teacher won't excite students.

Acknowledging the role of race in life and offering opportunities for students to explore these issues can enhance relationships and stimulate academic motivation. Many people might want to deny the role of race in daily life, but students generally know better. Power dynamics in the classroom impact student performance. Being aware of those dynamics can only make for better teaching . . . and better learning. Schools can be the one place that bridges the nation's racial divide, and that opportunity deserves attention. As Emma succinctly put it, "Although the ideas of dealing with race are as deep as any, it would be a severe injustice to this important topic if we did not delve into these depths, no matter how awkward they may be."

Homework needs a serious overhaul. Emphasis should be placed on *quality over quantity*. More homework is certainly harder, but not necessarily better. Assignments should emphasize student feedback and *application* of skills. Whereas top achievers see homework as a necessary burden in their road to college and successful careers, lower achievers see no such long-term benefit. All levels expressed an interest in homework that provided some meaning to their learning.

All children need advocates. Next to parents, teachers are the best advocates for all students. Students often feel powerless to impact their lives at school. Arguably the toughest yet most essential role for teachers involves advocating for those students who don't have strong advocacy at home. For those students who lack the self-confidence to stand out in a crowd and come to school *without* all the socioeconomic factors that auger success, including racial factors, the teacher represents the last chance for an advocate.

Investment in our teachers serves as an investment in our children. In order to develop the next generation of teachers, greater resources need to be available for those people with the desire to teach who lack the resources to achieve that goal.

Schools need to find ways to use the expertise of experienced teachers. Most teachers develop and hone their teaching skills over time. Schools need to provide young teachers with access to those teachers who have mastered their profession. Youthful energy and insights help to complement a veteran staff, but should not overshadow the expertise of older staff members.

Open up opportunities for students to speak with each other in class discussions. The medium of modern technology has fundamentally altered the messages between children. Schools need to provide an old-fashioned form of communication—people discussing their thoughts and feelings in an open forum.

Testing for student thinking and creativity must be the focus of standardized tests. Schools can no longer function like the factories that they replicated in the nineteenth century. That model has been outdated for decades. The global economy has created a demand for young people who can think critically and creatively. How they approach and utilize information will, in most cases, take precedence over memorizing information. That does not mean that memory has become obsolete; but much of what has been memorized can now be instantaneously obtained via the Internet. Testing for student memorization should be replaced with creative- and critical-thinking tasks.

Testing children's ability to find information and then work with it in critical and creative ways should replace reliance on some adult's version of what "everyone should know." Much of that common literacy should continue to be learned because it remains fundamental to being an informed and productive member of society. But young people are already reshaping the world in ways that most adults cannot comprehend. Standardized tests need to address that contemporary world.

Epilogue

Each day teachers are afforded a unique opportunity not only to expand learning but also to help shape respectful relationships in a world that increasingly seems to divide rather than unite people. Instead of confining and limiting those voices we need to hear them and respond to them. This book has dealt largely with voices focused on race. However, gender and class issues also significantly divide students and ultimately affect the educational lives of children. Those voices also need to be heard.

Children inherently want to learn, and they want to be heard. Classrooms that inspire both will produce students with enhanced critical-thinking skills and the ability to allow the United States to achieve its lofty goals of a nation predicated on *e pluribus unum*.

In my last year, I found myself being honored by Union College after having been nominated by Priscilla as a teacher of importance in her life. Speaking in front of my wife, college faculty, and students, I felt that very humbling, yet significantly rewarding, feeling that comes with teaching. Most teachers do their best work unseen and unacknowledged by anyone but the students in their classes. Few teachers, especially those of younger children, receive direct recognition from individual students. So this honor meant more than Priscilla could have imagined. On that day at Union College, at that moment in time, I felt what sustains teachers everywhere: the reward that comes from our students. Sometimes, they let us know that we made a difference.

I leave the final voice to Priscilla. I hope her words will help other students find their voices, not only on behalf of their needs and aspirations, but also on behalf of the teachers who made a difference in their lives. I also believe they will find that people *will care* about what they have to say. Priscilla's letter:

> I believe a student would be fortunate if in their entire educational career they were to encounter one teacher that would make a "significant difference" in their life. . . . Mr. Frio was such a teacher. Mr. Frio taught a class that was divided into three sections: Psychology, Race, and Crime. All three classes taught me so much about other people and opened my eyes, but the race class, in particular, has changed me as a person more than any class I have ever taken. I cannot even begin to put into words the way Mr. Frio impacted my thinking, nor do I think I will ever be able to write an essay that gives Mr. Frio the justice and credit he deserves for being an outstanding teacher.
>
> Before taking Mr. Frio's class I felt I was sensitive to other people's feelings and obvious prejudices; however, I learned I was naïve about the subtle injustices around me. I didn't see the racism, sexism, and other prejudices that were right in front of me. Prior to taking the class, I saw racism simply as minorities being denied jobs, or being subjected to racial slurs. However, I now

see that all the side comments, jokes, and stereotypes that ignorant people make about other races are so hurtful and disrespectful. Our class had only three students of races other than white, so it was often difficult for them to explain their feelings and views to a class of all white people.

To help some of us understand, Mr. Frio explained to us that women are also subjected to prejudices every day, but they are so conditioned to this injustice that they often don't even know when it is happening. To make his point he challenged the women in our class by making provoking comments about women and asked us to stand up to him. Not one of us did; we all sat silent. I am a very outspoken person and had previously spoken out in the class defending other topics, but even I found myself speechless.

Later that day I was so upset with myself for remaining silent about something I care so much about, I went to see Mr. Frio. I was crying and could barely talk, but I wanted him to know that sexism was a topic I was very passionate about. With the support of Mr. Frio I and several other women finally found our voices. Mr. Frio created an environment where we could truly express ourselves. He gave us the courage and strength to stand up and defend ourselves. His class was, by far, the most powerful class I have ever taken. There were times when students cried in class because they felt so strongly about certain topics. Often students got into heated arguments and debates that lasted long after class was dismissed. I eagerly attended every class; I couldn't wait to see what discussions we would become engaged in next.

Mr. Frio always made sure everyone was included and had a voice. I learned so much from him and my classmates because he created an environment that encouraged all points of view. Now that I'm in college I find myself surrounded primarily by white students with similar backgrounds. Often someone will say something offensive about a group of people not represented by anyone around us. Thanks to Mr. Frio I have found my voice to stand up for those not present and argue things like race, sex, class, religion, etc. I have a new respect for myself and discovered a new passion for equality.

Mr. Frio has changed the way I view people and society. I will take what I have learned with me for the rest of my life. Unfortunately for Wayland High School, Mr. Frio will be retiring in the spring. I am so grateful to have had the opportunity to learn from him. He deserves this recognition because he taught me, and all his students, to truly respect one another, which is the most valuable thing a person can learn.

Other Titles of Interest

OTHER TITLES OF INTEREST BY
ROWMAN & LITTLEFIELD EDUCATION

Innovative Voices in Education: Engaging Diverse Communities
Edited by Eileen Gale Kugler

White Urban Teachers: Stories of Fear, Violence, and Desire
By Audrey Lensmire

Global Issues in Education: Pedagogy, Policy, Practice, and the Minority Experience
Edited by Greg Wiggan and Charles Hutchison

Raising African-American Males: Strategies and Interventions for Successful Outcomes
By Theresa Harris and George Taylor

*Witnessing Whiteness: The Need to Talk About Race and
How to Do It, Second Edition*
By Shelly Tochluk

*Embracing Risk in Urban Education: Curiosity, Creativity, and Courage in the
Era of "No Excuses" and Relay Race Reform*
By Alice E. Ginsberg

Every Closed Eye Ain't Sleep: African American Perspectives on the Achievement Gap
By Teresa Hill